Reading and Writing for Argumentative Essays

英语议论文读写教程

丛书主编 张为民 张文霞
主　　编 刘梅华
副 主 编 王戈辉
编　　者 古秀玲　刘　宁　苏旦丽
　　　　 张荣曦　赵　珊　赵英男

清华大学出版社
北 京

English Reading and Writing for General Academic Purposes

通用学术英语读写系列教材

内 容 简 介

通用学术英语读写系列教材"的第二部，旨在训练、提高学生的学术英语议论文读写能
导学习者通过阅读议论性英语文章，了解该文体的特点和写作方法，学习学术语言的风
此外，通过研究和讨论文后的问题，对文章内容进行反思，培养批判性思维能力。全书
8个不同领域的话题，每单元包括议论文写作技巧讲解、议论文阅读、单元复习。每篇
计有相应的阅读、写作任务，以强化议论文阅读技能，扩大学术英语词汇量，巩固单元

究。举报：010-62782989，beiqinquan@tup.tsinghua.edu.cn。

目（CIP）数据

读写教程/刘梅华主编. —北京：清华大学出版社，2013.8（2021.8重印）

英语读写系列教材）

302-33229-9

Ⅱ.①刘… Ⅲ.①英语—议论文—阅读教学—教材 ②英语—议论文—写作—教材 Ⅳ.①H31

书馆CIP数据核字（2013）第163474号

学出版社
址：http://www.tup.com.cn, http://www.wqbook.com
址：北京清华大学学研大厦A座   邮   编：100084
：010-62770175   邮   购：010-62786544
者服务：010-62776969, c-service@tup.tsinghua.edu.cn
：010-62772015, zhiliang@tup.tsinghua.edu.cn
南印刷厂
书店
60mm   印   张：15.75   字   数：354千字
第1版   印   次：2021年8月第9次印刷

"通用学术英语读写系列教材"编委会

丛书主编：张为民　张文霞（清华大学）

总 序

学术英语学习旨在培养学生的学术交流能力，满足学生使用英语进行专业学习和发展的需要。中小学阶段英语教学的重点一般是培养学生用英语进行一般交流的能力，即侧重于一般英语教学。学术英语与一般英语既有联系，又有自己的特点。学术英语的学习既可以提高学生专业发展所需的语言知识和技能，同时也可以提高其一般英语的能力；它很大程度上涵盖了一般英语的学习，同时又可看作英语学习的更高阶段。学术英语学习包括两个层面的内容：一是技能层面（English for Academic Purposes）（如参加学术讲座、进行学术阅读需要的记笔记能力，论文写作、学术发言需要的概括能力等）；二是语言层面（Academic English）（如用学术语言写研究报告、研究论文的能力等）。学术英语是本科生、研究生用英语进行专业文献学习及研究交流所需要掌握的基本能力。

"通用学术英语读写系列教材"（English Reading and Writing for General Academic Purposes）针对教育部在《大学英语课程教学要求》（2007）中提出的英语较高要求和更高要求而编写。根据较高要求和更高要求，大学英语教学要注重培养学生的学术交流能力，要求学生能阅读所学专业的英语文献和资料，能用英语撰写所学专业的报告和论文。同时，本系列教材的编写也迎合全球化国际大环境对大学英语教学由一般英语转向学术英语的需要。

本系列教材的设计与编写主要依据两大原则：语言学习规律和高等教育特点。根据语言学习规律，语言输入为语言产出的基础，语言产出需与语言输入相结合，外语学习尤其如此。因此，本系列教材采用了以读促写、读写结合的编写理念。同时，掌握一门语言的读写能力遵循一定的先后顺序，如先学组词、造句、写段落，然后是记叙文、说明文、议论文等。在此基础上，进行更高层次的读写学习，即综述读写、论文读写等。另外，高等教育在很大程度上是专业教育，培养与专业相关的学术素养（如综述、议论、思辨、研究规范等）对学生而言至关重要。因此，大学英语教育应该顺应和符合学生的专业发展需求。具体而言，本科和研究生英语教育均需培养学生用英语完成说明文、议论文、文献综述和研究论文等不同语体的读写能力。

鉴于此，本系列教材1~4册分别围绕高等教育中最常用的四个学术语体进行设计与编写，即说明文、议论文、文献综述、研究论文。同时，这四册教材又针对高等教育对学生的学术素养要求，专门就常用的学术读写能力进行训练，包括学术阅读技能、学术词汇扩展、学术语言特点、学术文本特点、学术写作技巧（如paraphrasing）等。这些能力的训练贯穿于整个1~4册教材系列。

本系列教材是在教育全球化的新形势下为满足我国高校人才培养需求而开发的。教材

旨在为学生用英语顺利进行专业学习提供帮助和支撑，帮助学生掌握学术规范，提高学生的批判性和创造性思维，培养和提高学生的英语学术交流能力和专业学术素养，适用于本科生和研究生学习。我们相信，通过本系列教材的学习，学生不仅会进一步提高一般的英语交流能力，更能提高学术英语交流能力和跨文化学术素养。

感谢本系列教材的每一位编委专家为教材进行全面细致的审读，并提出宝贵的意见和建议，使得教材的编写更加契合广大院校培养优秀的研究型人才之目标，更加符合各高校英语教学向学术英语转型的要求。

丛书主编
2013 年 7 月

前 言

　　《英语议论文读写教程》是"通用学术英语读写系列教材"的第二部。议论文是大学生在学术阅读和学术写作过程中经常遇到的一种重要体裁，学生的学术水平在较大程度上取决于学生阅读、理解、评判和论述观点的能力。本教程重点突出不同的学术英语议论文写作技巧，从多角度阐述、训练议论文读写，旨在培养、提高中等英语水平学生的学术英语议论文读写能力。

适用对象和教学目标

　　本册教材适用对象是英语能力达到《大学英语课程教学要求》规定的"较高要求"的学生，或水平相当的英语学习者，旨在培养学生的学术英语议论文阅读和写作技能，为未来学术发展打下语言基础。具体教学目标如下：

- 运用和提高基础学术英语阅读技巧，如略读、寻读、记笔记等；
- 运用和提高基础学术英语写作技巧，如转述、概述、避免抄袭等；
- 掌握学术英语议论文写作技巧，如篇章组织、论据运用、合理论证、反驳技巧等；
- 了解学术英语文章的特点及学术英语和非学术英语的差别；
- 扩大学术英语词汇量，掌握并运用高频学术词汇。

内容安排

　　全书按照课文主题内容和写作特点分为 8 个单元，可以根据课时设置需要安排 4~6 个课时完成一个单元，一个学期完成全册内容的教学。每个单元分三大部分：

1. 议论文写作技巧讲解（Writing Skill Development）：

　　每个单元侧重议论文某个（些）特定的写作技巧，如运用数据、引用权威、合理论证、原因和结果、比较和对比、推理和归纳等；

2. 议论文阅读（Reading for Ideas）：

　　遵循阅读为写作准备语言和思想内容的原则，每单元所选三篇课文都集中体现了本单元的写作技巧，且围绕同一话题展开。每篇文章各有 800~1200 词左右。其中 Text A 为精读部分，Text B 和 Text C 为泛读部分，可由学生自学。通过精读和泛读，学生不仅能扩大学术英语词汇量，而且能够进一步熟悉学术英语的写作特点，掌握并熟练运用议论文各种写作技巧。

文章后的词汇表均为《大学英语课程教学要求》的纲内词汇，选词标准主要考虑词汇的 frequency（词汇在各种文章中出现的频率）、coverage（词汇取代其他词的能力）、needs and interest（学习者的需求及兴趣度）以及 familiarity（词汇的有用性和具体性）。词汇表中属于较高要求的单词标记为★，属于更高要求的单词标记为▲，超纲词汇不列入词汇表，其词意仅在文章中注明。

为了帮助学生更好地掌握和运用学术英语议论文阅读和写作技能，每篇阅读文章之后配有相应的练习。练习主要分为三大类：

议论文阅读训练：要求学生能够概括出文章的总论点，辨识出各分论点以及不同类型的论据，旨在帮助学生提高学术英语议论文阅读技能和扩大学术英语词汇量；

议论文写作训练：强化基础学术写作技巧，如转述、概述、避免抄袭等，旨在帮助学生巩固本单元的目标写作技巧；

段落写作：要求学生运用本单元的目标写作技巧完成特定题目的段落写作，也为单元复习中的篇章写作打下基础。

3. 单元复习（Unit Summary）：

全面复习、加强学生对该单元的理解和掌握。这一部分的篇章写作练习鼓励学生完成一篇完整文章的写作，其形式充分体现了过程写作和读写结合的教学理念。

教材特点

针对性强：本册着重议论文的读写，因此，每个单元侧重议论文的某个（些）写作技巧，该技巧不仅体现在该单元的每篇选文中，而且贯穿在该单元的练习中。

学术性强：本册所有选文均就某一话题提出观点、展开论证，行文规范，引用恰当，学术性强，为学生进行更高层次的学术写作（如文献综述写作、学术论文写作等）打下基础。

内容新颖，话题覆盖面广：本册涵盖八大不同领域的话题，如经济、工程、环境、哲学、信息工程、社会科学等，观点多样，内容丰富，涉及社会生活的方方面面。教学内容鲜活，具有国际性和时代感。

在编写本书的过程中，外籍教师 Diane Mcdowell 校对了本书的书稿，提出不少宝贵意见和建议，在此表示最诚挚的谢意。

由于编写时间仓促，编者热忱欢迎兄弟院校的使用者对本书的不足之处提出批评和指正。

编者
2013 年 3 月于清华园

Table of Contents

Unit 1

1. To know what an argumentative essay is;
2. To learn the basic structure of an argumentative essay;
3. To learn the basic components of an argumentative essay;
4. To be able to draft an outline with a clear structure and components for an argumentative essay.

Writing Skill Development

Basic Structure of an Argumentative Essay

What is an argumentative essay?

An argumentative essay makes a claim about a topic and justifies this claim with specific evidence. The claim could be an opinion, a policy proposal, an evaluation, a cause-and-effect statement, or an interpretation. The goal of the argumentative essay is to convince the audience that the claim is true based on the evidence provided.

Argumentative essay writing requires the author to investigate a topic, collect, and evaluate evidence, establish a position on the topic in a concise manner and show that he/she makes conclusions based on definite facts instead of on personal assumptions only.

The structure of an argumentative essay

➡ **A clear, concise and defined thesis statement that occurs in the first part of the essay**

The first part of an argumentative essay, which is generally understood as the introduction, is the broad beginning of the essay that fulfils the following tasks:

(a) *Set the context*—provide general information about the main idea, explaining the situation so the reader can make sense of the topic and the claims the author

makes and supports.

(b) *State why the main idea is important*—tell the reader why he/she should care about the issue and keep reading. The author's goal is to create a compelling, clear, and convincing essay people will want to read and act upon.

(c) *State the thesis/claim (thesis statement)*—compose a sentence or two stating the position the author will support with logos (sound reasoning: induction, deduction), pathos (balanced emotional appeal), and ethos (author credibility).

"Fixing" What Is Not Broken

[*Introduction*] [*Set the context*] Every pet owner knows that there are enormous responsibilities that go along with having a cat or dog. You must feed and exercise your pet, to keep it physically healthy; you must play with it, and keep it emotionally healthy too. You have to keep it safe from cars, people, or other animals, and you ought to protect other people, property, or pets from your own animal. There's another responsibility that not all pet owners think about, however: spaying or neutering, or "fixing". What does "fixing" your pet mean? Simply put, it means taking your pet to the vet for a quick, cheap surgery that will prevent your pet from ever becoming a mother or father. This surgery solves problems that pet owners know about, and some that they might not have considered before. [*Thesis statement*] In fact, I believe that all pet owners should be required to have their pets fixed.

Source: http://spot.pcc.edu.

➡ Clear and logical transitions between the introduction, body, and conclusion

Transitions are the links that hold the foundation of an essay together. Without logical progression of thought, the structure will collapse, and the reader is unable to follow the essay's argument. In other words, transitions tell readers what to do with the information presented to them.

Transitions should wrap up the idea from the previous section and introduce the idea that is to follow in the next section. Whether single words, quick phrases or full sentences, they function as signs for readers that tell them how to think about, organize, and react to old and new ideas as they read through what has been written (www.writingcentre.ubc.ca).

The organization of an argumentative essay includes two elements: (a) the order in which different parts of the discussion or argument are presented, and (b) the relationships constructed between these parts. Transitions cannot substitute for good organization, but they can make the organization clearer and easier to follow. Here are a few examples:

a. *In addition to this point,* there are many studies which establish a relationship between the income of one's parents and success in school.

b. *By contrast,* other passages of the poem suggest a totally different mood.

c. *This* emphasis on pharmaceutical intervention, *however,* brings with it real dangers. For example, the medication often brings immediately harmful side effects. *Moreover*, it can also create long-term addiction. Beyond that, there is the question of the expense. This being the case, one wonders why we are so keen to continue with this medication.

d. *Moreover,* rock 'n' roll music has exercised an important influence on civil rights in North America. In fact, in popular music since the 1950's, more than in any other activity (with the possible exception of professional sports), black people have won fame, fortune, and lasting status among the white middle-class.

Source: http://records.viu.ca.

As the examples suggest, transitions can help reinforce the underlying logic of an argument's organization by providing the reader with essential information regarding the relationship between the presented ideas. In this way, transitions act as the glue that binds the components of the argument or discussion into a unified, coherent, and persuasive whole.

➡ Body part with evidential support

Each paragraph should be limited to the discussion of one general idea. This allows for clarity and direction throughout the essay. In addition, such conciseness creates an ease of readability for the audience. It is important to note that each paragraph in the body of the essay must have some logical connection to the thesis statement in the opening paragraph. And each idea should be supported with evidence, whether factual, logical, statistical or anecdotal. The following are two examples:

The reasons for the lull suggest it should be temporary.

First, the tsunami in Japan sent its GDP tumbling and disrupted supply chains, and thus industrial output, around the world, particularly in April. But just as that slump shows up in the economic statistics, more forward-looking evidence points to a rebound. The summer production schedules of American car firms, for instance, indicate that the pace of annualized GDP growth there will accelerate by at least a percentage point.

Second, demand was dented by a sudden surge in oil prices earlier this year. More income is being shifted from cash-strapped consumers in oil-importing countries to producers who tend to sit on their treasures. Costlier fuel has knocked consumer confidence, particularly in gas-guzzling America. And there is still an uncomfortable possibility that further instability in the Arab world will send prices soaring again. Nonetheless, at least for now, the pressure is waning. America's average petrol price, though still 21% higher than at the beginning of the year, has started to fall. That should boost shoppers' morale (and their

spending).

Third, many emerging economies have tightened the monetary policy in response to high inflation. China's consumer-price inflation accelerated to 5.5% in the year to May. India's wholesale prices leapt by 9.1%. Slower growth is, in part, a welcome sign that their central banks have taken action, and that those measures are beginning to work. The bigger risk is that nervousness about a weakening world economy leads to a premature pause in the tightening. With monetary conditions still extraordinarily loose, such a loss of resolve would make higher inflation and an eventual crash far more likely.

Source: Sticky Patch or Meltdown, *The Economist*, June 16, 2011.

On the other end of the spectrum are metropolitan areas where prices still look bubbly. [*Evidential support*] In San Diego, the ratio was 22 at the end of last year. In northern and central New Jersey, it was 25, and it was 29 in Manhattan. In Silicon Valley and the nearby East Bay in California, the ratio was above 30.

Source: Rent or Buy, a Matter of Lifestyle, by David Leonhardt, *New York Times*, May 10, 2011.

An argumentative essay requires well-researched, accurate, detailed, and current information to support the thesis statement. Meanwhile, although it is not a must, argumentative essays should also consider and explain differing points of view regarding the topic. Depending on the length of the assignment, the author should dedicate one or two paragraphs of an argumentative essay to discussing conflicting opinions on the topic. In addition to explaining how these differing opinions are wrong outright, the author could also note how opinions that do not align with the thesis might not be well informed or how they might be out of date.

[*counter-argument*] Of course, some people will not agree with me. "I don't want to give my animal an unnecessary surgery," they will say. "Surgery is risky, too, and it's certainly expensive." [*rebuttal*] That idea shows ignorance. Spaying or neutering should be done as soon as you get your pet—when he or she is young and healthy—and it is almost 100% safe. Your animal is in much more danger if not fixed, for the urge to run away from home will put your pet in extremely dangerous situations. And almost all cities have a fund to help pay for the surgery. Just ask your vet or the local S.P.C.A. The cost can be as low as $10.

Source: http://spot.pcc.edu.

➡ Logic in argumentation

Logic is a formal system of analysis that helps authors invent, demonstrate, and prove arguments (www.articlesbase.com). There are two basic types of reasoning processes: deduction and induction.

Deduction begins with a general principle or premise and draws a specific conclusion from it. The strength and validity of a deductive argument depend upon three things: (a) there must be agreement about the general principle with which the argument begins; (b) the special application must be correct and clear, with no disputes about its validity; (c) the conclusion must be derived properly from putting these two together (www.articlesbase.com). Here is a simple example:

[*major premise*]	All people who smoke endanger their health.
[*minor premise*]	My father smokes.
[*conclusion*]	Therefore, my father is endangering his health.

Induction supports a general conclusion by examining specific facts or cases. The basis of all induction is the repeated observation, so that the facts about similar experiences accumulate to the point where one sees a repetitive pattern and can draw a conclusion about it (www.articlesbase.com). Having repeatedly observed in similar circumstances the same event or one very similar, the author draws a conclusion about the pattern he/she has seen. The following is a simple example:

[*specific fact*]	My father's teeth are yellowish and he's lost a considerable amount of weight.
[*specific fact*]	My father's no longer able to cycle his 25km every morning.
[*specific fact*]	Whenever my father exerts himself physically, he ends up coughing extremely hard.
[*conclusion*]	My father was endangering his health.

➡ **A conclusion that does not simply restate the thesis, but readdresses it in light of the evidence provided**

This is the part of the essay that will leave the most immediate impression on the mind of the reader. Therefore, it must be effective and logical. Do not introduce any new information into the conclusion; rather, synthesize the information presented in the body of the essay, restate why the topic is important, review the main points, and review the thesis (www.owl.english.purdue.edu). The author may also include a short discussion of more research that should be completed in light of his/her work.

Fed policy is determined by inflation and unemployment in the United States. But if Mr. Bernanke could discuss the exchange rate openly, he would probably tell you that [***Conclusion***] one way any monetary expansion helps a distressed economy is by weakening the dollar. That is taught in every introductory economics course, yet the Fed is asked to pretend it isn't true.

Source: Needed: Plain Talk About the Dollar, by **Christina D. Romer**, *Economic View*, **May 21, 2011.**

In general, an argumentative essay may consist of the following parts: introduction, support, counter-argument (optional), refutation (optional) and conclusion (www.writingcentre.ubc.ca). **Introduction** presents a general discussion of a problem and expresses the author's opinion in a thesis statement. **Support** uses different types of evidence to support the author's opinion/claim. **Counter-argument** includes a summary of the first two parts and introduces the strongest argument against the author's claim. **Refutation** explains why the counter-argument is wrong, which is often done in three steps: (a) start with a refutation sentence (*However...*); (b) support the opinion with evidence; (c) explain evidence. **Conclusion** presents a summary of the primary points and restatement of the thesis, and may also include recommendations for further actions in the area.

Reading for Ideas

Text Ⓐ

Drain or Gain?[1]

❶   When people in rich countries worry about migration, they tend to think of low-paid incomers who compete for jobs as construction workers, dishwashers or farm-hands. When people in developing countries worry about migration, they are usually concerned at the **prospect** of their best and brightest decamping (迁户) to Silicon Valley (硅谷) or to hospitals and universities in the developed world. These are the kind of workers that countries like Britain, Canada and Australia try to attract by using immigration rules that **privilege** college graduates.

❷   Lots of studies have found that well-educated people from developing countries are particularly likely to emigrate. By some estimates, two-thirds of highly educated Cape Verdeans (佛得角人) live outside the country. A big **survey** of Indian **households** carried out in 2004 asked about family members who had moved abroad. It found that nearly 40% of emigrants had more than a high-school education, compared with around 3.3% of all Indians over the age of 25. This "brain drain" has long bothered policymakers in poor countries. They fear that it hurts their economies, **depriving** them of much-needed skilled workers who could have taught at their universities, worked in their hospitals and **come up with** clever new products for their factories to make.

❸   Many now **take issue with** this view. Several economists believe that the brain-drain **hypothesis** fails to account for the effects of **remittances**, for the beneficial effects of returning migrants, and for the possibility that being able to migrate to greener

---

1 This article was taken from *The Economist*, May 26, 2011.

pastures induces people to get more education. Some argue that once these factors are **taken into account**, an exodus（尤指移民大批地离开）of highly skilled people could turn out to be a **net** benefit to the countries they leave. Recent studies of migration have found support for this "brain gain" idea.

4   The most obvious way in which migrants repay their homelands is through remittances. Workers from developing countries remitted a total of $325 billion in 2010, according to the World Bank. In Lebanon（黎巴嫩）, Lesotho（莱索托）, Nepal（尼泊尔）, Tajikistan（塔吉克斯坦）and a few other places, remittances are more than 20% of GDP （gross domestic product, 国内生产总值）. A skilled migrant may earn several **multiples** of what his income would have been had he stayed at home. A study of Romanian migrants to America found that the average emigrant earned almost $12,000 a year more in America than he would have made in his native land, a huge **premium** for someone from a country where income per person is around $7,500 (at market exchange rates).

5   It is true that many skilled migrants have been educated and trained partly **at the expense of** their governments. Some argue that poor countries should therefore rethink how much they spend on higher education. Indians, for example, often debate whether their government should continue to **subsidize** the Indian Institutes of Technology (IIT), its elite engineering schools, when large numbers of IIT graduates **end up** in Silicon Valley or on Wall Street. But a new study of remittances sent home by Ghanaian migrants suggests that on average they **transfer** enough over their working lives to cover the amount spent on educating them several times over. The study finds that once remittances are taken into account, the cost of education would have to be 5.6 times the official figure to make it a losing **proposition** for Ghana（加纳）.

6   There are more **subtle** ways in which the departure of some skilled people may aid poorer countries. Some emigrants would have been jobless had they stayed. Studies have found that unemployment rates among young people with college degrees in countries like Morocco（摩洛哥）and Tunisia（突尼斯）are several multiples of those among the poorly educated, perhaps because graduates are more demanding. Migration may lead to a more productive pairing of people's skills and jobs. Some of the benefits of this improved match then flow back to the migrant's home country, most directly via remittances.

7   The possibility of emigration may even have beneficial effects on those who choose to stay, by giving people in poor countries an **incentive** to invest in education. A study of Cape Verdeans finds that an increase of ten percentage points in young people's **perceived** probability of emigrating raises the probability of their completing secondary school by around eight points. Another study looks at Fiji（斐济）. A series of **coups**

beginning in 1987 was seen by Fijians of Indian origin as **permanently** harming their prospects in the country by limiting their share of government jobs and political power. This **set off** a wave of emigration. Yet young Indians in Fiji became more likely to go to a university even as the outlook at home **dimmed**, in part because Australia, Canada and New Zealand, three of the top destinations for Fijians, put more emphasis on attracting skilled migrants. Since some of those who got more education ended up staying, the skill levels of the resident Fijian population **soared**.

8   Migrants can also affect their home country directly. In a recent book about the Indian diaspora（离散人口）, Devesh Kapur of the University of Pennsylvania argues that Indians in Silicon Valley helped shape the **regulatory** structure for India's home-grown venture-capital（风险资本）industry. He also argues that these people helped Indian software companies break into the American market by vouching（担保、保证）for their quality. Migrants may finally return home, often with skills that would have been hard to **pick up** had they never gone abroad. The study of Romanian migrants found that returnees earned an average of 12%–14% more than similar people who had stayed at home.

9   Letting educated people go where they want looks like the brainy option.

📔 Words and Phrases

▲ coup	[ku:]	*n.*	政变
★ deprive	[di'praiv]	*vt.*	剥夺对某物的所有（或使用）
dim	[dim]	*vi.*	变暗淡，变模糊
household	['haushəuld]	*n.*	家庭，户
★ hypothesis	[hai'pɔθəsis]	*n.*	假设，前提
★ incentive	[in'sentiv]	*n.*	激励某人做某事的事物；诱因，动机
induce	[in'dju:s]	*vt.*	导致，引起
multiple	['mʌltipl]	*n.*	倍数
net	[net]	*a.*	纯的，净的，无虚价的
★ pasture	['pɑ:stʃə]	*n.*	牧草地，牧场
perceive	[pə'si:v]	*vt. & vi.*	意识到，察觉；理解
permanently	['pɜ:mənəntli]	*adv.*	永久地，耐久地，持久地
★ premium	['pri:miəm]	*n.*	费用，额外补贴
privilege	['privəlidʒ]	*n.*	（因财富和地位而享有的）特权
★ proposition	[ˌprɔpə'ziʃn]	*n.*	企业，事业

prospect	['prɔspekt]	n.	未来事件发生的可能性
★ regulatory	['regjələtəri]	a.	调整的
▲ remittance	[ri'mitns]	n.	（尤指邮汇）汇款，汇款额
			▲ remit vt. & vi. 汇款
soar	[sɔ:]	vi.	猛增
▲ subsidize	['sʌbsidaiz]	vt.	在财政上支持；补助，资助
subtle	['sʌtl]	a.	微妙的；巧妙的；敏感的
survey	['sɜ:vei]	n.	调查，调查表
transfer	[træns'fɜ:]	vt.	转移；调动；转让

at the expense of	以……为代价，在损失……的情况下
come up with	提出，想出；产生
end up	以……结束，最终成为
pick up	（无意地、不费劲地）得到；学会
set off	引起
take into account	重视；考虑，顾及
take issue with	提出异议

 **Exercises**

Part I. Understanding the text

1. Read the first three paragraphs of the essay and then answer the following questions.

1) What is the context of the issue that will be discussed in the essay?

2) In what aspects will an exodus of highly skilled people be "brain gain" for the countries they leave?

Argument	Aspects
An exodus of highly skilled people could turn out to be a net benefit to the countries they leave (brain gain).	_____ _____ _____

3) What is the thesis statement of this essay?

Part II. Writing skills development

2. Read Paragraphs 4–8 of the essay.

1) Read Paragraph 4 and do the following exercises.

a. The first sentence in a paragraph is often called a topic sentence. One key function of a topic sentence is to anticipate the ideas that follow. It helps readers to understand the focus and direction of the paragraph.

The topic sentence of Paragraph 4 is: _____

_____

b. What pieces of evidence are used to support the argument in Paragraph 4?

Argument	Evidence
The most obvious way in which migrants repay their homelands is through remittances.	(1) _____ _____ (2) _____ _____

2) Read Paragraph 5 and answer the following questions.

a. What is the argument of this paragraph?

b. How does the refutation work in this paragraph?

3) Read Paragraph 6 and find the evidence to support the argument "Some emigrants would have been jobless had they stayed."

4) Read Paragraphs 7 and 8 and find the evidence that are used to support the argument in each paragraph.

Argument	Evidence
Paragraph 7 _____ _____	(1) _____ (2) _____
Paragraph 8 _____ _____	(1) _____ (2) _____

Part III. Language focus

3. Choose the right word to complete each of the following sentences. Change the form where necessary.

coup	dim	induce	multiple	privilege
prospect	hypothesis	remit	soar	subsidize

1) He _____ some money to his mother.

2) We could not _____ the old lady to travel by air.

3) Old age has not _____ her memory.

4) His imagination resembled the wing of an ostrich and it enabled him to run, though not to _____.

5) Giving is not the _____ of the rich, but that of the sincere.

6) _____ descriptions are allowed in order to accommodate descriptions in different languages.

7) It's the old and the poor who suffer worst when _____ are cut.

8) I hope you can give this issue your immediate attention so that I can notify the _____ guests promptly.

9) Our _____ is that sitting in traffic jams costs us around $9 billion a year in lost output.

10) Haiti's first elected president was deposed in a violent military _____.

4. Paraphrase the following sentences.

> **Tips:**
>
> ❖ When paraphrasing a passage or a sentence, you express the meaning of the original text in a *different* way.
> ❖ When paraphrasing, you need to change both the *structure* and the *words* of the original text.
> ❖ When changing the structure, you may begin by starting at a *different place* in the passage and/ or sentence(s). You may also *break up* long sentences, *combine* short ones, *expand* phrases for clarity, or *shorten* them for conciseness.
> ❖ When changing the words, you may use *synonyms* or a *phrase* that expresses the same meaning.
> ❖ It's important to start by changing the structure, not the words, but you might find that as you change the words, you see ways to change the structure further.

1) Several economists believe that the brain-drain hypothesis fails to account for the effects of remittances, for the beneficial effects of returning migrants, and for the possibility that being able to migrate to greener pastures induces people to get more education.

2) A study of Romanian migrants to America found that the average emigrant earned almost $12,000 a year more in America than he would have made in his native land, a huge premium for someone from a country where income per person is around $7,500 (at market exchange rates).

3) The study finds that once remittances are taken into account, the cost of education would have to be 5.6 times the official figure to make it a losing proposition for Ghana.

Part IV. Writing

5. Now prepare to write an argumentative essay on *Emigration Is Brain Drain for China*. Work out an outline of your essay in the following format with a topic sentence for each paragraph (Note: Part 3 is optional).

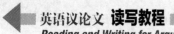
Part 1. Introduction (general discussion of a problem and thesis statement)

Part 2. Body (arguments that support your opinion)

Argument a: _____

Argument b: _____

Argument c: _____

Part 3. Body (counter-argument and refutation)

The strongest argument against your claim: _____

Why the counter-argument is wrong: (However, ...) _____

Part 4. Conclusion (summary of the primary points and restatement of the thesis)

Criteria for good argumentative writing:

1) **Task fulfillment:** Does the author achieve the writing purpose? Does the essay meet the requirements stated in writing prompts or instructions (like essay length, content, etc.)?

2) **Clear organization:** Is the overall argument clearly presented (in introduction and/or conclusion)? Does each paragraph have a topic sentence? Are the ideas clearly and logically organized?

3) **Effective argumentation:** Are all arguments supported with evidence? Does all the evidence support the overall argument? Is there any flaw in the reasoning?

4) **Conciseness:** Is there irrelevant evidence or redundant expressions?

5) **Originality:** Are the arguments new and original? Is the evidence fresh? Are all sources recognized to avoid plagiarism?

6) **Readability:** Are different types of evidence and rhetorical devices used in the writing? Does the author have a distinct personal style?

Text B

Rent or Buy, a Matter of Lifestyle[1] (Adapted)

By David Leonhardt[2]

❶   Real estate agents across the country are **aggressively making the case** that now is a good time to buy a house. **Mortgage** rates are near record lows and will probably rise in coming years. Home prices may not be done falling, but they probably don't have much further to go in most places either. Rents, on the other hand, seem **set to** increase, thanks to low vacancy rates（房屋空置率）.

---

1 This article was taken from *New York Times*, May 10, 2011.

2 David Leonhardt writes "Economic Scene," a weekly economics column, for *The New York Times* business section, looking at both the broad American economy and the economics of everyday life. Many of his recent columns have focused on effects of the economic downturn. In April 2011 Mr. Leonhardt was awarded the Pulitzer Prize for commentary.

❷　Individually, each of these points is **unobjectionable**. But it's important to remember the source. Real estate agents, like mortgage **brokers** and home builders, have a big financial **stake** in persuading people to buy homes. That's why many agents are always pushing home buying, whatever the rationale（理由，逻辑依据）of the moment happens to be.

❸　The truth is that you can make just as strong a case in many places for renting. For starters, neither mortgage rates nor rents are likely to rise rapidly. Even more important, house prices, relative to rents, remain higher than their long-term average, especially in much of California, the Pacific Northwest and the New York region. In these places, among others, renting is often cheaper than buying.

❹　As this year's spring buying season nears its peak, the relative **merits** of renting and buying are closer than they have been since the housing **bubble** began **inflating** almost a decade ago. So the best single piece of advice for most people is to make a decision based mainly on their stage of life, rather than on any complex financial calculations.

❺　If you think you are ready to settle in one place for at least five years, buying often makes a lot of sense. But if **the chances are** good that you will move again in the next few years, renting is usually the better bet. The various closing costs（产权转移费用）, including real estate agents' **fees**, are just too high. Owning a house also makes it much harder to move when you want to because selling a house is complicated.

❻　Within this basic **framework**, the numbers—specifically, something called rent ratios—are the next place to turn to. A rent ratio is the sale price of a house divided by the annual cost of renting an equivalent house. When the ratio is below 15, most people should **lean toward buying.**

❼　To see why, look at the Atlanta area, where the average ratio is now about 13. Combined with today's low interest rates, that ratio means that the typical monthly mortgage payment is several hundred dollars lower than the rent on an equivalent house. Over time, this difference helps **make up for** the other costs of owning, like closing costs and borrowing costs. And, yes, a mortgage costs money, despite the tax **deduction**. Only if home prices in Atlanta fall further and don't recover for years would most buyers today have reason for regret.

❽　On the other end of the **spectrum** are **metropolitan** areas where prices still look **bubbly**. In San Diego, the ratio was 22 at the end of last year. In northern and central New Jersey, it was 25, and it was 29 in Manhattan. In Silicon Valley and the nearby East Bay in California, the ratio was above 30.

❾　All these numbers are well down from their peaks from about five years ago. But they're still higher than they were in the decades before the housing bubble. They are also high enough to make the monthly costs of owning **steeper** than the costs of renting.

⑩   As **a rule of thumb**, a ratio above roughly 20 means that a monthly mortgage bill is higher than rent for a similar house. In Silicon Valley, the after-tax mortgage payment on a typical house might be $3,500—while the rent on the same house would be only about $2,500. The **arithmetic** of owning then gets mighty tough. **On top of** closing costs and mortgage costs, owners are also falling further behind renters each month.

⑪   When you look at the numbers this way, it's easy to conclude that the **excesses** of the housing bubble are mostly gone in much of the country. Yet you also start wondering whether New York, San Francisco, Seattle and a few other places still have a housing **crash** in their future.

⑫   I realize there are some important caveats（附加说明）here. **Affluent** people tend to want to own their houses, even when the dollars don't **make sense**. Yet the fact remains that a lot of New Yorkers and Californians, among others, are paying a hefty （数额巨大的）premium for the privilege of owning.

⑬   A crash **strikes** me as unlikely. But any potential homebuyers should know that real estate **exuberance**—irrational exuberance, it seems—has survived in at least a few places.

 Words and Phrases

▲ affluent	['æfluənt]	*a.*	富裕的，富足的
aggressively	[ə'gresivli]	*adv.*	侵略地；有进取心地；好争斗地
arithmetic	[ə'riθmətik]	*n.*	算术；计算
★ broker	['brəukə]	*n.*	（股票债券等的）经纪人；（买卖的）代理人
bubble	[bʌbl]	*n.*	泡；水泡；泡影
bubbly	['bʌbli]	*a.*	气泡的，冒泡的
crash	[kræʃ]	*n.*	（商业）失败，凋敝，崩溃，破产；瓦解
★ deduction	[di'dʌkʃn]	*n.*	扣除，减除
excess	['ekses]	*n.*	超过；超额量；多余量
▲ exuberance	[ig'zju:bərəns]	*n.*	活跃；愉快；茁壮
fee	[fi:]	*n.*	（加入组织或做某事付的）费；专业服务费，业务报酬；小费，赏钱
framework	['freimwɜ:k]	*n.*	构架；框架；（体系的）结构；组织

▲	inflate	[in'fleit]	vt. & vi.	使膨胀，使物价上涨
	merit	['merit]	n.	长处，优点，价值
★	metropolitan	[ˌmetrə'pɔlitən]	a.	大都会的，大城市的
★	mortgage	['mɔːgidʒ]	n.	抵押贷款
★	spectrum	['spektrəm]	n.	范围；系列
	stake	[steik]	n.	赌本；利益
	steep	[stiːp]	a.	（价格，需求）难以接受的；过高的
	strike	[straik]	vt. & vi.	给……以印象
	unobjectionable	[ˌʌnəb'dʒekʃənəbl]	a.	不会招致反对的；可以接受的
				objection *n.* 反对

----

a rule of thumb	经验法则
lean toward doing sth.	倾向于做某事
make sense	讲得通，有意义
make the case	提出理由证明
make up for	弥补
on top of	除……之外
set to	开始起劲地干
the chances are ...	大概是，很可能是

 **Exercises**

Part I. Understanding the text

1. Read the first three paragraphs of the essay.

1) Decide how the author supports the argument in the first paragráph.

Argument	Supports
Now is a good time to buy a house.	(1)_____
	(2)_____
	(3)_____

2) The second paragraph is a refutation against the argument made by real estate agents in the first paragraph. Explain the basic structure of the refutation as follows:

1—start with a refutation sentence	But…
2—support your opinion by evidence	
3—explain the evidence	

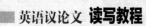

3) Decide how the author supports his argument in the third paragraph.

Argument	Supports
Now is a good time to rent a house.	(1) _____ (2) _____

2. Read the text again and work out the outline of the essay.

Introduction: _____

Body: _____

_____

_____

Conclusion: _____

Further thoughts: _____

Part II. Writing skills development

3. Read Paragraphs 4–10 and do the following exercises.

1) Fill in the diagram below according to Paragraphs 4 and 5.

If...

Argument:
Make decisions (as to buy or to rent) based on one's stage of life

If...

2) Fill in the diagram below according to Paragraphs 6–10.

Argument:

When the ratio is below 15—
_____

Evidence: _____
_____

When the ratio is above 20—
_____

Evidence: _____
_____

3) Fill out the table below according to Paragraphs 4–10.

	To Buy	To Rent
Years of staying in one place		
Rent ratios		

Part III. Language focus

4. Choose the right word to complete each of the following sentences. Change the form where necessary.

affluent	objection	crash	deduction	exuberance
inflate	merit	stake	steep	strike

1) Advancing technology and _____ make it easier to modify living conditions and the management of resource.

2) National pride is at _____ in next week's game against England.

3) These pressures have been largely unnoticed due to stock market _____.

4) In the days after the stock _____, it seemed logical that the market would drag New York City's prosperous economy down with it.

5) Adaptive re-use has in this case rescued a building of great historical and architectural _____ from the brink of disaster.

6) The country is now facing the most serious problems of soaring _____, rising prices and growing unemployment.

7) In addition, there is also snow king ski area in town which has some surprisingly _____ runs and is open for night skiing.

8) In certain cases, we recommend making itemized _____ which can reduce your taxable income.

9) There is no right to _____ against the public safety by anybody, anywhere, at any time.

10) The group _____ that the policy would prevent patients from receiving the best treatment.

5. Paraphrase the following sentences.

1) Real estate agents, like mortgage brokers and home builders, have a big financial stake in persuading people to buy homes.

2) As this year's spring buying season nears its peak, the relative merits of renting and buying are closer than they have been since the housing bubble began inflating almost a decade ago.

3) Combined with today's low interest rates, that ratio means that the typical monthly

mortgage payment is several hundred dollars lower than the rent on an equivalent house.

Part IV. Writing

6. **Now prepare to write an argumentative essay on *Rise or Fall: The Future of Real Estate in China*. Work out an outline of your essay in the following format with a topic sentence for each paragraph (Note: Part 3 is optional).**

Part 1. Introduction (general discussion of a problem and thesis statement)

Part 2. Body (arguments that support your opinion)

Argument a: _____

Argument b: _____

Argument c: _____

Part 3. Body (counter-argument and refutation)

The strongest argument against your claim: _____

Why the counter-argument is wrong: (However, …) _____

Part 4. Conclusion (summary of the primary points and restatement of the thesis)

Text ❸

Comeback Kid—America's Economy
Is Once Again Reinventing Itself[1] (Abridged)

❶   Almost the only thing on which Barack Obama and Mitt Romney, his Republican challenger, agree is that the economy is in a bad way. Unemployment is stuck above 8% and growth probably **slipped** below an annualized 2% in the first half of this year. Ahead lie the threats of a euro break-up, a slowdown in China and the "fiscal (国库的，财政的) cliff", a **withering** year-end combination of tax increases and spending cuts. President Obama and Mr. Romney disagree only on what would make things worse: re-electing a left-wing president who has regulated to death a private sector he neither likes nor understands; or **swapping** him for a rapacious(贪婪的)private-equity(私募股权投资基金)man **bent on** enriching the very people who caused the mess.

❷   America's economy is certainly in a **tender** state. But the pessimism of the presidential slanging-match(互相漫骂)misses something **vital**. Led by its inventive private

1 The article was taken from *The Economist*, July 14, 2012. http://www.economist.com/node/21558576?spc=scode&spv=xm&ah=9d7f7ab945510a56fa6d37c30b6f1709.

sector, the economy is remaking itself. Old weaknesses are being **remedied** and new strengths discovered, with an agility（轻快）that has much to teach **stagnant** Europe and dirigiste（国家干预经济的）Asia.

❸ America's **sluggishness stems** above all **from** pre-crisis excesses and the mis-shapen（畸形的）economy they created. Until 2008 growth relied too heavily on consumer spending and house-buying, both of them financed by foreign savings channeled through an **undercapitalized** financial system. Household debt, already nearly 100% of income in 2000, reached 133% in 2007. Recoveries always take years, as households and banks repair their balance-sheets（资产负债表）.

❹ Nonetheless, in the past three years that repair has proceeded fast. America's houses are now among the world's most undervalued: 19% below fair value, according to our house-price **index**. And because the Treasury and other regulators, unlike their euro-zone counterparts, chose to confront the **rot** in their financial system quickly, American banks have had to **write off** debts and raise equity faster than their peers. (Citigroup alone has **flushed** through some $143 billion of loan losses; no euro-zone bank has set aside more than $30 billion.) American capital ratios（资产率）are among the world's highest. And consumers have **cut back**, too: debts are now 114% of income.

❺ New strengths have also been found. One is a more dynamic export sector. The weaker dollar helps explain why the trade deficit has **shrunk** from 6% of GDP in 2006 to about 4% today. But other, more permanent, shifts—especially the growth of a consuming class in emerging markets—augur（预兆）well. A richer China has become the third-largest market for America's exports, up 53% since 2007.

❻ And American exporters are changing. Some of the products—Boeing jets, Microsoft software and Hollywood films—are familiar. But there is a **boom**, too, in high-value services (architecture, engineering and finance) and a growing "app economy", nurtured by Facebook, Apple and Google, which employs more than 300,000 people; its games, virtual **merchandise** and so on sell effortlessly across borders. **Constrained** by weakness at home and in Europe, even small companies are seeking a toehold（立足点）in emerging markets. American manufacturers are recapturing some markets once lost to imports, and pioneering new processes such as 3D printing.

❼ Meanwhile, what was once an Achilles heel[1] is becoming a competitive advantage. America has paid dearly for its addiction to imported oil. Whenever West Texas Intermediate[2] climbs above $100 per **barrel** (as it did in 2008, last year and again this year), growth suffers. But high prices have had an effect, **restraining** demand and stimulating

---

1. Achilles heel: a deadly weakness in spite of overall strength, that can actually or potentially lead to downfall.
2. West Texas Intermediate (WTI) 美国西德克萨斯轻质原油，是具有代表性的国际市场原油价格。

supply. Net imports of oil this year are **on track** to be the lowest since 1995, and America should eventually become a net exporter of gas.

8 America's **work-out** is not finished. Even when the results are more visible, it will leave many problems unsolved. Because the companies leading the process are so productive, they pay high wages but do not employ many people. They may thus do little to reduce unemployment, while **aggravating** inequality. Yet this is still a more balanced and **sustainable** basis for growth than what America had before—and a far better **platform** for prosperity than unreformed, elderly Europe.

9 What should the next president do to generate muscle in this new economy? First, do no harm. Not driving the economy over the fiscal cliff would be a start: instead, settle on a credible long-term deficit plan that includes both tax rises and cuts to **entitlement** programs. Second, the next president should fix America's ramshackle （破烂不堪的） public services. Even the most productive start-ups cannot help an economy held back by dilapidated （毁坏的） roads, the world's most expensive health system, underachieving （学习成绩不良的） union-dominated schools and a Byzantine （复杂难解的） immigration system that deprives companies of the world's best talents. Focus on those things, President Obama and Mr. Romney, and you will be surprised what America's private sector can do for itself.

Words and Phrases

★ aggravate	['ægrəveit]	*vt.*	加重（剧），使恶化；激怒，使恼火
barrel	['bærəl]	*n.*	桶；一桶之量
boom	[bu:m]	*n.*	隆隆声；繁荣；激增
▲ undercapitalized	[ˌʌndə'kæpitəlaizd]	*a.*	投资不足的
			capitalize *vt.* 投资于，提供资本给……
★ constrain	[kən'strein]	*vt.*	强迫，强使；限制，约束
entitlement	[in'taitlmənt]	*n.*	授权；应得权益；命名，被定名
★ flush	[flʌʃ]	*vt.*	（以水）冲刷，冲洗；冲掉，除掉
index	['indeks]	*n.*	索引；指数；指示；标志
▲ merchandise	['mɜ:tʃəndaiz]	*n.*	商品；货物
platform	['plætfɔ:m]	*n.*	台；站台；平台；纲领
remedy	['remədi]	*vt.*	改正，纠正；改进，补救；治疗
restrain	[ri'strein]	*vt.*	抑制，压抑；限定，限制；制止
★ rot	[rɔt]	*n.*	腐烂，腐朽

shrink	[ʃriŋk]	vt. & vi.	收缩，皱缩；（使）缩水；退缩，畏缩
slip	[slip]	vi.	滑；出错，变差
▲ sluggishness	['slʌgiʃnəs]	n.	萧条；呆滞；惰性，滞性
			▲ sluggish a. 怠惰的
▲ stagnant	['stægnənt]	a.	停滞的；萧条的
sustainable	[sə'steinəbl]	a.	可持续的；可以忍受的；可支撑的
★ swap	[swɔp]	vt. & vi.	交换
tender	['tendə]	a.	脆弱的；温柔的
vital	['vaitl]	a.	至关重要的，生死攸关的
▲ withering	['wiðəriŋ]	a.	使人畏缩的；使人害羞的；使人难堪的

bend on (doing)	一心做某事
cut back	减少
on track	在……道路上，走上正轨
stem from	来自，起源于；由……造成；出于
work-out	健身，锻炼
write off	购销；注销

 **Exercises**

Part I. Understanding the text

1. Read the first two paragraphs of the essay.

1) Fill out the table below according to Paragraph 1.

Argument	Evidence
Economy is in a bad way.	(1) _____
	(2) _____
	(3) _____
	(4) _____

2) Answer the following questions according to Paragraph 2.

   a. What writing skill is used in this paragraph?

   b. What is the thesis statement of this paragraph?

2. Read Paragraph 9 and answer the following questions.

1) What should the next president do to generate muscle in this new economy?

   First, _____

Second, _____

2) Does this paragraph work well as a conclusion of the essay?

Part II. Writing skills development

3. **Read Paragraphs 3–8 and fill out the table below.**

Argument	Evidence
(Paragraphs 3 and 4)	(1) America's houses are now among the world's most undervalued.
	(2)
	(3)
	(4)
	Type of evidence
	Writing technique
	contrast

Argument	Evidence
(Paragraph 5)	(1)
	(2)
	Type of evidence

Argument	Evidence
(Paragraph 6)	(1) Some of the products—Boeing jets, Microsoft software and Hollywood films—are familiar.
	(2)
	(3)
	(4) Small companies are seeking a toehold in emerging markets (3D)…
	Type of evidence

(continued)

Argument	Evidence		
(Paragraph 7)			
	Type of evidence		
	Writing technique		
Argument	**Writing technique**		
(Paragraph 8)			

Part III. Language focus

4. **Choose the right word to complete each of the following sentences. Change the form where necessary.**

aggravate	slip	capitalize	swap
remedy	rot	sluggish	stagnant

1) The government is eager to attract foreign _____.

2) The film was pretty _____.

3) There was a 50–50 chance that the economy could _____ back into recession.

4) Their money problems were further _____ by a rise in interest rates.

5) The group's international sales remained _____ compared to last year's 5% decrease.

6) An occasionally slightly _____ performance by the orchestra didn't seem to hinder the fluidity of movement on the stage.

7) I'll _____ my Michael Jackson tape for your Bruce Springsteen album.

8) It has been estimated that over 70% of the visual impairment present in people aged 65 and over is potentially _____.

5. **Paraphrase the following sentences.**

1) President Obama and Mr. Romney disagree only on what would make things worse: re-electing a left-wing president who has regulated to death a private sector he neither likes nor understands; or swapping him for a rapacious private-equity man bent on enriching the very people who caused the mess.

2) Until 2008 growth relied too heavily on consumer spending and house-buying, both of them financed by foreign savings channeled through an undercapitalized

financial system.

3) Even the most productive start-ups cannot help an economy held back by dilapidated roads, the world's most expensive health system, underachieving union-dominated schools and a Byzantine immigration system that deprives companies of the world's best talents.

Part IV. Writing

6. **Now prepare to write an argumentative essay on** *Is It Time to Shift from Real Estate to New Economic Growth Point for China*? **Work out an outline of your essay in the following format with a topic sentence for each paragraph (Note: Part 3 is optional).**

Part 1. Introduction (general discussion of a problem and thesis statement)

Part 2. Body (arguments that support your opinion)

Argument a: _____

Argument b: _____

Argument c: _____

Part 3. Body (counter-argument and refutation)

The strongest argument against your claim: _____

Why the counter-argument is wrong: (However, …)_____

Part 4. Conclusion (summary of the primary points and restatement of the thesis)

Unit Summary

In this unit, you have studied the basic structure of an argumentative essay. Now, do the following exercises to consolidate your knowledge.

1. Answer the following questions.

1) What is an argumentative essay?

2) What are the main parts of an argumentative essay?

3) Why should argumentative essays also consider and explain differing points of view regarding the topic?

4) What is counter-argument?

2. Read the following extracts and estimate which part (introduction, body, refutation or conclusion) of an argumentative essay they could be.

1) Yet doubts remain about Italy's public finances. More than €42 billion-worth of

the new measures has been postponed until after 2013, when a general election is due, so much will depend on the next government. Still, the legislature's prompt response to a crisis that had begun to envelop the country (and to terrify euro-zone leaders) appears to have won Italy some breathing space. By July 20th the yield gap between Italian and German benchmark bonds had dropped below three percentage points (though it remained worryingly high).

2) With the novelty of burgers and fries on the wane, and health concerns of such food rising, fast-food chains have been searching for ever more inventive ways to attract new customers and keep revenues rising. Such was the motivation behind McDonald's decision to develop a strategy to give 6,000-odd outlets across Europe a face-lift.

3) Product decisions also involve choices regarding brand names, guarantees, packaging and the services which should accompany the product offering. Guarantees can be an important component of the product offering. For example, the operators of the AVE, Spain's high-speed train capable of travelling at 300km.p.h. are so confident of its performance that they guarantee to give customers a full refund of their fare if they are more than five minutes late.

4) The extent to which the country's sophisticated export basket has been a direct consequence of its unorthodox policy regime is not clear. But it is not too much of a stretch to imagine that its industrial structure has indeed been shaped by policies of promotion and protection, just as in the cases of earlier East Asian tigers.

5) Indeed, Ford's future rests on strategies such as these. And through the clink of celebratory champagne glasses and purr of classic cars that will mark Ford's centenary, its leaders, shareholders and staff must be hoping that the start of its second century will herald a return to the glory days Ford experienced during the majority of its first 100 years.

6) There is a confused notion in the minds of many people, that the gathering of the property of the poor into the hands of the rich does no ultimate harm, since in whosever hands it may be, it must be spent at last, and thus, they think, return to the poor again. This is, of course a fallacy, and is not hard to expose.

3. **Write your essay: Use the skills you have learned in this unit to write a 300-word argumentative essay based on one of the three outlines that you worked out in the exercises of Texts A, B and C.**

Prewriting

Ask yourself: ✔ or ✗

What is the thesis statement of the essay?   ☐

Is the thesis statement obvious in Introduction and/or Conclusion?   ☐

How many parts will the essay have?   ☐

Is the main idea clear in each supporting paragraph?   ☐

Does the outline follow a logical sequence of ideas?   ☐

Revising

Review/peer review it with the following questions in mind: ✔ or ✗

Does the Introduction and/or Conclusion clearly present the thesis statement?   ☐

Are the ideas clearly and logically organized?   ☐

Is the main argument in each supporting paragraph supported with adequate evidence? ☐

Are the sentences grammatical and concise?   ☐

Is coherence within and across paragraphs adequately achieved?   ☐

4. **Use the proper form of the given word to complete each of the following sentences.**

1) He followed her into a _____ lit kitchen. (dim)

2) The current economic crisis is _____ by high oil prices. (induce)

3) Whenever citing _____ works by the same author, the best policy may be to incorporate either the author or the title—or both—into your introductory sentence, thereby shortening the parenthesis. (multiple)

4) It is the church that is associated with elitist grammar schools and the socially _____ . (privilege)

5) I chose to work abroad to improve my career _____ . (prospective)

6) The sale has been held up because the price is _____ to be too high. (reckon)

7) Many immigrants regularly _____ money to their families. (remittance)

8) His _____ voice cuts straight to the heart. (soar)

9) European farmers are planning a massive demonstration against farm _____ cuts. (subsidize)

10) Currently, consumers do not feel as _____ as they did in 2004, but neither are they trading down. (affluence)

11) During the 1980s, people were menaced by double-digit _____ , trade union power and the cold war. (inflate)

12) He said he had done nothing wrong to _____ a criminal investigation. (merit)

13) He has _____ his political future on an election victory. (stake)

14) The road climbs _____ , with good views of Orvieto through the trees. (steep)

15) What _____ me as interesting is how much we judge other people by the

clothes they wear. (strike)

16) Our intention is to _____ the company by any means we can. (capital)

17) This shall be your sole _____ in these circumstances. (remedy)

18) The company has responded _____ to these changes in technology. (sluggish)

19) Mass movements are often a factor in the awakening and renovation of _____ societies. (stagnancy)

20) Despite _____ by the White House, the Senate voted today to cut off aid. (objective)

Unit 2

Engineering

Learning Objectives

1. To get familiar with different kinds of reliable sources for effective argumentation;
2. To be able to identify the use of different kinds of reliable sources in argumentative writing;
3. To be able to use reliable sources such as statistics, facts, research results and illustrative incidents in one's own argumentative writing.

Writing Skill Development

Supporting Evidence and Effective Argumentation (1)

Use of Reliable Sources (statistics, facts, quotation, illustrative incidents, etc.)

A persuasive writer has to present concrete evidence to support his/her argument, which is made up of facts, accurate statistics, reliable authority/sources, and illustrative incidents (Pierson et al., 2007).

Fact

A fact is a verifiable truth and cannot be argued, thus it can be used to support one's argument. In the following example, the author uses the lack of natural resources as a fact to support the argument that Japan's ardent pursuit of nuclear energy has sprung from a deep sense of vulnerability.

[Argument] Japan's ardent pursuit of nuclear energy has sprung from a deep sense of vulnerability.

[Fact] Lacking coal, oil, natural gas, or other fossil fuels, Japan, particularly after the oil crises of the 1970s, has seen nuclear power as a means of providing energy security. And it has built a new generation of centrifuges for uranium enrichment in a bid to ensure that it is not vulnerable to a cutoff in supply of nuclear fuel, even if its main providers—countries like France and the Netherlands—seem pretty trustworthy.

Source: Japan's Nuclear Crisis: The Fine Line Between Security and Insecurity, by Miles, A. Pomper, *Crazy English Reader*, 2011, 113, 15-17.

Statistics

Based on objective evidence, statistics, as special facts based on numerical evidence, are also effective evidence in persuasive writing. As in the following sample, the author successfully supports his argument by using the statistics issued by the National Association of Colleges and Employers.

> *[Argument]* Unpaid internships are a cheap way for universities to provide credit or help companies skirt a nebulous area of labor laws.
>
> *[Statistics]* Statistics from the National Association of Colleges and Employers showed that of 700 colleges, 95% allowed the positing of unpaid internships in campus career centers and on college Web sites. And of those colleges, only 30% provided their students with academic credits for those unpaid internships; the rest, evidently, were willing to overlook potential violations of labor laws.
>
> Source: Unpaid Interns, Complicit Colleges, by Ross Perlin, *Crazy English Reader*, 2011, 113, 10-13.

Research results

Research results are hard evidence that powerfully supports/proves an argument, as done in the following example.

> *[Argument]* It is impossible for a living cell or a molecule of protein to come into being all by itself.
>
> *[Research result]* On a study conducted by a team of leading mathematicians and biological evolutionary researchers came up with the startling result, proving that the mathematical probability of a living cell or a molecule of protein to come into being all by itself is absolutely nil!
>
> Source: www.buzzle.com/articles/arguments-against-evolution.html.

Examples

Suitable examples can be as powerful as facts and statistics to support one's argument. For instance, several examples are listed to support the viewpoint that several features didn't exactly feel like news that evening.

> *[Argument]* Several features didn't exactly feel like news.
>
> *[Example]* Surprisingly, only one portion of the news this evening from 6 to 6:30 repeated exactly what we had already seen during the 5:30 to 6 segment. Billed as a "follow-up", it was a videotaped redundancy. There were, however, several features that didn't exactly feel like news. "Covering Connecticut" amounted to several five- or ten-second blurbs on what prominent people had done that day across the state. "People in the News" was mostly about the shenanigans of Hollywood types, about a new film called *Primary Colors* that seems to mock the White House scandals and about the star of *Titanic* being upset because some pictures of him, naked, were being published by a magazine. There was the nightly announcement of the

winning Lottery Numbers (perhaps this is, indeed, important news for some people!), and two segments about St. Patrick's Day parties going on in the capital city—lots of people drinking lots of beer. A "Health Beat" segment told us about pheromones and perfumes and "Business Beat" told us something about Kathie Lee Gifford's sweatshops.

Source: http://grammar.ccc.comment.edu/grammar/composition/examples.htm.

Reliable authority/sources (quotation)

Another common type of convincing support for one's argument is to cite an authority/expert in the relevant area. The evidence is stronger if the cited authority/expert is well known. The author of the following example cited a director's words as evidence to support the idea that some economists and tax reform advocates don't think households making more than $250,000 are rich enough to be considered as millionaires.

[Argument] Some economists and tax reform advocates are questioning whether those households making more than $250,000 are rich enough to be worthy of the same tax bracket as millionaires.

[Reliable authority/source] "The very round nature of it suggests that it's arbitrary," said Roberton Williams, a senior fellow at the Tax Policy Center and the deputy assistant director for tax analysis at the Congressional Budget Office from 1998 to 2006. "There's nothing magical about $250,000 per year. It has no economic basis."

Source: Rich and Sort of Rich, by Andrew Ross Sorkin, *New York Times*, 2011, 14.

Illustrative incidents

Relevant illustrative incidents, or personal experiences, lend powerful support to one's argument. For example, by using illustrative incidents, the writer of the following sample convincingly supports his/her opinion against genetic engineering for ill purposes.

[Argument] I am against the use of genetic engineering to create monstrous creatures.

[Illustrative incidents] Remember *Dren* from the 2009 sci-fi movie *Splice*? A shudder runs down my spine every time I visualize that genetically engineered monstrous creation of the overly ambitious scientist couple in that movie! Agreeing that genetic engineering opens the doors to a lot of scientific breakthroughs, especially in the domain of medicine and developing cures for terminal and degenerative diseases, you never know when too much curiosity to find out what it feels like to play God may lead to such a predicament as shown in the aforementioned movie! No, don't misunderstand me here. I am not against genetic engineering—only as far as it is used for curing diseases and making the world a better place for all of nature's creatures. However, I am staunchly against the use of genetic engineering for selfishly forwarding human progress at the expense of nature and for playing with genes to create monstrous creatures or to sacrifice the natural aspects of life—the basic flaws—that make humans what they are.

Source: http://www.buzzle.com/articles/arguments-against-genetic-engineering.html.

Reference:

Pierson, H., Kumar, S., Lin, Z., & Neu, P. (2007). *New Perspective Graduate Series: Reading, Writing, and Rhetoric for the 21ˢᵗ Century.* Beijing: Education Press.

Reading for Ideas

Text A

Altering the Forces of Nature: Genetic Engineering on Animals[1]

❶ I remember the time when I first saw glowing fishes at the local fish markets in Taiwan, I felt two different emotions. One was pure excitement from seeing these **elegant** creatures, while the other was an indescribable feeling of discomfort. They caught my eyes not only because I knew they were genetically engineered, but because they were simply **stunning**. Our modern society focuses its attention on these "stunning" results from **genetic** engineering practices, which in many cases, with animals as experimental subjects, have helped provide insight into groundbreaking discoveries in medicine, **commerce**, and agriculture. With the new advances in biomedical technology **followed up** by medical breakthroughs, the **conflict** begins when **ethical** considerations are **drawn upon** as **moral** guidelines. Most researchers and lab scientists agree that genetic engineering on animals will **lead to** medical breakthroughs, while some agree that it should be **banned** as an immoral method for medical purposes.

❷ In 2007, a stem cell experiment **cured** sickle cell anemia (镰状细胞性贫血) in mice by genetically replacing a damaged piece of DNA. Karan Kaplan from *Los Angeles Times* describes that researchers used a technique in which adult cells were "reprogrammed" into **embryonic** cells which had not yet specified themselves to a particular organ or **tissue** as **replacements** for diseased or damaged cells. These **artificially** developed cells are called induced pluripotent stem cells (诱导式多能干细胞), or iPS cells. To develop iPS, it requires an **activation** of four genes that are found dormant (休眠的；静止的) in adult cells but active in embryos. Once those genes are activated, the cells essentially "forget" that they were once, say, liver cells, or muscle cells, and they then behave like embryonic stem cells. This new method of research is considered "flawless" (无瑕疵的) and "works beautifully" (Kaplan, 2007) because it **ensures** that

---

1 This essay was retrieved from http://blogs.saschina.org/aplangpd/2010/04/07/altering-the-forces-of-nature-genetic-engineering-on-animals.

the cells will not be **rejected** since they **derive** from patients' own cells. The experiment involves extraction (取出；抽出) of mice tail cells genetically **infected** with sickle cell anemia and transforming these cells into iPS cells. They used a type of virus to turn on the four dormant genes to correct the genetic flaw (瑕疵) by replacing a few nucleotides (核苷；核甘酸). However, a major consequence of this method is that it creates a c-Myc gene which has a **tendency** to create **tumors**. But scientists found a way to completely delete it once the replacement process had been made. This procedure was done on three 12-week rats and twelve weeks later, the mice were producing normal cells, all **virtually** sound, and improving body weight and **respiratory capacity**. It was also noted that no tumors had appeared. This **innovative** experiment **establishes** "a platform for any one of dozens of human genetic blood diseases, not just sickle cell anemia" (Kaplan, 2007). Genetic engineering, as demonstrated by this lab's results, has **potential** for future successes in medicine and in curing **terminal** human genetic diseases **prior to** this new discovery.

❸　　Although animal genetic engineering **generates** some of the most exciting new human discoveries for future uses, investigation have **revealed** that it has many harmful effects. Genetic engineering poses serious **challenges** on human health, animal rights, and the future of agriculture. Greta Gaard examines how milk from genetically engineered cows is harmful and the process to create these "pharm" animals (基因动物) harms them. She states that "in the current industrial system of factory farming, cows are production machines." Polisac or recombinant bovine growth hormone (rBGH) (重组牛生长激素) is a manufactured hormone (激素，荷尔蒙) that, when **injected** into cows, increases the amount of milk produced by 10 to 15 percent. Although it is similar to a natural hormone found in cows and different only by one amino acid (氨基酸), "a cow's life **span** is cut from 20 to 25 years down to five or less when the rBGH hormone is injected into its system" (Haugen, 2009). This is a major issue of ethics when animal rights are considered. The rBGH hormone has also proved to be more harmful to growing children than to adults. And children in general consume more milk than adults. Because children are more **vulnerable** to hormones and chemicals than adults, many become more **susceptible** to cancer and have an **altered onset** of puberty (青春期) (Haugen, 2009). As revealed by research, "Girls who menstruate (女性例假) before the age of 12 are at a higher risk of **contracting** breast cancer later in life" (Haugen, 2009). It may be true that rBGH cows may alleviate world hunger because the hormone increases milk production. But the case seems to be counterintuitive (违反直觉的). As more cows are bred to match the milk consumption rate, feeding **livestock** becomes more important than feeding people. Since 80% of the corn and 95% of the oats (燕麦) grown in the US are being fed to animals, an increase of livestock will provide less food for people of the nation (Haugen, 2009).

❹   As seen, genetic engineering on animals is a **complex controversy**. Any research that will be conducted must be fully supported by both sides and facts should be **addressed** before a product is made. Typically all ethical issues should be considered and made public before any research is conducted upon living livestock and the end re-sult will **yield** groundbreaking successes for both sides. The stem cell research on iPS cells is an excellent new way to address the ethics behind stem cell research because it does not kill an **innocent** animal and yet provides a new cure to the world of medicine.

References:

Haugen, D. M. (2009). Milk from Genetically Engineered Cows Is Harmful. *Genetic Engineering (Opposing Viewpoints)*. Farmington Hills, MI: Greenhaven Press.

Kaplan, K. (2007). Stem Cell Method Finds Cure. *Los Angeles Times*, 7.

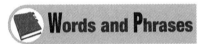 **Words and Phrases**

★ activation	[ˌækti'veiʃn]	*n.*	激活；活化作用
			★ activate *vt.& vi.* 刺激；使活动；使活泼；使产生放射性
address	[ə'dres]	*vt.*	处理；从事；忙于；演说；写姓名地址
		n.	地址；演讲；致辞
alter	['ɔ:ltə]	*vt. & vi.*	改变，更改；修改
artificially	[ˌɑ:ti'fiʃəli]	*adv.*	人工地，人为地，不自然地
ban	[bæn]	*vt.*	禁止；取缔
		n.	禁令；禁忌
▲ beverage	['bevəridʒ]	*n.*	饮料
capacity	[kə'pæsəti]	*n.*	能力；容量；生产力
challenge	['tʃælindʒ]	*n.*	质疑，怀疑；挑战
		vt.	向……挑战
★ commerce	['kɔmɜ:s]	*n.*	贸易；商业
complex	['kɔmpleks]	*a.*	复杂的；合成的
		n.	复合体；综合设施
conflict	['kɔnflikt]	*n. & vi.*	冲突，矛盾；斗争；争执
contract	[kən'trækt]	*vt. & vi.*	感染；收缩；订约
	['kɔntrækt]	*n.*	合同；婚约

controversy	[ˈkɔntrəvɜːsi]	n.	争论；论战；辩论
cure	[kjuə]	vt. & vi.	治疗；治愈
derive	[diˈraiv]	vt. & vi.	源于；起源；得自
elegant	[ˈeligənt]	a.	高雅的，优雅的；讲究的
▲ embryonic	[ˌembriˈɔnik]	a.	胚胎的；像胚胎的
			▲ embryo n. 胚胎；晶胚；初期
ensure	[inˈʃuə]	vt.	保证，确保；使安全
establish	[iˈstæbliʃ]	vt.	建立；创办；安置
▲ ethical	[ˈeθikl]	a.	伦理的；道德的
			▲ ethic n. 伦理；道德规范
generate	[ˈdʒenəreit]	vt.	使形成；发生；生殖
genetic	[dʒiˈnetik]	a.	遗传的；基因的；起源的
			gene n. 基因
infect	[inˈfekt]	vt.	感染，传染
★ inject	[inˈdʒekt]	vt.	注射；注入
innocent	[ˈinəsnt]	a.	无辜的；无罪的；无知的
▲ innovative	[ˈinəveitiv]	a.	革新的，创新的
▲ livestock	[ˈlaivstɔk]	n.	家畜，牲畜
moral	[ˈmɔrəl]	a.	道德的；精神上的；品性端正的
			immoral a. 不道德的；邪恶的
★ onset	[ˈɔnset]	n.	开始，着手；发作；进攻
potential	[pəˈtenʃl]	n.	潜能；可能性
		a.	潜在的；可能的
prior	[ˈpraiə]	a.	优先的；在先的，在前的
		adv.	在前，居先
reject	[riˈdʒekt]	vt.	排斥；抵制
replacement	[riˈpleismənt]	n.	更换；复位；代替者
▲ respiratory	[riˈspiətəri]	a.	呼吸的
reveal	[riˈviːl]	vt.	泄露；显示
span	[spæn]	n.	跨度，跨距；范围
		vt.	跨越；持续；以手指测量
★ stunning	[ˈstʌniŋ]	a.	使人晕倒的；极好的；震耳欲聋的
			★ stun vt. 使震惊；打昏；使印象深刻
★ susceptible	[səˈseptəbl]	a.	易受影响的；易感动的；容许……的
tendency	[ˈtendənsi]	n.	倾向，趋势；癖好

terminal	['tɜːmɪnl]	*a.*	晚期的；终点的；末端的
		n.	末端；终点；终端机
tissue	['tɪʃuː]	*n.*	组织；纸巾
▲ tumor	['tjuːmə]	*n.*	肿瘤；肿块
virtually	['vɜːtʃuəli]	*adv.*	实际上，实质上；虚拟
★ vulnerable	['vʌlnərəbl]	*a.*	易受攻击的；易受伤害的
yield	[jiːld]	*vt. & vi.*	产生，出产；提供；屈服；让步
		n.	产量；产出；收益

draw upon	利用；开出；总结
follow up	跟踪；坚持完成；追究，追查
lead to	导致；通向
prior to	在……之前；居先

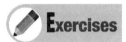

Exercises

Part I. Understanding the text

1. **Study the title of Text A.**
   - What are the key words in the essay title?
   - Why do you think they are the key words?

2. **Spend 10 minutes browsing the essay and work out the outline of the essay, with reference to the following:**
   - Thesis statement/main argument
   - Supporting ideas

   After you have finished, discuss your outline with your partner.

Part II. Writing skills development

3. **Read the following paragraphs of Text A and decide the argument and the type of evidence used therein: facts, statistics, research results, examples, reliable authority/sources, or illustrative incidents, etc.**

   1) Read Paragraph 2 and decide its argument and the type of evidence used to support the argument.

      Argument: _____

      Type of evidence: _____

   2) Read Paragraph 3 and decide its argument and the type of evidence used to

support the argument.

Argument: _____

Type of evidence: _____

4. **Read the text again and discuss with your partner how coherence within and across paragraphs is achieved.**

Part III. Language focus

5. **Complete the following sentences with the words you've learned in Text A in proper forms. The first letter of each word is given.**

1) Some researchers believe that genetic engineering on animals should be b_____ as an immoral method for medical purposes.

2) A new technique has been discovered to use adult cells as r_____ for diseased or damaged cells.

3) Once a_____, the cells will behave like embryonic stem cells and forget what they once were.

4) The new method ensures that no applications will be r_____ without being reviewed.

5) Lab results demonstrate that genetic engineering has p_____ for future successes in medicine and in curing human genetic diseases.

6) P_____ to this new discovery, people had long believed that genetic diseases couldn't be cured.

7) Empirical research r_____ that animal genetic engineering has many forms of harmful effects.

8) C_____ on the environment, human health, animal rights, and the future of agriculture must be endured if genetic engineering is to be further developed.

9) Generally speaking, children are more v_____ to many kinds of diseases and thus should be given special protection.

10) Since both proponents and opponents can support themselves with facts and data, whether genetic engineering is good remains a c_____.

6. **Paraphrase the following sentences.**

1) With the new advances in biomedical technology followed up by medical breakthroughs, the conflict begins when ethical considerations are drawn upon as moral guidelines.

2) Because children are more vulnerable to hormones and chemicals than adults, many become more susceptible to cancer and have an altered onset of puberty.

3) Typically all ethical issues should be considered and made public before any

research is conducted upon living livestock and the end result will yield ground-breaking successes for both sides.

Part IV. Writing

7. **The first sentence in a paragraph is often called a topic sentence. One key function of a topic sentence is to anticipate the ideas that follow. It helps readers to understand the focus and direction of the paragraph. Now discuss with your partner on what information might follow each of the following sentences:**

   - Genetic engineering on animals faces challenges led by animal rights activists.
   - Genetic engineering on animals is a complex controversy.

8. **Now imagine you are going to write a paragraph on** *The Use of Genetic Engineering in Medicine*, **which following sentence would you choose as the topic sentence and what type of evidence would you use to develop it/support the argument?**

   - Genetic engineering is useful in medicine.
   - Genetic engineering helps cure diseases but faces challenges.
   - There are many uses made of genetic engineering in medicine, each having its own advantages and disadvantages.

   Now discuss your ideas with your partner and give reasons.

9. **Write out the paragraph discussed above, with reference to the following phrases and sentence structures.**

Research results	• … a stem cell experiment done by researchers has cured sickle cell anemia… • Genetic engineering, as demonstrated by this lab's results, has potential for… • Research says that… (Haugen, 2009).
Statistics	• …, increases the amount of milk produced by 10 to 15 percent. • Since 80% of the corn and 95% of the oats grown in the US are being fed to animals, …
Quotes	• Karan Kaplan… describes that… this… research is considered "flawless" and "works beautifully" (Kaplan, 2007)… • Greta Gaard examines… She states that…
Illustrative incidents	• I remember the time when I first saw…

> **Suggested writing steps:**
> - Write the first draft alone.
> - Peer review each other's writing.
> - Revise your first draft.

Text B

Genetically Modified Foods: A Solution to World Hunger or Potential Health Threat?[1]

❶   Genetically modified foods have recently entered the spotlight as a proposed so-lution to some of the most **pressing global** problems, including an ever-increasing population and larger **wealth divisions**, as they create larger, more **pest** and weed **resistant** crops that produce more food and fiber per acre. This practice, however, has been argued as being unhealthy, unethical, and threatening to the **current** natural crop production. Examining both sides of the argument reveals that genetically modified crops are **beneficial in the short term** to farmers' outputs and income, but their long term effects are **scarcely** known and should therefore be considered more carefully.

❷   The select amount of information we currently have **access** to **with regards to** genetically modified crops is limited to only a few studies, but **a host of** anecdotal (轶事的) evidence suggests that there is nothing immediately harmful or dangerous about the production of modified food. In fact, the Council for Biotechnology Informa-tion (CBI) (2001) quotes a 2002 study by the National Center for Food and Agricultural Policy found that 6 of the largest biotech crops planted in the United States, including soybeans, corn, cotton, and canola, "produced an additional 4 billion pounds of food and fiber on the same acreage, improved farm income by $1.5 billion, and reduced pes-ticide use by 46 million pounds." The CBI strategically **concedes** that biotechnology "is not the single solution for feeding a growing population," but, understanding that envi-ronmentally concerned citizens **constitute** a large portion of their audience, makes an **appeal** that GE (genetically engineered) crops will be **essential** in growing "more food in a sustainable way that does not **deplete** existing farmland" and keeping existing wil-derness area from going "under the plow."

❸   Although **confronted** with a plethora (过多;过剩) of statistics that gives testa-ment (证据;证明) to the ability of genetically engineered crops to produce greater

---

1 This essay was retrieved from http://blogs.saschina.org/aplangpd/2010/04/07/genetically-modified-foods-a-solution-world-hunger-or-potentially-health-threat.

crop yields than their non-engineered **counterparts**, many of the opponents of GE crops **stress** that even though the immediate outputs are promising, there is the danger of unforeseen（无法预料的）future **consequences**. The foremost issue which Brian Tokar, a member of the Institute for Social Ecology and author of several articles and books on genetic engineering, addresses is the intellectual property war now fought over seeds and plants. When large corporations like Mosanto began shifting their "technological interventions" to focus on acquiring new "patented seed varieties, as well as the particular chemicals with which those seeds were 'designed' to grow" (Tokar, 2001), they were able to control large portions of the agriculture business. Many countries in Africa and Europe, however, have rejected the **import** of such genetically "manufactured" crops for another **valid** concern that the newly introduced GE crops would **contaminate** their own local varieties. In contrast to CBI's claim that genetic engineering can be a major factor in overcoming world hunger, Tokar (2001) dispels（驱散，驱逐）this statement as "the most **pervasive** of the **numerous** false hopes that the developers of this technology have **aroused**." In fact, he instead argues that GE crops are "undermining food security and the survival of land-based peoples" by reducing the gene pool of crops worldwide. As the dangerous effects of smoking were not known until hundreds of years after the start of cultivation of the tobacco plant, Tokar implies that biotech crops could **have** serious health **impacts on** humans, as "very few laboratories around the world have the funds to carry out experiments on GE food effects," and "agribusiness corporations have **tremendous** economic and political leverage（杠杆作用；手段）over the **priorities** in agricultural research," so there might be side effects to eating genetically modified foods we have not yet discovered.

❹　　The collection of statistics presented by the CBI proves to be quite impressive upon first glance and promising towards finding a solution to feeding the world's ever-growing population. Upon further reconsideration, however, one must wonder whether or not the genetic technology will be **monopolized** by **giant** industry, supplying the crops to only the highest **bidder**, or whether or not the lack of future **diversity** in the global crop gene pool will lead to an **ecological crisis**, or whether or not consuming genetically modified foods will have some unforeseen impact on humans. Although GE crops can post staggering（令人惊讶的）short term yields, there are too many unknown consequences of genetically **modifying** foods to **promote** them before more extensive research is done.

Reference:

Tokar, B. (2001). Genetically Modified Foods Are Dangerous. In J. D. Torr (ed.), *Ge-*

netic Engineering: Opposing Viewpoints. Detroit: Greenhaven Press.

 **Words and Phrases**

access	['ækses]	*n.*	机会，权利；通路；通到
	[æk'ses]	*vt.*	存取；到达；进入；使用
appeal	[ə'pi:l]	*n.*	呼吁，请求；吸引；上诉
		vt. & vi.	呼吁，恳求；上诉；有吸引力，迎合爱好
arouse	[ə'rauz]	*vt. & vi.*	激发；引起；唤醒；鼓励
beneficial	[ˌbeni'fiʃl]	*a.*	有益的，有利的；可享利益的
bidder	['bidə]	*n.*	出价人，投标人
			bid *vt. & vi.* 投标；出价；吩咐
concede	[kən'si:d]	*vt. & vi.*	承认；让步；容许
confront	[kən'frʌnt]	*vt.*	面对；面临；处理，对付
consequence	['kɔnsikwəns]	*n.*	结果；后果；重要性
constitute	['kɔnstitju:t]	*vt.*	组成，构成；建立；任命
contaminate	[kən'tæmineit]	*vt.*	污染；弄脏
★ counterpart	['kauntəpɑ:t]	*n.*	职位（或作用）相当的人；对应的事物
crisis	['kraisis]	*n.*	危机；危急关头；危难时刻；病危期
current	['kʌrənt]	*a.*	当前的；现在的；流通的，通用的；流行的
		n.	水流；气流；电流；趋势；潮流
▲ deplete	[di'pli:t]	*vt.*	耗尽，用尽；使衰竭，使空虚
▲ diversity	[dai'vɜ:səti]	*n.*	多样性；差异
			▲ **diversify** *vt.* 使多样化，使变化；增加产品种类以扩大
division	[di'viʒn]	*n.*	除法；部门；分割
★ ecological	[ˌi:kə'lɔdʒikl]	*a.*	生态的；生态学的
essential	[i'senʃl]	*a.*	基本的；必要的；本质的；精华的
		n.	本质；要素；要点；必需品
giant	['dʒaiənt]	*a.*	巨大的；巨人般的
		n.	巨人；巨兽；伟人
global	['gləubl]	*a.*	全球的；球形的；总体的
impact	['impækt]	*n.*	巨大影响；强大作用；撞击；冲击力
	[im'pækt]	*vt. & vi.*	有影响，有作用；冲击；撞击

import	['impɔ:t]	*n.*	进口；输入的产品；引进
		vt.	输入，进口，引进
modify	['mɔdifai]	*vt. & vi.*	调整，使更适合；缓和；修饰
▲ monopolize	[mə'nɔpəlaiz]	*vt.*	垄断；独占；拥有……的专卖权
numerous	['nju:mərəs]	*a.*	许多的，很多的
★ pest	[pest]	*n.*	害虫；有害之物；令人讨厌的人
★ pervasive	[pə'veisiv]	*a.*	遍布的；弥漫的
pressing	['presiŋ]	*a.*	紧迫的；迫切的；恳切的
			press *vt. & vi.* 压；按；逼迫
priority	[prai'ɔrəti]	*n.*	优先；优先权；优先考虑的事
promote	[prə'məut]	*vt.*	促进；提升；推销
resistant	[ri'zistənt]	*a.*	抵抗的，反抗的；顽固的
scarcely	['skeəsli]	*adv.*	缺乏地，不足地；稀有地
stress	[stres]	*vt.*	强调；用重音读
		n.	紧张；压力；强调；重音；重读
tremendous	[trə'mendəs]	*a.*	极大的，巨大的；惊人的
valid	['vælid]	*a.*	有效的，有根据的；正当的
wealth	[welθ]	*n.*	财富；大量；富有

a host of	许多，一大群；众多，大量
have impacts on...	对……有影响
in the short term	从短期来看；就眼前来说
with regard(s) to	关于；至于

 **Exercises**

Part I. Understanding the text

1. **Study the title of Text B.**
   - What are the key words in the essay title?
   - Why do you think they are the key words?

2. **Spend 10 minutes browsing the essay and work out the outline of the essay, with reference to the following:**
   - Thesis statement/main argument
   - Supporting ideas

After you have finished, discuss your outline with your partner.

Part II. Writing skills development

3. **Read the following paragraphs of Text B and decide the argument and the type of evidence used therein, facts, statistics, research results, examples, reliable authority/sources, or illustrative incidents, etc.**

1) Read Paragraph 2 and decide its argument and the type of evidence used to support the argument.

   Argument: _____

   Type of evidence: _____

2) Read Paragraph 3 and decide its argument and the type of evidence used to support the argument.

   Argument: _____

   Type of evidence: _____

4. **Read the text again and discuss with your partner how coherence within and across paragraphs is achieved.**

Part III. Language focus

5. **Complete the following summary of the text using the words you've learned in Text B. The first letter of each word is given.**

   It is proposed that genetically 1) m_____ foods can solve some of the most 2) p_____ problems such as an ever-increasing population and larger 3) w_____ divisions in the world. The few studies available up to now suggest that there is nothing immediately harmful or dangerous about the production of modified food. Moreover, biotech crops can produce 4) t_____ greater crop yields and reduce pesticide use than their non-engineered 5) c_____. Even so, many opponents believe that there is the danger of unforeseen future 6) c_____. For example, large corporations might control large portions of the agriculture business, and GE crops might 7) c_____ local varieties and reduce the gene pool of crops worldwide. As very few labs in the world can afford to do research on GE food effects, biotech crops could have serious health 8) i_____ on humans. Thus, even though GE crops 9) a_____ to many people in that they might solve the problem of feeding the world's ever-growing population and are 10) b_____ in many other aspects, they must be cautiously treated before more research is done.

6. **Paraphrase the following sentences.**

1) Examining both sides of the argument reveals that genetically modified crops are beneficial in the short term to farmers' outputs and income, but their long term

effects are scarcely known and should therefore be considered more carefully.

2) Although confronted with a plethora of statistics that gives testament to the ability of genetically engineered crops to produce greater crop yields than their non-engineered counterparts, many of the opponents of GE crops stress that even though the immediate outputs are promising, there is the danger of unforeseen future consequences.

3) Many countries in Africa and Europe, however, have rejected the import of such genetically "manufactured" crops for another valid concern that the newly introduced GE crops would contaminate their own local varieties.

Part IV. Writing

7. **Read the text again and study the following phrases and sentence structures used to support arguments.**

Research results	• The Council for Biotechnology Information (CBI) (2001) quotes a 2002 study... that...
Statistics	• ..., produced an additional 4 billion pounds of food and fiber on the same acreage, improved farm income by $1.5 billion, and reduced pesticide use by 46 million pounds.
Quotes	• The CBI strategically concedes that biotechnology "is not the single solution for feeding a growing population," ... • When large corporations... began shifting their "technological interventions" to focus on acquiring new "patented seed varieties, as well as..." (Tokar, 2001), ...
Examples	• When large corporations like Mosanto began shifting their...
Analogy	• As the dangerous effects of smoking were not known until hundreds of years after the start of cultivation of the tobacco plant, Tokar implies that biotech crops could have serious health impacts on humans, ...

8. **Discuss with your partner on what information you might expect to follow each of the following sentences:**
   • Genetic engineering can be a major factor in overcoming world hunger.
   • There are side effects of eating genetically modified foods.

9. **Use the following research results to write a paragraph which develops the following topic sentence:**
   Tall buildings should be forbidden in cities.

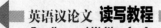
- High rise buildings may cause environmental problems like high wind velocities in open spaces around them, as well as extended shadows over nearby houses and open spaces (Helios, 1999, 2000).
- The construction cost of high-rise buildings is steep (Tan, 1999, Gat, 1995).

Suggested writing steps:

- Write the first draft alone.
- Peer review each other's writing.
- Revise your first draft.

Text Ⓒ

Genetic Engineering and Cloning[1]

❶ What are the principal, ethical issues and experimental procedures used in genetic engineering and cloning? Should cloning be allowed to continue?

❷ In the 1970's, scientists discovered that **strands** of DNA could be cut using special enzymes (酶), which could cut out genetic combinations. DNA contains information about genes particular organisms hold. **Duplicates** of genes are also possible through genetic engineering and are very useful for medical purposes. Advances in technology have raised issues such as animal and human cloning. These issues have caused many different sided arguments.

❸ Some people feel that cloning should be banned, however never seeming to see its medical value. There are already **drug** and medicine manufactures all over the world that are working on products that can be produced in cows' milk or even sheep or goats' milk when the **trait** is cloned. Right now they are trying to produce vaccines (牛痘苗) against malaria (疟疾；瘴气), antibodies (抗体) against HIV, as well as proteins (蛋白质) to treat haemophilia (血友病), muscle disease, **internal** intestinal (肠的) infections, rheumatoid (风湿症的) arthritis (关节炎), cystic fibrosis (囊胞性纤维症) and emphysema (气肿；肺气肿). These same companies are also working on proteins to help **digest** fat and proteins to serve as **nutritional supplements** for **infants**, as well as different proteins, which are found in human blood and in cows' milk. None of these treatments would be possible in the future if cloning were banned.

❹ The safety of genetic engineering is something that presents much concern. The current **precautions** and **previous** precautions of the biotechnological industry can

---

1 This article was retrieved from http://www.123HelpMe.com/view.asp?id=13184.

clear up the safety issue. The FDA and State Governments **impose** limits such as the illegalization of human cloning and limits on other genetic engineering processes. The only **legal** forms of genetic engineering that are used today are in vitro fertilization（体外授精）, artificial insemination（授精；受胎）, and sperm banks（精子库）.

5 The moral question of genetic engineering is answered by looking at the advances in medicine. Today the advancements in medicine are **evolving** at an extremely high rate. If the science of genetic engineering is wrong, then so are the rest of the advances in medicine. The reason is because genetic engineering is just another form of medical advancement. Gene **manipulation** is not going to be used for any other purposes except for the treatment and **elimination** of diseases. The one thing that people need to realize is the potential of genetic engineering. Try to **visualize** what parents of a child dying from a disease like multiple sclerosis（硬化；细胞壁硬化）think about the benefits of genetic engineering. Do they think that it is morally wrong or right? They think that it is right because it is going to save their child's life.

6 Genetic diseases **affect** a large proportion of our population. A genetic disease is an illness **passed on** through genes, such diseases include cystic fibrosis, Huntington's disease（亨廷顿氏舞蹈病）and sickle cell anaemia. These diseases can cause paralysis（麻痹；无力）, mental **deteriorating**, and physical deformity（畸形）, all leading to death. Some genetic diseases can be **detected** by prenatal（产前的；胎儿期的）tests but others such as Huntington's can only be detected in early adulthood. Genetic engineering is being used all over the world to help and cure these fatal（致命的）diseases.

7 There is an article from the "Times" that is about a middle aged man who is suffering from Huntington's disease. There are no cures at present but stem cell **therapy** was suggested to replace **defective** cells in the brain, which led to the symptoms of Huntington's. This therapy worked on this man. The man and his wife encourage the research into stem cell and hope that one day it will lead to treatment for Huntington's.

8 Some benefits are used in medicine today, but the real benefits will come as genes can be altered more. The real benefit that will help mankind is when bioengineers will be able to replace a cancer or defective gene with a gene that does not have an error in its genetic **code**. "The new science of genetic engineering aims to take a **dramatic** shortcut in the slow process of **evolution**." What is meant by the previous quote from Stableford is that scientists hope to take a gene from an organism and change it so that it will **be immune to** certain diseases and free from cancer. For example, many years ago small pox（天花）was widely spread. Today it is almost nonexistent, because of the evolution of man. The only problem with this was it took hundreds of years for our genetic code to **adapt** and make our bodies fight it.

9 Plants are also being genetically engineered. This type of genetic engineering is more commonly accepted, but why? It is no different for a plant to be able to **fight off** pests than it is for a human to be able to fight off diseases. This is a **contradiction**, because society is saying that it is all right for a plant to be genetically engineered but not a human.

10 Many people also think that this new biotechnology is letting scientists and doctors play god. These doctors are not trying to recreate human science; they are just trying to **perfect** its flaws. Doctors and scientists have already helped diabetics（糖尿病，糖尿病患者）with their **synthetic** insulin（胰岛素）, and unfertile（不能生育的）parents are now able to have children. Those that oppose genetic engineering because doctors are trying to play god, do not realize what genetic engineering has already **contributed** to our world. Society should research issues before forming an **ignorant** opinion.

11 One example of cloning is "Dolly". Dolly was the first ever mammal（哺乳动物）cloned from a cell of an adult animal. Dolly is an example of asexual（无性生殖的）reproduction. Unfertilised eggs were taken from a sheep and were reconstructed. These reconstructed eggs were cultured for 6 days and **inserted** into a surrogate（代孕的）ewes（母羊）. Dolly the lamb was born 148 days later. Dolly was produced after 277 failures. What happened to them? There are many experiments that were "genetic **disasters**". The Beltsville pig was one of the many genetic hiccups（打嗝；灾难）.

12 After the success of cloning "Dolly", fears about cloning led to a total ban on the cloning of humans in many countries. The advance in technology is moving fast, already people can pay to decide what sex their unborn child will be. In 20 years, scientists believe we will be able to design our babies, even if the technology is only **available** for the rich. Gene therapy will **enable** parents to choose eye colour, hair colour, build, etc. Even the **temperament** of the child could be decided. Gene therapy is illegal at the moment because people should not be able to create the perfect child, but they should be able to correct a gene in a child if it has a chance of being born with Down syndrome（唐氏症）. The safety precautions are **in effect** in order to save the lives of unborn babies. Gene therapy cannot be used on humans until it is perfected and there is little or no chance of failure. These sciences are not perfect but give it a few years and it will be a great benefit to the human race.

13 There are many doctors who prepared to make the first human clone such as Professor Severino Antinori. However there are many doctors who feel the procedure would be unsafe such as Dr. Harry Griffin (who worked on the dolly project). I myself feel that it would be immoral to clone humans just **for the sake of** it. It is unsafe to clone humans, it took 277 attempts to clone Dolly. Imagine the loss of 277 human lives, it would be a **scandal**. The **overwhelming reaction** from most people was that human cloning should not be done. The fear that people have toward genetic engineering is not new to science. Ever since the beginning of science, man has been afraid of the unknown. Space travel and flying were not widely accepted until the twentieth century and was completely **absurd** just one hundred years ago. Today they are widely accepted and are used every day. Genetic engineering is in the first stage of its discovery and will **emerge** in the twenty first century and will be as accepted as are flying and space travel. The people of the world should **ease up** on holding back the evolution of science and realize its possibilities for future generations.

Words and Phrases

★ absurd	[əb'sɜːd]	*a.*	荒谬的；可笑的
adapt	[ə'dæpt]	*vt. & vi.*	使适应；改编
affect	[ə'fekt]	*vt. & vi.*	影响；感染；侵袭
available	[ə'veiləbl]	*a.*	可获得的；可购得的；有空的
code	[kəud]	*n.*	代码，密码；编码；法典
		vt. & vi.	编码；制成法典
contradiction	[ˌkɔntrə'dikʃn]	*n.*	矛盾；不一致；反驳
contribute	[kən'tribjuːt]	*vt.*	贡献，出力；投稿；捐献
★ defective	[di'fektiv]	*a.*	有缺陷的；有缺点的；有毛病的
detect	[di'tekt]	*vt.*	发现；察觉；探测
★ deteriorate	[di'tiəriəreit]	*vt. & vi.*	恶化，变坏
digest	[dai'dʒest]	*vt. & vi.*	消化；领会；领悟
	['daidʒest]	*n.*	文摘；摘要
disaster	[di'zɑːstə]	*n.*	不幸；灾难，灾祸
dramatic	[drə'mætik]	*a.*	突然的；令人吃惊的；戏剧的
drug	[drʌg]	*n.*	药；毒品
★ duplicate	['djuːplikət]	*n.*	副本；复制品
	['djuːplikeit]	*vt. & vi.*	复制；重复
elimination	[iˌlimi'neiʃn]	*n.*	消除；除去；淘汰
			eliminate *vt.* 消除；排除
emerge	[i'mɜːdʒ]	*vi.*	出现；浮现；暴露；摆脱
enable	[i'neibl]	*vt.*	使能够，使成为可能
evolution	[ˌiːvə'luːʃn]	*n.*	演变；进展；进化

evolve	[i'vɔlv]	*vt. & vi.*	发展，进化；逐步形成
ignorant	['ignərənt]	*a.*	无知的；愚昧的
impose	[im'pəuz]	*vt. & vi.*	把……强加于；迫使；推行；强制实行
infant	['infənt]	*n.*	婴儿；幼儿
		a.	婴儿的；幼稚的；初期的；未成年的
insert	[in'sɜ:t]	*vt.*	插入；嵌入
internal	[in'tɜ:nəl]	*a.*	内部的；内在的；国内的
legal	['li:gl]	*a.*	法律的；合法的；法定的
			illegal *a.* 非法的；违法的
manipulation	[mə,nipju'lei∫n]	*n.*	操作；操纵；使用
			manipulate *vt.* 操纵；操作
★ nutritional	[nju'tri∫ənl]	*a.*	有营养的；滋养的
			★ **nutrition** *n.* 营养，营养品
★ overwhelming	[,əuvə'welmiŋ]	*a.*	压倒性的；势不可挡的
perfect	[pə'fekt]	*vt.*	使完美；使完善
	['pɜ:fikt]	*a.*	完美的；最好的；精通的
precaution	[pri'kɔ:∫n]	*n.*	预防，警惕；预防措施
previous	['pri:viəs]	*a.*	先前的；以往的；稍前的
reaction	[ri'æk∫n]	*n.*	反应，回应；抗拒；阻碍；化学反应
scandal	['skændl]	*n.*	丑闻；丑行；流言飞语
★ strand	[strænd]	*n.*	股，缕；部分，方面
		vt.	使搁浅；使滞留
supplement	['sʌpləment]	*n.*	补充物；添加物；增刊
		vt.	补充，增补
synthetic	[sin'θetik]	*a.*	合成的，人造的
		n.	合成物
★ temperament	['temprəmənt]	*n.*	气质，性情，性格
therapy	['θerəpi]	*n.*	治疗，疗法
trait	[treit]	*n.*	特性，特点；品质
★ visualize	['viʒuəlaiz]	*vt. & vi.*	想象，设想；构想；使形象化

be immune to	对……有免疫力；不受……的影响
clear up	清理；整理；打扫；放晴
ease up	缓和；放松；减轻
fight off	击退；排斥；竭力避免

for the sake of	为了；为了……的利益
in effect	实际上；生效
pass on	传递；继续；去世

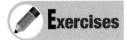 **Exercises**

Part I. Understanding the text

1. **Study the title of Text C.**
   - What are the key words in the essay title?
   - Why do you think they are the key words?

2. **Spend 10 minutes browsing the essay and work out the outline of the essay, with reference to the following:**
   - Thesis statement/main argument
   - Supporting ideas

   After you have finished, discuss your outline with your partner.

Part II. Writing skills development

3. **Read the following paragraphs of Text C and decide the argument and the type of evidence used therein: facts, statistics, research results, examples, reliable authority/sources, or illustrative incidents, etc.**

   1) Read Paragraph 3 and decide its argument and the type of evidence used to support the argument.

      Argument: _____

      Type of evidence: _____

   2) Read Paragraph 4 and decide its argument and the type of evidence used to support the argument.

      Argument: _____

      Type of evidence: _____

   3) Read Paragraphs 5–7 and decide its argument and the type of evidence used to support the argument.

      Argument: _____

      Type of evidence: _____

   4) Read Paragraph 10 and decide its argument and the type of evidence used to support the argument.

Argument: _____

Type of evidence: _____

4. **Read the text again and discuss with your partner how coherence within and across paragraphs is achieved.**

Part III. Language focus

5. **Choose the right word from the four choices to complete each of the following sentences.**

1) We need to take in certain proteins to _____ fat every day.

   A. digest   B. duplicate   C. manufacture   D. confront

2) With the help of cloning, some medicine manufacturers in the world are now working on products against _____ intestinal infections.

   A. external   B. valid   C. internal   D. susceptible

3) _____ research revealed that genetically modified food could be both beneficial and harmful to human beings.

   A. Prior   B. Previous   C. Legal   D. Giant

4) A series of measures taken by the biotechnological industry helps _____ the safety issue.

   A. rely on   B. clear up   C. lead to   D. follow up

5) Since genetic diseases _____ a large proportion of our population, genetic engineering is worth research.

   A. infect   B. manipulate   C. emerge   D. affect

6) Up to now, some genetic diseases can be _____ by prenatal tests but others can only be diagnosed in early adulthood.

   A. detected   B. cured   C. eliminated   D. impacted

7) It still remains a controversy why some people are _____ to certain diseases such as small pox.

   A. ignorant   B. beneficial   C. perfect   D. immune

8) To create an account on a website, one must have a username and a _____ made up of several numbers and/or letters.

   A. source   B. reaction   C. code   D. therapy

9) It usually takes a long time for a person to _____ to a new environment; it takes even longer time for a gene to do so to a new body.

   A. adapt   B. impose   C. contribute   D. enable

10) Diseases that are _____ through genes can cause serious consequences such as paralysis, mental deteriorating, physical deformity, and death.

   A. fought off   B. passed on   C. accounted for   D. eased up

6. Paragraph the following sentences.

1) Some people feel that cloning should be banned, however never seeming to see its medical value.

2) If the science of genetic engineering is wrong, then so are the rest of the advances in medicine.

3) It is no different for a plant to be able to fight off pests than it is for a human to be able to fight off diseases.

Part IV. Writing

7. Discuss with your partner on what information you might expect to follow each of the following sentences:

- Cloning has value in medicine.
- Genetic diseases affect a large proportion of our population.

8. Read the text again and study the following phrases and sentence structures used to support arguments.

Statistics	• Dolly the lamb was born 148 days later. Dolly was produced after 277 failures.
Quotes	• The FDA and State Governments impose limits… • In 20 years, scientists believe…
Examples	• Some genetic diseases can be detected… but others such as Huntington's can only be detected in early adulthood… • There is an article from the "Times" that is about a middle aged man…. • For example, many years ago small pox was widely spread. • One example of cloning is "Dolly".
Analogy	• If the science of genetic engineering is wrong, then so are the rest of the advances in medicine. • It is no different for a plant to be able to fight off pests than it is for a human to be able to fight off diseases. • Genetic engineering is in the first stage of its discovery and will emerge in the twenty first century and will be as accepted as is flying and space travel.

9. Use the following statistics to write a paragraph which develops the following topic sentence:

No advance in genetic engineering is easy.

- DNA was discovered more than 130 years ago in 1869. Some 74 years passed before scientists recognized its function.

- Dolly was produced after 277 failures.

Suggested writing steps:

- Write the first draft alone.
- Peer review each other's writing.
- Revise your first draft.

Unit Summary

In this unit, you have practiced supporting arguments with reliable sources such as fact, statistics, research results, examples, quotations, illustrative incidents, etc. Now, do the following exercises to consolidate your knowledge.

1. How do you explain the following terms?

1) Facts and statistics

2) Research result

3) Quotation

4) Illustrative incidents

2. Identify the function of the underlined sections in each extract below.

1) Federal, state, and local governments employed about <u>12% of engineers in 2008.</u>
<u>About 6%</u> were in the Federal Government, mainly in the U.S. Departments of Defense, Transportation, Agriculture, Interior, and Energy, and in the National Aeronautics and Space Administration. Many engineers in State and local government agencies worked in highway and public works departments. <u>In 2008, about 3% of engineers</u> were self-employed, many as consultants.

2) Is genetic engineering permissible when applied to human beings, or, even more, at least in some cases obligatory, or rather it has to be forbidden? Some authors, in particular in the utilitarian tradition, have a very positive attitude toward genetic engineering. <u>John Harris, for example</u>, finds it not only tolerable, but also admirable in some cases.

3) <u>Ackerman, being part of the liberal tradition of political thought, says</u> that each

member of the political society must be allowed to choose his or her system of goals and values by himself or herself. This statement is relevant to the topic of genetic engineering because genetic manipulations are an example of choice of goals and values that will be obtained or affirmed in the future (by changing people we can choose that the future world will be a world of affirmation of music talent, or sport talent, etc.).

4) <u>Scientific observation states</u> that any organism can give birth to or reproduce another organism of the same species. Sometimes, genetic mutations may occur that might make the offspring appear physically or otherwise different from the parent(s) and such mutation, with extremely rare exceptions, is usually in the form of a genetic disorder or disfiguration. The mutated offspring being better than the parents is not a common phenomenon. Going by this observation, only a sporadic burst of progressive mutations can lead to the inception of creatures better equipped for survival than its previous generations. This is where the foundations of the theory of natural selection receive a mighty blow!

3. **Write your essay: Use the skills you have learned to write an argumentative essay on any topic related to engineering. At this stage, you shall be able to write an essay of 200 to 250 words.**

Prewriting

Work out the outline of the essay and ask yourself: ✔ or ✘

What is the overall stance/argument of the essay?	☐
Is the overall stance/argument obvious in Introduction and/or Conclusion?	☐
Is the main idea clear in each supporting paragraph?	☐
How many paragraphs will the essay have?	☐
Does the outline follow a logical sequence of ideas?	☐

Writing

Write the first draft alone.

Revising

Once you have the first draft of your paper completed, (peer) review it with the following questions in mind: ✔ or ✘

Does the Introduction and/or Conclusion clearly present the overall argument?	☐
Are the ideas clearly and logically organized?	☐
Is the main argument in each supporting paragraph supported with adequate evidence?	☐
Are the sentences grammatical and concise?	☐
Is coherence within and across paragraphs adequately achieved?	☐
After that, please revise your first draft.	☐

4. Match the following words (a–t) to their definitions (1–20). Make sure you have fully understood them.

Words	Definitions
a. create	1. a situation in which people, groups or countries are involved in a serious disagreement or argument
b. alter	2. to make a disease or an illness spread to a person, an animal or a plant
c. address	3. weak or easily hurt physically or emotionally
d. ban	4. to be used instead of something/somebody else; to do something instead of somebody/something else
e. challenge	5. to make somebody/something different; to become different
f. conflict	6. to make or produce goods in large quantities, using machinery
g. consume	7. to produce or provide something such as a profit, result or crop
h. infect	8. to change something slightly, especially in order to make it more suitable for a particular purpose
i. manufacture	9. to make something known to others
j. replace	10. to think about a problem or a situation and decide how to deal with it
k. reveal	11. to be the parts that together form something
l. vulnerable	12. happening now, of the present time
m. yield	13. to forbid something officially
n. confront	14. an urgent and deeply felt request for money, help or information, especially one made by a charity or by the police
o. modify	15. to use something, especially fuel, energy or time
p. constitute	16. a time of great danger, difficulty or uncertainty when problems must be solved or important decisions must be made
q. appeal	17. a statement or an action that shows that somebody refuses to accept something and questions whether it is right, legal, etc.
r. current	18. to change something to make it suitable for a new use or situation
s. crisis	19. to make somebody face or deal with an unpleasant or difficult person or situation
t. adapt	20. to make something happen or exist

Science

Writing Skill Development

Supporting Evidence and Effective Argumentation (2)

Cause and Effect

In some argumentative essays, the evidence is supported by causes or effects. The cause is to explore the reasons of an event and the effect concentrates on the results of an event on society, nature, etc.

Words and phrases indicating cause and effect

since, because, because of, as, for, on account of, due to, as a result, consequently, therefore, thus, so, hence, in that, result from/in, prove, support, confirm, attest to, etc.

Formats for the cause and effect relation

- One effect happens as a result of one cause.
- One effect happens as a result of Cause A, Cause B, Cause C…
- One cause brings about an effect.
- One cause brings about Effect A, Effect B, Effect C…

Please read the following paragraph and find out the cause and effect relation in it.

"In recent decades, cities have grown so large that now about 50% of the Earth's population lives in urban areas. There are several reasons for this occurrence. First, the increasing industrialization of the nineteenth century resulted in the creation of many factory jobs, which tended to be located in cities.

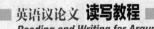

These jobs, with their promise of a better material life, attracted many people from rural areas. Second, there were many schools established to educate the children of the new factory laborers. The promise of a better education persuaded many families to leave farming communities and move to the cities. Finally, as the cities grew, people established places of leisure, entertainment, and culture, such as sports stadiums, theaters, and museums. For many people, these facilities made city life appear more interesting than life on the farm, and therefore drew them away from rural communities."

Source: http://essayinfo.com/essays/cause_and_effect_essay.php.

The following chart summaries the main ideas of the above paragraph and helps you understand the relationships better.

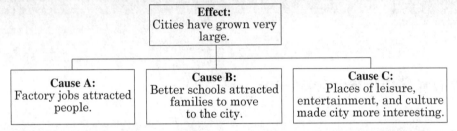

Cause-and-effect relationships are common in our daily lives, so paragraphs of the essays are often developed by the cause-and-effect relationship existing between two or more subjects. In the writing, we try to trace causes or predict effects or explain the chain of cause-and-effect. As for the arrangement of such writings, it seems convenient to state the effect first and then explain the causes. The reverse order, however, is to be preferred when one cause leads to various effects. Sometimes, causes and effects are arranged in this way: a cause first, then an effect, which serves again as a cause of another effect because there is a chain of cause-and-effect. Here are two examples:

Example 1:

The introduction of new varieties of rice and wheat in Asia and Latin America has been known as the "Green Revolution". Its direct effects of introducing high-yielding varieties of food grains have been modest, but its *indirect effects* have sometimes been significant. The new technology has led to *changes in crop pattern and in methods of production.* It has accelerated *the development of a market-oriented, capitalist agriculture.* It has encouraged the growth of wage labor, and thereby helped to create or augment a class of agriculture laborers. It has increased the power of landowners, and this in turn has been associated with *a greater polarization of classes and intensified conflict.*

Example 2:

It is natural for young people to be critical of parents at times and to blame them for most of the misunderstandings between them. Young people often irritate their parents with their choices in clothes and hairstyles, in entertainers and music. This is not their motive. *They feel cut off from the adult world* into which they have not yet been accepted. So they create a culture and society of their own. Then, if it turns out that their music or entertainers or vocabulary or clothes or hairstyles irritate their parents, *this gives them additional enjoyment.* They feel that they are superior, at least in a small way, and that they are leaders in style and taste.

Example 1 analyzes the effects. The writer focuses on the indirect effects of the introduction of new varieties of food grains, which are: the change in crop pattern and in methods of production; the development of a market-oriented capitalist agriculture; and a greater polarization of classes and intensified conflict. In Example 2, the writer gives the reasons why young people often irritate their parents with their choices in clothes and hairstyles. The first reason is that young people feel that they are cut off from the adult world, so they want to create a society of their own. The second reason is that their choices in clothes and hairstyles will give them additional enjoyment because of the feeling of superiority.

Please read the following paragraph and find out the cause and effect relation in it.

Only three strategies are available for controlling cancer: prevention, screening, and treatment. As for lung cancers, the main strategy must be prevention. There are four reasons why the prevention to lung cancer is of such overwhelming importance. Firstly, the disease is extremely common, causing more deaths than any other type of cancer nowadays. Secondly, it is generally incurable. Thirdly, effective, practicable measures to reduce its incidence are already reliably known. And finally, reducing tobacco consumption will also have a substantial impact on many other diseases.

Strategies for writing argumentative essays in terms of cause and effect

When writing an argumentative essay supported by cause and effect, you'd better keep the following suggestions in mind (http://lrs.ed.uiuc.edu/students/fwalters/cause. html):

1) Focus on immediate and direct causes. Limit yourself to causes that are directly related to the main effect, as opposed to remote and indirect causes, which have little impact on the main effect.

2) You also need to notice or to establish a proper relation between the direct causes and indirect causes, major causes and minor causes, major and minor effects.

3) Transitional words, phrases and even sentences are significant in showing the relationship between causes and effects, so try to use them in the writing.

4) Though the argument is mainly supported by cause and effect in an argumentative essay which is dedicated to the analyses of reasons and outcomes, rich materials, examples, and statistics, etc. are also needed to prove the idea.

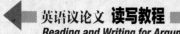
5) Distinguish between causes and effects. To determine causes, ask, "Why did this happen?" To identify effects, ask, "What happened because of this?" The following is an example of one cause producing one effect:

 Cause —You are out of gas.

 Effect —Your car won't start.

Sometimes, many causes contribute to a single effect or many effects may result from a single cause. But, it can be very complicated in many situations. The following is an example of a chain reaction:

Thinking about friend… forgot to buy gas… car wouldn't start… missed math exam… failed math course.

Reading for Ideas

Text Ⓐ

Can Animals and Plants Adapt to Global Warming?[1]

❶ Humans are transforming the global environment. Great swathes of temperate forest (大片辽阔的温带森林) in Europe, Asia and North America have been cleared over the past few centuries for agriculture, **timber** and urban development. Tropical forests are now in danger. Human-assisted species invasions of pests, competitors and **predators** are rising **exponentially**, and over-**exploitation** of fisheries, and killing of forest animals, **to the point of collapse** (濒临崩溃的边缘), continues to be the rule rather than the exception.

❷ Driving this has been a six-fold expansion of the human population since 1800 and a 50-fold increase in the size of the global economy. The great modern human enterprise was built on exploitation of the natural environment. Today, up to 83% of the Earth's land area is under direct human influence and we entirely dominate 36% of the bioproductive surface (可生长生物的地表). Up to half the world's freshwater runoff (径流) is now captured for human use. More **nitrogen is** now **converted into reactive** forms by industry than all by all the planet's natural processes and our industrial and agricultural processes are causing a continual build-up of long-lived greenhouse gases to levels **unprecedented** in at least the last 800,000 years.

---

1 This essay was retrieved from *EMBO* reports2, 165-168(2001). http://www.skepticalscience.com/Can-animals-and-plants-adapt-to-global-warming.htm.

❸   Clearly, this planet-wide domination by human society will have implications for biological diversity. Indeed, a recent review on the topic, the 2005 Millennium Ecosystem Assessment report, drew some **bleak** conclusions—60% of the world's ecosystems are now degraded and the extinction rate is now 100 to 1,000 times higher than the "background" rate of long spans of geological time. For instance, a study I conducted in 2003 showed that up to 42% of species in the Southeast Asian region could be **consigned to** extinction by the year 2100 due to deforestation (森林开伐) and habitat **fragmentation** alone.

❹   Given these existing pressures and upheavals (巨变), it is a reasonable question to ask whether global warming will make any further meaningful contribution to this mess. Some, such as the **sceptics** S. Fred Singer and Dennis Avery, see no danger at all, maintaining that a warmer planet will be beneficial for mankind and other species on the planet and that "**corals**, trees, birds, mammals, and butterflies are adapting well to the routine reality of changing climate." Also, although climate change is a concern for conservation biologists, it is not the focus for most researchers (at present), largely I think because of the severity and immediacy of the damage caused by other threats.

❺   Global warming to date has certainly affected species' **geographical** distributional ranges and the timing of breeding, migration, flowering, and so on. But extrapolating (外推；推断) these observed impacts to predictions of future extinction risk is challenging. The most well known study to date, by a team from the UK, estimated that 18% and 35% of plant and animal species will **be committed to** extinction by 2050 due to climate change. This study, which used a simple approach of estimating changes in species geographical ranges after fitting to current bioclimatic conditions, caused **a flurry of** debate. Some argued that it was overly optimistic or too uncertain because it left out most ecological detail, while others said it was possibly overly **pessimistic**, based on what we know from species responses and apparent resilience (恢复力) to previous climate change in the **fossil** record.

❻   A large number of ancient mass extinction events have indeed been strongly linked to global climate change, including the most **sweeping** die-off that ended the Palaeozoic Era (古生代), 250 million years ago. Yet in the more recent past, during the Quaternaryglacial (第四纪冰河时代) cycles spanning the last million years, there were apparently few climate-related extinctions. This curious paradox of few ice age extinctions even has a name—it is called "the Quaternary Conundrum (第四纪难题)".

❼   Over that time, the globally averaged temperature difference between the depth of an ice age and a warm interglacial (间冰期的) period was 4°C to 6°C. Most species appear to have persisted across these multiple glacial–interglacial cycles. This can be inferred from the fossil record, and from genetic evidence in modern species. In Europe and North America, populations shifted ranges southwards as the great northern hemisphere ice sheets advanced, and reinvaded northern realms when the glaciers retreated.

8 However, although the geological record is essential for understanding how species respond to natural climate change, there are a number of reasons why future impacts on biodiversity（生物多样性）will be particularly severe:

9 Human-**induced** warming is already rapid and is expected to further accelerate. The IPCC（政府间气候变化专门委员会）storyline **scenarios** imply a rate of warming of 0.2°C to 0.6°C per decade. By comparison, the average change from 15 to 7 thousand years ago was 0.005°C per decade, although this was occasionally punctuated by short-lived **abrupt** climatic **jolts**, such as the Younger Dryas（新仙女木期）.

10 A low-range optimistic estimate of 2°C of 21st century warming will shift the Earth's global mean（平均）surface temperature into conditions which have not existed since the middle Pliocene（上新世中叶）, 3 million years ago. More than 4°C of atmospheric heating will take the planet's climate back, within a century, to the largely ice-free world that existed prior to about 35 million years ago. The average "species' lifetime" is only 1 to 3 million years. So it is quite possible that in the comparative geological instant of a century, **planetary** conditions will be transformed to a state unlike anything that most of the world's modern species have encountered.

11 As noted above, it is critical to understand that ecosystems in the 21st century have lost resilience. Most habitats are already degraded and their populations depleted. For millennia our impacts have been localized although often severe, but during the last few centuries we have **unleashed** physical and biological transformations on a global scale. In this context, synergies（协同作用）from global warming, ocean acidification（酸化；成酸性）, habitat loss, habitat fragmentation, invasive species, chemical pollution are likely to lead to cascading extinctions. For instance, over-harvest, habitat loss etc. will probably enhance the direct impacts of climate change and make it difficult for species to move to undamaged areas or to maintain a "**buffer**" population size. One threat reinforces the other, or multiple impacts play off on each other, which makes the overall impact far greater than if each individual threats occurred in isolation (Brook et al., 2008).

12 Past adaptation to climate change by species was mainly through shifting their geographic range to higher or lower latitudes, or up and down mountain **slopes**. There were also evolutionary responses—individuals that were most tolerant to new conditions survived and so made future generations more **intrinsically** resilient. Now, because of the points described above, this type of adaptation will, in most cases, simply not be possible or will be inadequate to cope. Global change is simply too pervasive and occurring too rapidly. Time's up and there is nowhere for species to run or hide.

Reference:

Brook, B. W., Sodhi, N. S. & Bradshaw, C. J. A. (2008). Synergies Among Extinction Drivers Under Global Change. *Trends in Ecology and Evolution*, 23, 453-460.

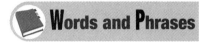

Words and Phrases

abrupt	[əˈbrʌpt]	a.	突然的；唐突的；陡峭的；生硬的
★ bleak	[bliːk]	a.	荒凉的；阴冷的；黯淡的，无希望的
▲ buffer	[ˈbʌfə]	n.	缓冲器，减震器；缓冲区
		vt.	缓冲
collapse	[kəˈlæps]	vi.	倒塌；瓦解；暴跌
		vt.	使倒塌，使崩溃；使萎陷
		n.	倒塌；失败；衰竭
▲ coral	[ˈkɔrəl]	n.	珊瑚；珊瑚虫
		a.	珊瑚色的；珊瑚的
exploitation	[ˌeksplɔiˈteiʃn]	n.	开发，开采；利用；广告推销
▲ exponentially	[ˌekspəˈnenʃəli]	adv.	以指数方式
			▲ exponent n. 指数，幂
fossil	[ˈfɔsl]	n.	化石；僵化的事物；顽固不化的人
		a.	化石的；陈腐的，守旧的
fragmentation	[ˌfrægmenˈteiʃn]	n.	破碎；分裂；存储残片
			fragment n. 碎片，碎块
geographical	[ˌdʒiːəˈgræfikl]	a.	地理的；地理学的
			geography n. 地理（学）
induced	[inˈdjuːst]	a.	感应的；诱发型
★ intrinsically	[inˈtrinsikli]	adv.	本质地；固有地；内在地
▲ jolt	[dʒəult]	vt.	使颠簸；使摇动；使震惊
		n.	颠簸；摇晃；震惊；严重挫折
nitrogen	[ˈnaitrədʒən]	n.	[化] 氮
pessimistic	[ˌpesiˈmistik]	a.	悲观的，厌世的；悲观主义的
★ planetary	[ˈplænətri]	a.	行星的
▲ predator	[ˈpredətə]	n.	食肉动物；掠夺者；捕食者

reactive	[ri'æktiv]	a.	反动的；反应的；电抗的
			react vi.（作出）反应；反对；起化学反应（作用）
★ scenario	[si'nɑ:riəu]	n.	情节；剧本；方案
★ sceptic	['skeptik]	n.	怀疑论者；疑虑极深的人
slope	[sləup]	n.	倾斜；斜率；斜坡；扛枪姿势
		vi.	倾斜；逃走
		vt.	扛；倾斜；使倾斜
sweeping	['swi:piŋ]	n.	扫除；垃圾
		a.	扫荡的；彻底的；广泛的
timber	['timbə]	n.	木料；木材
▲ unleash	[ʌn'li:ʃ]	vt.	解开……的皮带；解除……的束缚；发动
		vi.	不受约束；自由自在；放荡不羁
★ unprecedented	[ʌn'presidəntid]	a.	空前的；史无前例的

a flurry of	一阵
be committed to	致力于；委身于；以……为己任
be converted into	使转变；把……转化成
consign to	交付给
to the point of	达到……的程度

Exercises

Part I. Understanding the text

1. Study the title of Text A.

- What are the key words in the essay title?
- Why do you think they are the key words?

2. Spend 10 minutes browsing the essay and work out the outline of the essay, with reference to the following:

- Thesis statement/main argument
- Supporting ideas

After you have finished, discuss your outline with your partner.

Part II. Writing skills development

3. Read the essay and find out the "effect" of the following "cause".

Cause: Today, up to 83% of the Earth's land area is under direct human influence and we entirely dominate 36% of the bioproductive surface. Up to half the world's freshwater runoff is now captured for human use. More nitrogen is now converted into reactive forms by industry than all by all the planet's natural processes and our industrial and agricultural processes are causing a continual build-up of long-lived greenhouse gases to levels unprecedented in at least the last 800,000 years and possibly much longer.

Effect: _____

Part III. Language focus

4. Find the correspondent words to the following interpretations from the essay.

1) to fall down or inward suddenly; cave in; to break down suddenly in strength or health and thereby cease to function

2) to move or dislodge with a sudden, hard blow; strike heavily or jarringly

3) sudden or unexpected

4) belonging to a thing by its very nature

5. Choose the right word to complete each of the following sentences. Change the form where necessary.

arid	deplete	exponential	unleash	resilient
bleak	sceptic	jolt	consign	pessimistic

1) Mankind must take care not to_____the earth of its natural resources.

2) The child was_____to his uncle's care, so you needn't worry anymore.

3) She was_____ by the betrayal of her trusted friend. She was so miserable.

4) The government must still convince the_____that its policy will work.

5) People tend to become_____and lose confidence in adverse circumstances.

6) It seems to me that these plants will not root in such_____ soil.

7) He'll get over it—young people are amazingly_____ .

8) Thousands of trees were planted on the_____ hillside last year.

9) The Populations in India are growing at an_____ rate.

10) Usually enormous forces are_____in thunderstorms.

6. Paraphrase the following sentences.

1) Humans are transforming the global environment. Great swathes of temperate forest in Europe, Asia and North America have been cleared over the past few centuries for agriculture, timber and urban development.

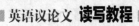
2) For instance, a study I conducted in 2003 showed that up to 42% of species in the Southeast Asian region could be consigned to extinction by the year 2100 due to deforestation and habitat fragmentation alone.

3) Human-induced warming is already rapid and is expected to further accelerate.

4) The global warming will shift the Earth's global mean surface temperature into conditions which have not existed since the middle Pliocene.

Part IV. Writing

7. **Discuss with your partner on what information you might expect to follow each of the following sentences:**

1) Humans are transforming the global environment.

2) Human-induced warming is already rapid and is expected to further accelerate.

8. **Read the text again and study the following phrases and sentence structures used to support arguments.**

Research results	• Indeed, a recent review on the topic, the 2005 Millennium Ecosystem Assessment report, drew some bleak conclusions—…
Statistics	• Today, up to 83% of… dominate 36% of the bioproductive surface.
Quotes	• …S. Fred Singer and Dennis Avery, … maintaining that… that "corals, trees, birds, mammals, and butterflies are adapting well to the routine reality of changing climate"…
Examples	• For instance, a study I conducted in 2003 showed that…

9. **Try to use the methods above and write a paragraph which develops the following topic sentence:**

Economic globalization has a strong impact on the development of China.

> **Suggested writing steps:**
>
> • Write the first draft alone. (You can argue this topic from the positive or negative perspective).
> • Peer review each other's writing.
> • Revise your first draft based on the peer feed back.

Text B

Intermittent Exercise—Factors That Effect Performance[1]

❶   Participation in sports and recreational activities often requires individuals to perform repeated **bursts** of all-out effort with short recovery **intervals**.

❷   This type of movement pattern is usually seen in the multiple sprint (短跑；冲刺) sports such as soccer, rugby, hockey and basketball.

❸   In these sports, the periods of maximal exercise last only a few seconds (usually up to 6) and are randomly **punctuated** by longer periods of rest or lower **intensity** activity such as standing still, walking or jogging. During actual play, this unpredictable mixture of sprint and **endurance** activities imposes unique demands on the energy supply systems of the body and the early onset of **fatigue** is a common experience.

❹   Fatigue is **manifested** by the inability of the participant to perform maximally and **deterioration** in the **execution** of motor skills even at submaximal exercise intensities. Consequently, the energy demands and the degree of fatigue experienced during **intermittent** exercise can vary considerably depending upon the intensity and duration of each exercise period, the time allowed for recovery, the exercise intensity during recovery, and finally the **preceding** number of high intensity exercise **bouts**.

❺   In most of the multiple sprint sports it would be considered **advantageous for** a player to be able to maintain high-intensity running performance especially during the later stages of the game. Training improves performance in many ways and not least of course, by delaying the early onset of fatigue. In practice, however, this activity pattern, which demands a combination of sprint and endurance running over a relatively long time, requires a large energy production which **is associated with** a large **consumption** of energy fuels. During sprint running, the energy needed by the working muscles for **contraction** must be provided at a very high rate. This is achieved mainly through the anaerobic (厌氧的) degradation of two **compounds** stored in the muscles, namely phosphocreatine (PCr, 磷酸肌酸) and glycogen (糖原) leading to lactic (乳的；乳汁 的) **acid** formation. Phosphocreatine breaks down rapidly **at the onset of** maximal exercise but can provide enough energy for only 5–10 seconds. Muscle glycogen is also **utilized** very rapidly at the onset of maximal exercise although there is a **progressive** decline in energy **provision** from this fuel. Consequently, as maximal exercise continues for several seconds performance begins to decline even in the presence of adequate

---

1 The essay was written by Georgios C. Gaitanos, extracted from *Understanding English for Science and Technology* of Science Press.

PCr and the **accumulation** of products of anaerobic metabolism (新陈代谢) such as lactic acid.

6 During recovery from maximal exercise, PCr is resynthesized (再合成) from energy which **is derived** almost **exclusively from** aerobic metabolism. Resynthesis of PCr is a relatively rapid process during recovery. In contrast, **removal** of lactic acid from the muscle is a much slower process taking several minutes. Thus, when considering performance during repeated brief periods of maximal exercise, recovery duration becomes a very important **variable**. The influence of recovery duration on performance during this type of exercise has been extensively examined.

7 It has been shown that when performing repeated 6-second sprints with 30, 60 and 120 seconds of recovery intervals, performance was **impaired** less with the longer recovery interval. This can be explained by the greater resynthesis of PCr and removal of lactic acid from the muscle that occurs during the longer intervening recovery periods.

8 It should be pointed out, however, that performance during repetitive maximal exercise is also dependent upon sprint distance and the preceding number of sprints. For example, if one attempts to cover 600m by doing forty 15m sprints (3 sec) every 30 seconds, no decrease in performance is observed during each sprint. In contrast, if the same distance is covered by doing fifteen 40m (6 sec+) sprints every 30 seconds, then a significant decrease in performance is observed after only three sprints. It becomes apparent therefore, that 30s are long enough to recover from approximately 3s bouts of sprint running, but not when the duration of sprints is extended to approximately 6s. These findings may indicate that in the 15m sprints **trial** there is an adequate resynthesis of PCr during each 30s recovery period. In contrast, in the 40m sprints there is **insufficient** PCr resynthesis and muscle is not able to recover from the increased energy demands during this short recovery interval. It seems therefore, that the **availability** of PCr might be one of the most likely limitations to muscle performance during repeated brief bouts of maximal exercise.

9 As mentioned above, degradation of muscle glycogen also makes a significant contribution to energy provision during repeated brief periods of maximal exercise. However, the rate at which glycogen is utilized declines as the number of bouts is increased. Given the limited glycogen stores of the body, it is important for games players to maintain, preserve and increase their glycogen reserves to meet the heavy metabolic demands during competition and training that leads to a **pronounced** utilisation of glycogen. In addition, these players unlike most endurance athletes, often compete with insufficient time between games for **optimal** recovery, as in a **tournament** situation. For these reasons, a high **carbohydrate** diet consumed at appropriate times before and after exercise (7–10g/kg body weight daily) has to become accepted practice among players. In soccer, for example, players who start the match with low glycogen concentration in the leg muscles, cover a shorter distance and sprint significantly less, particularly in the second half, compared with players who have initially normal glycogen levels prior to the match. In addition consumption of 6% carbohydrate solution during **prolonged** high-intensity intermittent running **spares** muscle glycogen utilization. Thus, it is clearly advantageous for an athlete who participates in multiple sprint sports to increase carbohydrate consumption before, during and after exercise to cope with heavy training and competition.

⑩ Recently, oral creatine **supplementation** has been shown to increase the resting concentration of PCr in muscles, and the rate of PCr resynthesis following maximal exercise. This would, in theory be advantageous when performing repeated bouts of maximal exercise with short recovery intervals. Although there is insufficient research information regarding the effectiveness of this nutritional supplement as a precompetition ergogenic (机能增进的；生力的) aid during actual play, it is possible that players may benefit during training **drills** which are designed to improve the capacity to perform high-intensity exercise repeatedly with relatively short recovery periods between bouts of exercise.

⑪ In conclusion, when repeated sprints are performed with short recovery intervals, the decline in performance is associated with a decline in energy provision from PCr. In this respect creatine supplements may benefit performance. During more prolonged intermittent exercise, however, glycogen **depletion** is also a potential factor contributing to fatigue. Thus, a high carbohydrate diet before, during and after this type of exercise is recommended as an effective nutritional strategy for optimal performance.

📖 Words and Phrases

accumulation	[əˌkjuːmjuˈleiʃn]	n.	积聚，累积；堆积物
acid	[ˈæsid]	n.	酸；< 俚 > 迷幻药
		a.	酸的；讽刺的；刻薄的
★ availability	[əˌveiləˈbiləti]	n.	可用性；有效性；实用性
▲ bout	[baut]	n.	较量；发作；回合；一阵
burst	[bɜːst]	vt. & vi. & n.	爆发，突发；爆炸
▲ carbohydrate	[ˌkɑːbəuˈhaidreit]	n.	糖类；碳水化合物
compound	[ˈkɔmpaund]	vt.	混合；合成；掺合
		n.	化合物；复合词；混合物

		a.	复合的；混合的
consumption	[kən'sʌmpʃn]	n.	消费；消耗
contraction	[kən'trækʃn]	n.	收缩，紧缩；缩写式；害病
▲ depletion	[di'pliːʃn]	n.	消耗；放血；损耗
★ deterioration	[diˌtiəriə'reiʃn]	n.	恶化；退化；堕落
drill	[dril]	n.	钻子；钻孔机；播种机；训练
		vt. & vi.	钻孔；训练
endurance	[in'djuərəns]	n.	忍耐；持久；耐久；忍耐力
exclusively	[ik'skluːsivli]	adv.	专有地；排外地；唯一地
			exclusive a. 高级的；独有的；排他的
			n. 独家新闻
★ execution	[ˌeksi'kjuːʃn]	n.	执行，实行；完成；死刑
fatigue	[fə'tiːg]	n.	疲劳，疲乏；杂役
		vt.	使疲劳；使心智衰弱
		vi.	疲劳
		a.	疲劳的
impaired	[im'peəd]	a.	受损的
			impair vt. 损害，损伤，削弱
intensity	[in'tensəti]	n.	强烈；强度；亮度；紧张
★ intermittent	[ˌintə'mitənt]	a.	间歇的，断断续续的
intervals	['intəvls]	n.	间隔；音程
insufficient	[ˌinsə'fiʃnt]	a.	不足的，不充足的
		n.	不足
			sufficient a. 足够的，充分的
★ manifest	['mænifest]	vt.	证明，表明；显示
		vi.	显示，出现
		a.	明白的；显然的，明显的
▲ optimal	['ɔptiməl]	a.	最理想的；最佳的
preceding	[pri'siːdiŋ]	a.	在前的；前述的
			★ precede vt. 在……之前，先于
			★ precedent n. 先例，范例，判例；惯例
progressive	[prə'gresiv]	a.	进步的；先进的
		n.	改革论者；进步分子
★ prolonged	[prə'lɔŋd]	a.	延长的；拖延的；持续很久的
pronounced	[prə'naunst]	a.	断然的；显著的；讲出来的

			pronounce *vt.* 发音；宣布，宣判
provision	[prə'viʒn]	*n.*	供应品；准备；条款；规定
		vt.	供给……食物及必需品
			▲ provisional *a.* 暂时的，临时的
★ punctuate	['pʌŋktʃueit]	*vt.*	不时打断；强调；加标点于
		vi.	加标点
removal	[ri'mu:vl]	*n.*	移动；免职；排除；搬迁
spare	[speə]	*vt.*	节约，吝惜；饶恕；分出，分让
		vi.	饶恕，宽恕；节约
		a.	多余的；瘦的；少量的
		n.	剩余；备用零件
★ supplementation	[,sʌplimen'teiʃn]	*n.*	补充；增补
			★ supplementary *a.* 增补的，补充的
▲ tournament	['tuənəmənt]	*n.*	比赛；锦标赛，联赛
trial	['traiəl]	*n.*	试验；磨炼；审讯；努力
		a.	审讯的；试验的
utilize	['ju:təlaiz]	*vt.*	利用
			★ utilization *n.* 利用
variable	['veəriəbl]	*a.*	易变的，多变的；可变的；变异的
		n.	可变物，可变因素；[数] 变量

at the onset of...	在……的最初
be advantageous for	对……有利
be associated with	和……联系在一起，与……有关
be derived from...	源自于……，来自，由……得到

 **Exercises**

Part I. Understanding the text

1. **Study the title of Text B.**
   - What are the key words in the essay title?
   - Why do you think they are the key words?

2. **Spend 10 minutes browsing the essay and work out the outline of the essay, with reference to the following:**

   - Thesis statement/main argument
   - Supporting ideas

   After you have finished, discuss your outline with your partner.

Part II. Writing skills development

3. **Read the essay and find out the "causes" for the following "effects".**

   1) **Effect:** When considering performance during repeated brief periods of maximal exercise, recovery duration becomes a very important variable.

      Causes: _____

   2) **Effect:** The availability of PCr might be one of the most likely limitations to muscle performance during repeated brief bouts of maximal exercise.

      Causes: _____

   3) **Effect:** A high carbohydrate diet consumed at appropriate times before and after exercise has to become accepted practice among players.

      Causes: _____

4. **Read the text again and discuss with your partner how coherence within and across paragraphs is achieved.**

Part III. Language focus

5. **Choose the right word to complete each of the following sentences. Change the form where necessary.**

consume	accumulate	available	intense
interval	endure	utilize	

   1) By buying ten books every month, he soon _____ a good library.

   2) Keys are _____ on application to the principal.

   3) Its findings provide the scientific foundation for rational _____ of land.

   4) Chinese economy is developing rapidly and the Chinese government encourages individual _____.

   5) The announcement says that latecomers will not be admitted until the _____.

   6) Both the boy and the girl vowed their love would _____ forever.

   7) He fell down and hurt his left leg seriously and the pain increased in _____.

6. **Paraphrase the following sentences.**

   1) In practice, however, this activity pattern, which demands a combination of sprint and endurance running over a relatively long time, requires a large energy produc-

tion which is associated with a large consumption of energy fuels.

2) As mentioned above, degradation of muscle glycogen also makes a significant contribution to energy provision during repeated brief periods of maximal exercise.

3) For these reasons, a high carbohydrate diet consumed at appropriate times before and after exercise (7–10g/kg body weight daily) has to become accepted practice among players.

Part IV. Writing

7. Discuss with your partner what information you might expect to follow each of the following sentences:

1) It should be pointed out, however, that performance during repetitive maximal exercise is also dependent upon sprint distance and the preceding number of sprints.

2) In most of the multiple sprint sports it would be considered advantageous for a player to be able to maintain high-intensity running performance especially during the later stages of the game.

8. Now imagine you are going to write a paragraph on popularity of sports in U.S. Now talk with your partner about the possible causes and effects and try to be logical and ordered.

9. Write out the paragraph discussed above with cause and effect relationship. You can employ some other methods used in the essay.

Contrast	• PCr is resynthesized from energy... Resynthesis of PCr is a relatively rapid process... In contrast, removal of lactic acid from the muscle is a much slower process...
Statistics	• It has been shown that when performing repeated 6-second sprints with 30, 60 and 120 seconds of recovery intervals... • In addition consumption of 6% carbohydrate solution...
Examples	• For example, if one attempts to cover 600m by doing...

Suggested writing steps:

- Write the first draft alone.
- Peer review each other's writing.
- Revise your first draft.

Text C

Stem Cell Research—Why Is It Regarded as a Threat?[1]

—An investigation of the economic and ethical arguments made against research with human embryonic stem cell

1　The British House of Lords voted on January 22, 2001 to **ease** restrictions on the use of human embryonic **stem** cells. Researchers in the UK are now allowed to use early stage human embryos for **therapeutic** purposes, mainly to **retrieve** stem cells. This decision comes amidst a heated debate regarding the medical and economic potential of stem cell research as against its ethical **pitfalls**. The scientific, legal, ethical and philosophical arguments have been discussed extensively (Colman & Burley, 2001).

2　What I wish to discuss is why the prospect of stem cell therapy has been greeted, in quite widespread circles, not as an **innovation** to be welcomed but as a threat to be resisted. In part, this is the characteristic reaction of Luddites, who regard all technological innovation as threatening and look back **nostalgically** to a **fictitious**, golden, pre-industrial past. There are, however, also serious arguments that have been made against stem cell research; and it is these that I would like to discuss.

Stem cell technologies would be very expensive and available only to rich countries and to rich people.

3　It is indisputable that most novel medical technologies are expensive. However, they usually get cheaper as the scale on which they are used increases. A good example is bone marrow（骨髓）transplantation, which initially was extremely expensive. A few decades later, bone marrow transplantation has become a routine procedure that is cheap enough to be used for the treatment of numerous diseases as more patients are treated, as the manufacturing process becomes more efficient and as patents **expire**.

4　There is, however, a further argument against this particular threat. One of the major financial problems of health care since World War II has been that major advances in **clinical** research resulted in ways of controlling diseases rather than curing them. The elderly and many **chronically** ill people in the First World now live a life of high quality. But this depends on the long-term administration of drugs to treat a number of conditions including high blood pressure, diabetes（糖尿病）, rheumatoid（风湿的）arthritis（关节炎）and asthma（哮喘）. Consequently, the cost of health care in these countries has dramatically increased over the last few decades. Even for diseases such as Parkin-

---

1 This article was written by Peter Lachmann, president of the Academy of Medical Sciences in London.

son's disease(帕金森综合症)that cannot be adequately controlled, continuous therapy is given over many years to relieve **symptoms**. Stem cell therapy may indeed lead to cures for many **ailments**. It may become possible to cure Parkinson's disease with **grafts** of brain cells. It is also likely that diabetes will be curable using stem cell treatment. It may also be possible to achieve at least something approaching a cure for cardiovascular(心血管的)diseases by replacing damaged endothelial(内皮的)cells in the blood vessels or the cardiomyocytes(心肌细胞)in the heart itself. If these promises hold true, stem cell therapy might result in a reduction in the overall cost of healthcare as a number of currently incurable diseases are cured.

Stem cell research would deviate efforts from other health strategies.

❺　　It is difficult to tell in advance what type of research will give rise to what type of benefit. The fundamental research from which stem cell technology originated came from studies in developmental biology whose **utility** could not have been foreseen. Furthermore, current research into the mechanisms of cellular reprogramming and into the growth requirements of different cell lineages (血统；家系) will not only advance scientific knowledge, but is also likely to become of widespread value in clinical medicine.

❻　　These two preceding arguments are essentially economic. The following are predominantly ethical and should therefore be given greater weight. But before considering them, it is worth remembering Onora O'Neill's eloquent warning against declamatory or polemical ethics at the Millennium Festival of Medicine. Ethics is a subject grounded in philosophy and religion. Ethics cannot be determined by polling people and asking them what they think is right or wrong and simply accepting the view of the majority. It does require support from logically and philosophically coherent arguments.

Somatic (躯体的；肉体的) cell nuclear transfer is immoral as it involves creating embryos only to destroy them.

❼　　The essential problem here is to decide at what stage of development a human embryo acquires the interests—and the rights to protect these interests—that characterize a human being, i.e. when does an embryo become part of humanity? This is a problem that has occupied a great deal of theological and philosophical attention and the arguments have been extensively discussed (Dunstan, 1990; Dunstan & Seller, 1988).

❽　　One **principal** condition is regarded as sufficient to confer interests and the right to defend them—sentience (感觉能力，知觉). Sentience here is defined as the ability to form any links with the outside world. Until an organism has a rudimentary (基本的；初步的) central nervous system and some sense receptors—be it for pain, touch, smell, taste, sight or sound—it cannot form any contact with the outside world and there-

fore is not sentient. It therefore does not seem possible to attribute sentience to a pre-**implantation** embryo, or indeed even to an implanted embryo until it has developed some form of nervous system and sense organs.

❾   The **medieval** church **took the view** that an embryo acquired a soul, or it became animatus, at the same time that it became formatus, i.e. when it acquired recognizable human form. The medieval church held that the abortion（流产）of an embryo that was neither formatus nor animatus was only a **fineable offence**; and it was only after an embryo had become animatus that abortion became a mortal sin. At the core of the refusal of the Roman Catholic Church to countenance（支持）embryo research is a **doctrine** by Pope Pius IX, who declared in 1869 that an embryo acquires full human status at fertilization.

❿   But women lose large numbers of pre-implantation embryos throughout their reproductive life. These embryos are not **mourned**, they are not given **burial** and no one says prayers for them. The intra-uterine（子宫内的）**coil** is designed to prevent implantation of embryos and, again, is not regarded as being morally reprehensible（应该谴责的）.

⓫   Further difficulties for the view that full human status is acquired at fertilization arise from advances in reproductive biology. Somatic cell nuclear transfer does not involve fertilization and thus turns the Pius IX doctrine ad absurdum, since it makes it possible to see in any somatic cell whose nucleus can be introduced into an oocyte（卵母细胞）, the potential for giving rise to a complete human being. When reprogramming of cells becomes better understood, it may be possible to convert somatic cells into embryos without the need for an oocyte. If, ultimately, any somatic cell has the potential of being grown into a complete embryo and, **subsequently**, into a human being, it would logically mean that we should **ascribe** a moral status to every cell in the body—a concept that is clearly ridiculous.

⓬   The view that an embryo does not acquire the status of a human being until it is obviously of human form with a central nervous system and organs, or even until it is delivered, is more defensible on philosophical grounds than is stating that human status is acquired at fertilization. Of course, any decision relating to the particular point in development at which an embryo acquires full human status must be partially **arbitrary**. There are other cases where there is blurring at the interface of two categories or where distinctions are made slightly arbitrarily. The fact that making distinctions can sometimes be difficult is not an argument for making fundamentalist distinctions or making no distinction at all.

Eventually, an "immortal" population could evolve and that would create its own moral problems.

⑬   This proposal derives from John Harris who is sufficiently impressed by the promises of stem cell therapy to believe that we may have to face a population that can live two or even more centuries (Harris, 2000). Success on that sort of scale seems a long way off—but it would be an accolade（荣誉）to medicine to have that set of problems to face!

⑭   I wish to close with another quotation from the *Microcosmographica Academica*: "There is only one reason for doing something; the rest are arguments for doing nothing." The Luddites can always produce a variety of more or less **plausible** arguments for resisting technological innovation. But without innovation we would not have moved on from the Stone Age to the Computer Age in only 100 generations. The present arguments for doing nothing are no more potent than all preceding ones.

References:

Colman, A. & Burley, J. C. (2001). A Legal and Ethical Tightrope. *EMBO Reports*, 2, 2.

Cornford, F. M. (1908). *Microcosmographica Academica*. Cambridge: Bowes & Bowes.

Dunstan, G. R. (1990). *The Human Embryo: Aristotle and the Arabic and European Traditions*. Exeter: University of Exeter Press.

Dunstan, G. R. & Seller, M. J. (1988). *The Status of the Human Embryo: Perspectives from Moral Tradition*. Oxford: King Edward's Hospital Fund for London & Oxford University Press.

Hamilton, W. D., Axelrod, R. & Tanese, R. (1990). Sexual Reproduction as an Adaptation to Resist Parasites. *Proc. Natl Acad. Sci.*, 87, 3566–3573.

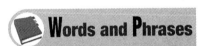

Words and Phrases

▲ ailment	['eilmənt]	*n.*	小病；不安
arbitrary	['ɑ:bitrəri]	*a.*	任意的；武断的；专制的
★ ascribe	[ə'skraib]	*vt.*	归因于；归咎于
burial	['beriəl]	*n.*	埋葬；葬礼；弃绝
		a.	埋葬的
★ chronically	['krɔnikli]	*adv.*	慢性地；延续很长地
clinical	['klinikl]	*a.*	临床的；诊所的
coil	[kɔil]	*vt.*	盘绕，把……卷成圈
		n.	卷；线圈

		vi.	成圈状
★ deviate	['di:vieit]	*vi.*	越轨；脱离
		vt.	使偏离
★ doctrine	['dɔktrin]	*n.*	教义；学说；主义；信条
ease	[i:z]	*vt.*	减轻，缓和；使安心
★ expire	[ik'spaiə]	*vi.*	终止；期满；死亡；呼气
		vt.	呼出（空气）
fictitious	[fik'tiʃəs]	*a.*	虚构的；假想的；假装的；编造的
fineable	['fainəbl]	*n.*	终曲
		a.	可罚款的（=finable）
▲ graft	[grɑ:ft]	*vt. & vi.*	嫁接；移植；贪污
		n.	嫁接；移植；渎职
▲ implantation	[ˌimplɑ:n'teiʃn]	*n.*	移植；灌输；鼓吹
			▲ implant *vt.* 移植；灌输
★ innovation	[ˌinə'veiʃn]	*n.*	创新，革新；新方法
★ medieval	[ˌmedi'i:vl]	*a.*	中世纪的；仿中世纪的；老式的
★ mourn	[mɔ:n, məun]	*vt. & vi.*	哀悼；忧伤；服丧
▲ nostalgically	[nɔ'stældʒikəli]	*adv.*	怀乡地；恋旧地
			▲ nostalgic *a.* 怀旧的，引起对往事怀恋的
offence	[ə'fens]	*n.*	攻击；违反；犯罪；过错
▲ pitfall	['pitfɔ:l]	*n.*	缺陷；陷阱，圈套；诱惑
plausible	['plɔ:zəbl]	*a.*	貌似真实的，貌似有理的；花言巧语的
principal	['prinsəpl]	*n.*	校长；资本；委托人，当事人；主犯
		a.	首要的；最重要的
★ retrieve	[ri'tri:v]	*vt.*	重新得到；恢复；检索
		vi.	找回猎物
		n.	检索；恢复；取回
			★ retrieval *n.* 取回；补偿
stem	[stem]	*n.*	茎；干；船首；血统
		vt.	除去……的茎；给……装柄；阻止；逆行
subsequently	['sʌbsikwəntli]	*adv.*	随后，其后；后来
symptom	['simptəm]	*n.*	征兆；症状
therapeutics	[ˌθerə'pju:tiks]	*n.*	疗法；治疗学
utility	[ju:'tiləti]	*n.*	效用；实用；功用；公共设施
		a.	有多种用途的；通用的；实用的

take the view	持某种观点

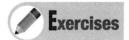 **Exercises**

Part I. Understanding the text

1. **Study the title of Text C.**
   - What are the key words in the essay title?
   - Why do you think these are the key words?

2. **Spend 10 minutes browsing the essay and work out the outline of the essay, with reference to the following:**
   - Thesis statement/main argument
   - Supporting ideas

   After you have finished, discuss your outline with your partner.

Part II. Writing skills development

3. **Read the whole essay again and find out the "causes" for each "effect".**

   1) **Effect:** There are difficulties for the view that embryo acquires full human status at fertilization.

      Causes: _____

   2) **Effect:** Somatic cell nuclear transfer turns the Pius IX doctrine ad absurdum.

      Causes: _____

4. **Read the text again and discuss with your partner how coherence within and across paragraphs is achieved. And try to find some transitional sentences in the essay.**

Part III. Language focus

5. **Choose the right word to complete each of the following sentences. Change the form where necessary.**

deviate	potent	arbitrary	expire
retrieve	graft	fictitious	plausible

   1) Non-Korean scholars criticize that they made _____ interpretations for historical sources which depended on whether they suited their nationalistic beliefs or not.

2) It is proved that this statement seemed slightly to _____ from the truth.

3) The chairman of the company knows that the lease has _____ and he has to seek sponsorship again.

4) He is not an honest man and he always greets people with _____ enthusiasm.

5) Burns can often be cured by _____ on skin from another part of the same body.

6) I should like to _____ my umbrella which I left in the car.

7) Both ideas sound _____ and there was no way of telling in advance who was right.

8) The chemical teacher told us that the extract from the bark was a _____ blend of active compounds.

6. Paraphrase the following sentences.

1) The British House of Lords voted on January 22, 2001 to ease restrictions on the use of human embryonic stem cells.

2) If these promises hold true, stem cell therapy might result in a reduction in the overall cost of healthcare as a number of currently incurable diseases are cured.

3) But without innovation we would not have moved on from the Stone Age to the Computer Age in only 100 generations.

Part IV. Writing

7. Discuss with your partner on what information you might expect to follow each of the following sentences:

1) One principal condition is regarded as sufficient to confer interests and the right to defend them—sentience.

2) Further difficulties for the view that full human status is acquired at fertilization arises from advances in reproductive biology.

8. Read the text again and study the following phrases and sentences used to support arguments.

Definition	• Sentience here is defined as the ability to form any links with the outside world.
Quotes	• I wish to close with another quotation from the *Microcosmographica Academica*: ...
Examples	• A good example is bone marrow transplantation... • But this depends on the long-term administration of drugs to treat a number of conditions including high blood pressure, diabetes, rheumatoid arthritis and asthma.

(continued)

Interpretation	• The essential problem here is to decide at what stage of development… i.e. when does an embryo become part of humanity? • The medieval church took the view that… i.e. when it acquired recognizable human form.

9. **Use the following statistics and other methods as needed to write a paragraph which develops the following topic sentence:**

Smoking cigarettes is bad for your health.

- According to World Health Organization, in developed countries, smoker's account for 90% of those who get cancer.

- Among the patients who have coronary heart disease (冠心病) and hypertension (高血压), 75% of them have smoking history.

> **Suggested writing steps:**
> - Write the first draft alone.
> - Peer review each other's writing.
> - Revise your first draft.

Unit Summary

In this unit, you have practiced using causes and effects in argumentative essays to prove ideas. Now, do the following exercises to consolidate your knowledge.

1. Identify the causes and effects in the following paragraphs.

1) Times Square is the unquestionable center of entertainment in New York City. There are nearly a hundred Broadway theaters and Off-Broadway stages. People can choose many kinds of musicals from internationally well-known classical to lively and unusual productions. Besides Broadway theaters, there are a lot of movie theaters in which most recent Hollywood first-run films are shown. People can see different popular films and spend a whole day in these theaters. Moreover, during lunchtime, there are some street performances such as Jazz and Hard Rock. People crowd the street and listen to ethnic and experimental music with special sound effects. As a result, no one feels bored in Times Square as it brings her or him a rich variety of entertainment like Broadway musicals, movies and street shows.

2) The explanation for the phenomenon of the rising teenage suicide rate involves many complicated factors. Some attribute the rise to an overemphasis on early success, others point to mounting peer pressure, and still others to confusion over changing social values.

2. Match the following words (a–j) to their definitions (1–10). Make sure you have fully understood them.

Words	Definition
a. abrupt	1. readily perceived by the eye or understanding; evident
b. intrinsical	2. stopping or ceasing for a time; alternately ceasing and beginning again
c. deplete	3. most favorable or desirable; best
d. intermittent	4. to interrupt at intervals
e. manifest	5. belonging to a thing by its very nature
f. punctuate	6. created, taken, or assumed for the sake of concealment; not genuine
g. optimal	7. to turn aside, as from a route, way, course, etc.; to depart or swerve, as from a procedure, course of action, or acceptable norm
h. fictitious	8. sudden or unexpected
i. retrieve	9. to decrease seriously or exhaust the abundance or supply of
j. deviate	10. to recover or regain; to bring back to a former and better state; restore

3. Complete the following sentences with the words above.

1) Being chronically angry, frustrated, or apprehensive can _____ your physical resources.

2) The _____ level of investment depends on a country's stage of development.

3) Thinking can indirectly and resumptively reflect _____ attribute and inherent rule of existence in the function of human brain.

4) Did you hear the _____ sound outside?

5) The former football star says he went into a hotel room to _____ sports memorabilia belonging to him.

6) Though the novel is _____, we can see the truth of human nature through those writing.

7) Nobody denies the _____ disaster of the past four years.

8) The _____ change of schedule gave me lots of trouble.

9) Children should not _____ too much from the topic that has been chosen.

10) The staccato of the dancer's heels against the floor, and the sharp bursts of clapping _____ the singer's haunting wail.

4. **Try to write out all the possible causes of the following effect.**

   Fast-food consumption in China keeps increasing a lot these years.

5. **List all the possible effects of the following cause.**

   China opens her gate to the whole world in the 1970s.

6. **Write your essay: Use the skills you have learned to write an argumentative essay on the effects of global warming in your daily life. At this stage, you shall be able to write an essay of 200 to 250 words.**

   Prewriting

   Work out the outline of the essay and ask yourself: ✔ **or ✘**

   What is the overall stance/argument of the essay?   ☐
   Is the overall stance/argument obvious in Introduction and/or Conclusion? ☐
   Is the main idea clear in each supporting paragraph?   ☐
   How many paragraphs will the essay have?   ☐
   Does the outline follow a logical sequence of ideas?   ☐

   Writing

   Write the first draft alone.

   Revising

   Once you have the first draft of your paper completed, (peer) review it with the following questions in mind: ✔ **or ✘**

   Does the Introduction and/or Conclusion clearly present the overall argument? ☐
   Are the ideas clearly and logically organized?   ☐
   Is the main argument in each supporting paragraph supported with adequate evidence? ☐
   Are the sentences grammatically correct and concise?   ☐
   Is coherence within and across paragraphs adequately achieved?   ☐

   After that, please revise your first draft.

Writing Skill Development

Supporting Evidence and Effective Argumentation (3)

Comparison and Contrast

What are comparison and contrast?

Using comparison and contrast involves looking at both similarities and differences. As soon as you begin to compare two things, you usually begin to contrast them as well, for rarely are two things alike in all respects. Comparison brings similar things together for examination, to see how they are alike, whereas contrast is a form of comparison that emphasizes their differences (McWhorter, 2000). For example, when you compare and contrast two houses, you consider how they are similar (in terms of layout, size, building materials) and how they are different. Analyzing similarities and differences is a common and useful decision-making skill by weighing (or comparing) options and alternatives.

The purpose of comparison and contrast

Writers use comparison and contrast for two purposes (McWhorter, 2000):

1) To draw distinctions among related subjects. In many instances, comparison is used to eliminate confusion. Many people, for instance, mistake an *optician* who makes and sells eyeglasses for an *optometrist* who performs eye examinations and prescribes lenses. Comparison can pair extended definitions to show readers

the difference, for example, between air-cooled and water-cooled engines, African and Indian elephants, or cross-country and downhill skiing. When drawing distinctions writers explain differences between similar subjects but do not choose one over the other.

2) To recommend a choice between two things. For example, TV commercials compare competing products, political campaign brochures urge voters to support a candidate over his or her rival, articles in medical journals argue that one drug is more effective than the other, business proposals recommend one computer program or one security service over competitors, and government studies assert that one air-quality standard is preferable to another.

The organization of comparison and contrast

When developing an argumentative essay supported by comparison and contrast, you must be sure that your subjects share enough common points for meaningful discussion (Connelly, 1997). This means that you should not try to compare and contrast things so completely different that you will not have any basis of comparison. For example, you would not try to support your viewpoint by arguing that the tourist industry is better than the banking system.

In addition, comparison and contrast have to be carefully limited, especially when comparing and contrasting broad or complex subjects. For example, if you are comparing differences between two presidents, you might focus your comparison on their relations with the press, the way they handled crises, or their trade polices.

Perhaps the most frustrating problem while writing argumentative essays supported by comparison and contrast is organizing ideas. Without careful planning, you may find yourself awkwardly switching back and forth between subjects. Your reader may have difficulty following your train of thought and may confuse one subject with another.

There are two ways to organize comparison and contrast in argumentative writing: in sequence (point by point or alternating method), and in chunks (subject by subject or block method) (McWhorter, 2000).

➡ Point-by-point organization

In sequencing, the items are compared point by point. Suppose you want to compare two used cars (Car A and Car B), after brainstorming ideas, you decide to compare the following aspects: price, body type, gas mileage, and engine size. You would first discuss the price of each car, then their body type, then gas mileage, and finally engine size. You would go back and forth between the two cars, noting similarities and differences

between them on each of the four points of comparison. You can visualize the pattern as shown in Graph 1.

Graph 1: A point-by-point comparison and contrast

```
                        ┌─────────┐
                   ┌───►│  Car A  │
┌─────────┐        │    └─────────┘
│  Price  │────────┤    ┌─────────┐
└─────────┘        └───►│  Car B  │
     │                  └─────────┘
     ▼                  ┌─────────┐
                   ┌───►│  Car A  │
┌─────────┐        │    └─────────┘
│Body type│────────┤    ┌─────────┐
└─────────┘        └───►│  Car B  │
     │                  └─────────┘
     ▼                  ┌─────────┐
                   ┌───►│  Car A  │
┌─────────┐        │    └─────────┘
│Gas mileage│──────┤    ┌─────────┐
└─────────┘        └───►│  Car B  │
     │                  └─────────┘
     ▼                  ┌─────────┐
                   ┌───►│  Car A  │
┌─────────┐        │    └─────────┘
│Engine size│──────┤    ┌─────────┐
└─────────┘        └───►│  Car B  │
                        └─────────┘
```

Example 1

Though my hometown and my college town are twins since they have several things in common, the essential features of the two cities make them different. My hometown Gridlock and my college town Subnormal are all located in rural areas and their population is close to each other, the composition of the residents and their life vary considerably. Gridlock is surrounded by many acres of farm which are devoted mainly to growing corn and soybeans. As 73% of the residents are retirees, they live a comparatively relaxed and enjoyable life. On the contrary, in Subnormal where 52% of middle-aged people and 39% of young men work full time, life is always stressful and challenging there. In addition, Gridlock contains a college campus, Neutron College, whose research is primarily directed in Environmental Policy program and does not seem to have much immediate influence on the life of the locals. Subnormal is similar to Gridlock in that it also boasts a beautiful college campus called Quark College, but it is well known for its Finance and Computer Science. Since 68% of graduates go into these fields, they earn an average of 56%–60% more than similar people in Gridlock. Consequently, despite the similarities they bear, they are basically not the same type of the cities.

This paragraph uses a point-by-point organization: the writer moves back and forth between his two subjects (Gridlock and Subnormal), comparing them on the basis of several key points or characteristics to argue that they are actually different.

The point-by-point method tends to emphasize details and specifics. It often works better for lengthy technical papers. It keeps both subjects current in the readers' mind as the specific facts, statistics, and quotes about A and B appear side by side. It is also helpful when addressing multiple readers who may be interested in only a portion of the paper. However, argumentative essays organized in point-by-point manner about abstract subjects might be difficult to develop because many important details about one subject may have nothing in common with the other subject.

➡ Subject-by-subject organization

In chunking or in the subject-by-subject organization, each object of comparison is presented separately. You would first discuss all points of comparison about Car A (its price, body type, gas mileage, and engine size) before moving on to Car B (see Graph 2).

Graph 2: A subject-by-subject comparison and contrast

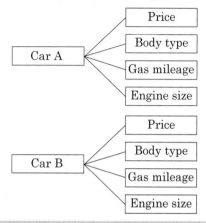

Example 2

Though my hometown and my college town are twins since they have several things in common, the essential features of the two cities make them different. My hometown Gridlock and my college town Subnormal are all located in rural areas and their population is close to each other, the composition of the residents and their life vary considerably. Gridlock is surrounded by many acres of farm which are devoted mainly to growing corn and soybeans. As 73% of the residents are retirees, they live a comparatively relaxed and enjoyable life. In addition, Gridlock contains a college campus, Neutron College, whose research is primarily directed in Environmental Policy program and does not seem to have much immediate influence on the life of the locals. On the contrary, in Subnormal where 52% of middle-aged people and 39% of young men work full time, life is always stressful and challenging there. Subnormal is similar to Gridlock in that it also boasts a beautiful college campus called Quark College, but it is well known for its Finance and Computer Science. Since 68% of graduates go into these fields, they earn an average of 56%–60% more than similar people in Gridlock. Consequently, despite the similarities they bear, they are basically not the same type of the cities.

This passage still argues for the view that Gridlock and Subnormal are essentially different, but adopting a subject-by-subject organization of comparison and contrast. Namely, the author describes the key points of Gridlock first and then moves on to those of Subnormal.

The subject-by-subject method is often preferable for short expository papers. When writing an argumentative essay, comparison and contrast are often used side by side with other types of evidence to support the view(s).

Integrating comparison and contrast into an argumentative essay

While some argumentative essays may use comparison and contrast as the primary pattern of development, in most cases, comparison and contrast are integrated into argumentative essays as a type of evidence. They can be particularly effective in argumentative essays intending to be persuasive. Please use the following tips to incorporate comparison and contrast into argumentative essays supported by different types of evidence (McWhorter, 2000).

1) Determine the purpose of the comparison and contrast. What will it contribute to your argumentative essay?

2) Introduce the comparison and contrast clearly. Tell your readers how it supports the main point of the argumentative essay. Do not leave it to readers to figure out why the comparison is included.

3) Keep the comparison and contrast short and to the point. An extended comparison will distract readers from the overall point of your argumentative essay.

4) Organize the points of the comparison and contrast. Even though it is part of a large essay, the comparison and contrast should follow a point-by-point or subject-by-subject organization.

If you use point-by-point method, keep the following suggestions in mind:

- Work back and forth between your two subjects, generally mentioning the subjects in the same order. If both subjects share a particular characteristic, then you may want to mention the two subjects together.

- Arrange your points of comparison carefully; start with the clearest, simplest points and then move on to more complex ones.

If you use subject-by-subject method, keep the following suggestions in mind:

- Be sure to cover the same points for both subjects.

- Cover the points of comparison in the same order in both halves of your essay.

- Write a clear statement of transition whenever you switch from one subject to the other.

5) Use transitions. Transitional words and expressions are especially important in easing the flow into the comparison and contrast and then back to the essay's primary pattern of development. They can alert readers to the organization of the argumentative essay as well as to shifts between subjects or to new points of comparison. An argumentative essay lacking transitions sounds choppy and unconnected. Some useful transitional words include *similarly, in contrast, on the one hand, on the other hand,* and *not only...but also,* etc.

References:

Connelly, M. (1997). *The Sundance Reader*. San Diego: Harcourt Brace Jovanovich Publishers.

McWhorter, K. T. (2000). *Successful College Writing*. Boston, New York: Bedford/St. Martin's.

Reading for Ideas

Text A

iPads and Kindles Are Better for the Environment Than Books

By Brian Palmer

❶ With Apple and Amazon's touting (兜售) their e-readers like iPad and Kindle, some bookworms are bound to wonder if tomes-on-paper (纸版巨著，大部头书) will one day become **quaint relics**. But the question also arises, which is more environmentally friendly: an e-reader or an old-fashioned book?

❷ Environmental analysis can be an endless balancing of this vs. that. Do you care more about **conserving** water or avoiding toxic chemical usage? **Minimizing** carbon dioxide **emissions** or **radioactive** nuclear waste? But today the Lantern (华盛顿邮报 的一个专栏) has good news: There will be no Sophie's Choice[1] when it comes to e-books. As long as you consume a healthy number of titles, you read at a normal pace and you don't **trade in** your **gadget** every year, perusing (细读，精读) electronically will lighten your environmental impact.

❸ If the Lantern has taught you anything, it's that most consumer products make their biggest scar on the Earth during manufacture and transport, before they ever get into your greedy little hands. Accordingly, green-minded consumers are usually-although not always—**better off** buying fewer things when possible. Reusable cloth diapers (尿布), for example, are better than **disposables**, because the environmental costs of manufacture and transport **outweigh** those of washing.

❹ Think of an e-reader as the cloth diaper of books. Sure, producing one Kindle

---

1 Sophie's Choice: 两难的选择，或说没有选择。Sophie's Choice 是作家 William Styron1979 年出版的小说，1982 年 被改编成同名电影。小说描述波兰女子 Sophie 在第二次世界大战期间的悲惨遭遇。其中一个场景是纳粹要把她的一 个孩子送去集中营，她必须在她的一双儿女中选择一个。(A 1979 novel written by William Styron, depicts a mother at wits' end, faced with a forced decision in which all options have equally negative outcomes.)

is tougher on the environment than printing a single **paperback** copy of "Pride and **Prejudice**". But every time you download and read an electronic book, rather than purchasing a new pile of paper, you're **paying back** a little bit of the carbon dioxide and water **deficit** from the Kindle production process. The actual operation of an e-reader represents a small percentage of its total environmental impact, so if you run your device into the ground, you'll **end up** paying back that debt many times over. (Unless, of course, reading "Pride and Prejudice" over and over again is enough for you. Then, **by all means**, buy it in print and enjoy.)

5   According to the environmental consulting firm Cleantech, which **aggregated** a series of studies, a single book generates about 7.5 kilograms (almost 17 pounds) of carbon dioxide **equivalents**. (That's the value of all its greenhouse gas emissions expressed in terms of the impact of carbon dioxide.) This figure includes production, transport and either **recycling** or disposal.

6   Apple's iPad generates 130 kilograms of carbon dioxide equivalents during its lifetime, according to company estimates. Amazon has not released numbers for the Kindle, but Cleantech and other analysts put it at 168 kilograms. Those analyses do not indicate how much additional carbon is generated per book read (as a result of the energy required to host the e-bookstore's servers and power the screen while you read), but they do include the full cost of manufacture, which likely **accounts for** the **lion's share** of emissions. (The iPad uses just three watts of electricity while you're reading, far less than most light bulbs.) If we can trust those numbers, then, the iPad pays for its CO_2 emissions about one-third of the way through your 18th book. You'd need to get halfway into your 23rd book on Kindle to get out of the environmental red.

7   Water is also a major consideration. The U.S. newspaper and book publishing industries together consume 153 billion gallons of water annually, according to figures by the nonprofit group Green Press Initiative included in the Cleantech analysis. It takes about seven gallons to produce the average printed book, while e-publishing companies can create a digital book with less than two cups of water. (Like any other company, e-book publishers consume water through the paper they use and other office activities.) Researchers estimate that 79 gallons of water are needed to make an e-reader. So you come out on top, water-wise, after reading about a dozen books.

8   E-readers also have books beat on toxic chemicals. The production of ink for printing releases a number of **volatile** organic compounds（有机化合物）into the atmosphere, including hexane（己烷）, toluene（甲苯）and xylene（二甲苯）, which contribute to smog and **asthma**. Some of them may also cause cancer or birth defects. Computer production is not free of hard-to-pronounce chemicals, to be sure, but both the iPad and the Kindle **comply with** Europe's RoHS[1] standards, which ban some of the scarier chemicals that have been involved in electronics production. E-readers do, however, require the **mining** of **nonrenewable** minerals, such as columbite-tantalite （铌钽铁矿）, which sometimes come from politically unstable regions. And experts can't seem to agree on whether we're at risk of exhausting the world's supply of lithium （锂）, the lifeblood of the e-reader's battery.

9　If you're not ready to **plunk down** $139 for a Kindle or $499 for an iPad, or if you just love the feel of dead tree between your fingers, there's one thing you can do to significantly ease the environmental impact of your reading: Buy your books online. Brick-and-mortar （实体的） bookstores are very inefficient because they stock more books than they can sell. Between a quarter and a third of a bookstore's volumes will ultimately be shipped back to the publisher and on to recycling centers or landfills （垃圾填筑地）.

10　An even better option is to walk to your local library, which can spread the environmental impact of a single book over an entire community. Unfortunately, libraries are underutilized. Studies suggest that fewer than a third of Americans visit their local library at least once a month, and fewer than half went in the last year. Libraries report that the average community member checks out 7.4 books per year—far less than the three per month consumed on e-readers—and more than a third of those items were children's books.

11　As such, it is clear that iPads and Kindles are better for the environment than books. Of course, you could also stop reading altogether. But then how would you know how much carbon you saved?

Words and Phrases

★ aggregate	['ægrigət]	vt.	使聚集，使积聚；总计达
▲ asthma	['æsmə]	n.	哮喘
★ conserve	[kən'sɜːv]	vt.	节约，节省；保护，保藏，保存
deficit	['defisit]	n.	不足额；赤字；亏空；亏损
disposable	[di'spəuzəbl]	a.	一次性的，可任意处理的
		n.	一次性物品
★ emission	[i'miʃn]	n.	排放；辐射；排放物
equivalent	[i'kwivələnt]	a.	相等的，相当的，等效的；等价的，等

---

1 RoHS 是由欧盟立法制定的一项强制性标准，它的全称是《关于限制在电子电器设备中使用某些有害成分的指令》 (Restriction of Hazardous Substances)。

积的；[化学] 当量的

★ gadget	['gædʒit]	n.	小玩意；小配件；小装置
mine	[main]	vt. & vi.	在……中开采，开采
★ minimize	['minimaiz]	vt.	把……减至最低数量（程度）；对（某事）做最低估计
★ nonrenewable	[ˌnɔnri'nju:əbl]	a.	不可再生的；不可更新的
outweigh	[ˌaut'wei]	vt. & vi.	比……重要
★ paperback	['peipəbæk]	n.	平装本，平装书
prejudice	['predʒudis]	n.	偏见
▲ quaint	[kweint]	a.	（由于老式而）诱人的，奇特的
★ radioactive	[ˌreidiəu'æktiv]	a.	放射性的
recycle	[ri:'saikl]	vt.	回收利用；使再循环
		vi.	重复利用
▲ relic	['relik]	n.	遗迹；古董
▲ volatile	['vɔlətail]	a.	易变的，不稳定的；挥发的

---

account for	说明（原因、理由等）；导致；（在数量、比例上）占……
better off	比较富裕；情况好转
by all means	一定，务必
comply with	服从
end up	（以……）结束；最终成为；最后处于
lion's share	最大的一份，最好的一份
pay back	偿还；报复；报答；偿付
plunk down	付给
trade in	用（旧物）贴换新物；出售，经营

 **Exercises**

Part I. Understanding the text

1. **Study the title of Text A.**

   ● What are the key words in the essay title?

   ● Why do you think they are the key words?

2. Outlining: Read the essay quickly and summarize the author's main supporting ideas (usually suggested in topic sentences) and compare them with the list of ideas you have produced on iPads and Kindles. Do you think the points presented by the author are justifiable and convincing enough? Why or why not?

Part II. Writing skills development

3. Read the text and identify types of evidence used in the article.

4. Familiarize yourself with the following phrases and sentence structures of comparison and contrast, and then try to add more examples from the essay to the list.

Comparison	Reusable cloth diapers, for example, **better than** disposables, because *the environmental costs of manufacture and transport* **outweigh** *those of washing.*
Contrast	But the question also arises, *which is more environmentally friendly:* an e-reader **or** an old fashioned book?

5. Does the comparison and contrast in the essay make a recommendation? If so, what makes the chosen subject superior to others? What evidence is offered?

Part III. Language focus

6. Try to match the words to their corresponding denotations in the two columns below.

a. equivalent	1) to protect something and prevent it from changing or being damaged
b. impact	2) to reduce to the smallest possible amount, extent, size, or degree
c. aggregate	3) to be a particular amount when added together
d. defect	4) evaporating readily at normal temperatures and pressures
e. deficit	5) intended to be used once or for a short time and then thrown away
f. disposable	6) the difference between the amount of something that you have and higher amount that you need
g. volatile	7) a fault or a lack of something that means that something or someone is not perfect
h. conserve	8) having the same value, purpose, job, etc. as a person or thing of a different kind
i. minimize	9) the effect or influence that an event, situation, etc. has on someone or something

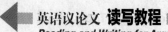

7. Paraphrase the following sentences.

1) As long as you consume a healthy number of titles, you read at a normal pace and you don't trade in your gadget every year, perusing electronically will lighten your environmental impact.

2) They do include the full cost of manufacture, which likely accounts for the lion's share of emissions.

3) If you're not ready to plunk down $139 for a Kindle or $499 for an iPad, or if you just love the feel of dead tree between your fingers, there's one thing you can do to significantly ease the environmental impact of your reading.

Part IV. Writing

8. Write an essay (about 300 words) on either of the following topics, using comparison and contrast to illustrate your idea(s).

1) "E-books (including iPads, Kindles and digital books) should or should not replace printed books". Use supporting evidence to illustrate your view. You are encouraged to use expressions and ideas from the text such as "if Tomes-on-paper will one day become quaint relics" (Paragraph 1) as well as your own insights.

2) It is a common practice in universities for students to evaluate their teachers' work at the end of each semester. There is a belief in society that teaching is a form of service because teachers are selling knowledge. Therefore it makes no big difference between teaching and service offered by waiters. Do you agree? Use specific reasons and examples to support your idea.

In-depth discussion with your partners

- *What are the similarities and differences between teaching and service offered by waiters?*
- *Do you think it is a good idea for teachers to be evaluated only by students?*
- *Do you value the opportunity of evaluating your teacher(s)?*
- *What do you think might be some of its positive and negative sides?*

Text B

Stop Blaming the Internet[1]

❶ There is an increasing amount of blame being placed on the Internet as the source of corruption in teenagers and children. One source of fear comes from news articles

---

1 This essay was taken from http://www.123HelpMe.com/view.asp?id=10447.

concerning youth that are making explosives from the easily found instructions on the web. There has been a flood of reaction to children finding **recipes** for explosives on the Internet. However, in blaming the Internet parents are ignoring the fact that children were making explosives long before the web existed.

2 The source of some children's knowledge of making pipe bombs is actually from a book. The *Anarchist's Cookbook*, published in 1971, was, and still is, the source for these bomb recipes and other recipes for **mischievous** behavior long before the Internet searches provided the answers. Actually, many of the sites I found that give bomb-making recipes, cite this book as the source. One site actually gives the whole book in a zip file, which can be downloaded onto your PC.

3 So parents might ask, how did children get access to this book, before the web? Despite what parents think, children will go through much trouble to get the information they are interested in. If children wanted to learn how to make a pipe bomb, they mail-ordered the book to get the answers just as easily as they would search for the subject on the web. Facility in getting information does not necessarily **preclude** using information that one normally would not use. Julia Wilkins in her article, "Protecting Our Children from Internet Smut（淫秽内容）: Moral Duty or Moral Panic?" quotes Lisa Schmeiser, a researcher of on-line pornography—who testifies to children's **ingenuity**. Schmeiser says, "There will be children who circumvent（设法避开）passwords, surfwatch software, and seemingly innocuous（无害的）links to find the 'adult' material. But these are the same kids who would visit every convenience store in a five mile **radius** to find the one stocking of Playboy" (Wilkins, 1997). In other words, Internet access is not the only source for "**indecent**" material; children will always find a way to see what they are not supposed to see.

4 Mainly, the burden being placed on the Internet is a **displacement** of the blame that should be put on the parents themselves. The cause for **deviant** behavior in children often is not the result of media, but lack of parental guidance and support. As Wilkins (1997) suggests, "the easiest solution [to blocking access to 'indecent material' on the Internet] is to keep the family computer in a well-traveled space, like a living room, so that parents can monitor what their children download." One friend of mine, who prefers to stay anonymous, built a pipe bomb as an adolescent, before the Internet existed, and admitted in **retrospect** that he did it because he could; with both parents working and him home alone, he was able to do what he wanted.

5 Most importantly, by focusing on the "evils of the Internet," politicians and **legislators**, parents and the media are all **straying** away from the more pressing issues. The main issue is violence and deviance among adults themselves—not the electronic "**brainwashing**" media. Mike Males writes about this issue in his article entitled, "Stop Blaming Kids and TV". As he says, "All sides seem to agree that **fictional** violence, sex on the screen, Joe Camel, beer-drinking frogs, or naked bodies on the Internet pose a bigger threat to children than do actual beatings, rape or parental **addictions**." Males gives **incredible** statistics which prove that deviance among adults towards children is greater than deviance attributed to the electronic media. He says how the Institute for Alternative Media emphasizes, "the average American child will witness 200,000 acts of TV violence by the time that child graduates from high school." He goes on to say that, "None of these varied interests note that during the eighteen years between a child's birth and graduation from high school, there will be fifteen million cases of real violence in American homes **grave** enough to require hospital emergency treatment." He also refers to the 150-page study from Carnegie scholars, "Great Transitions: Preparing **Adolescents** for a New Century," which according to Males, devotes only two sentences to household violence.

❻ The biggest problem then concerning the Internet is the way the media and others are blowing the issue out of proportion. As Wilkins says in her article, we are not doing our "moral duty" through **censoring** the Internet; rather we are creating "moral panic" in our **preoccupation** with Internet censorship. She goes on to say, "Through **sensationalized** reporting, certain forms of the behavior become classified as deviant." This seems to **resonate** well with the issue at hand; children have in the past been looking at pornography and playing with explosive material, but now the news media has succeeded in making this behavior seem the result of corruptive material-hence deviant behavior. Wilkins goes on to say that, "It is important to bear in mind that children are still a minority of Internet users." So, in reality, the problem not only is misdirected, but it is not nearly as big a problem as the news makes it out to be.

❼ Wilkins also gives the example of the *Time* magazine article that according to her sparked the debate on Internet censorship. The article published on July 3, 1995 and placed on the cover, entitled, "On a Screen Near You: Cyberporn", printed false statistics, which later were used in a **Congressional** hearing on Internet Censorship. The main statistic quoted was from Marty Rimm's report from the *Georgetown University Law Journal* in which he stated that a whopping（巨大的）83.5% of the Internet graphics are pornographic, when it actually is less than 1% (Males, 1997). We cannot unquestionably believe statistics even if they are from a **reputable** magazine like *Time*. So do not blame the Internet without all the facts—there is much more to the issue of corruption of youth than the Internet.

References:

Males, M. (1997). Stop Blaming Kids and TV. *The Progressive*, 61(10), 26.

Wilkins, J. (1997). Protecting Our Children from Internet Smut: Moral Duty or Moral Panic? *The Humanist*, 57(5), 6.

Words and Phrases

addiction	[ə'dikʃn]	*n.*	沉溺，上瘾
★ adolescent	[ˌædə'lesnt]	*a.*	青春期的
		n.	青少年
brainwashing	['breinwɔʃiŋ]	*n.*	洗脑
★ censor	['sensə]	*vt. & vi.*	检查
congressional	[kən'greʃənl]	*a.*	议会的，国会的；会议的
★ deviant	['di:viənt]	*a.*	不正常的，离经叛道的
★ displacement	[dis'pleismənt]	*n.*	置换，转位，移动
fictional	['fikʃənl]	*a.*	虚构的，小说的
grave	[greiv]	*a.*	严重的
incredible	[in'kredəbl]	*a.*	难以置信的，惊人的
indecent	[in'di:snt]	*a.*	下流的，不妥当的
▲ ingenuity	[ˌindʒə'nju:əti]	*n.*	心灵手巧；独创性；精巧
★ legislator	['ledʒisleitə]	*n.*	立法者
▲ mischievous	['mistʃivəs]	*a.*	调皮的，恶作剧的；有害的
★ preclude	[pri'klu:d]	*vt.*	阻止，排除
▲ preoccupation	[ˌpri:ɔkju'peiʃn]	*n.*	全神贯注
★ radius	['reidiəs]	*n.*	半径范围，半径；桡骨
★ recipe	['resipi, 'resəpi]	*n.*	秘诀；食谱；药方
reputable	['repjutəbl]	*a.*	受好评的；有声望的；规范的
▲ resonate	['rezəneit]	*vt. & vi.*	共鸣，共振
▲ retrospect	['retrəuspekt]	*n.*	回顾，追溯
★ sensationalized	[sen'seiʃənəlaizd]	*a.*	引起轰动的，骇人听闻的
★ stray	[strei]	*vi.*	偏离

 **Exercises**

Part I. Understanding the text

1. **Study the title of Text B.**
   - What are the key words in the essay title?
   - Why do you think they are the key words?

2. **Outlining: Spend 10 minutes browsing the essay and summarize the author's main supporting ideas (usually suggested in topic sentences) with reference to the following:**
   - Thesis statement/main argument
   - Supporting ideas

   Are you convinced by the author? Why or why not?

Part II. Writing skills development

3. **Read the essay and identify the types of evidence used in the article.**

4. **Read the essay again, try to locate examples of the use of comparison and contrast in the author's argumentation, and then discuss how this helps support the main argument of the essay.**

5. **Study the following phrases and sentence structures used to support arguments, and try to find more examples from the essay to expand the list.**

Comparison & Contrast	• There has been a flood of reaction to… However, in blaming something; somebody is ignoring the fact that…
	• …was, and still is, …long before…
	• So someone might ask, how did…, before…?
Quotes	• Schmeiser says, …
	• As Wilkins suggests, …

Part III. Language focus

6. **Choose the right word to complete each of the following sentences. Change the form where necessary.**

stray	circumvent	preclude	corruption	anarchist
deviant	resonate	adolescent	sensationalize	anonymous

1) Their immediate focus is on eliminating high-level _____ and bribery.

2) Rosalind has put forward new proposals that _____ with many voters.

3) Black skin alone does not _____ Barack Obama from standing as a president.

4) Grover, you can't disobey the law, but you can try to _____ it.

5) His adorable son changed from a friendly and cheerful young boy into a confused _____.

6) The media often _____ crime.

7) Similarly, becoming a hermit and avoiding contact with other people would be considered _____ behavior but it is not criminal.

8) The lecture is beginning to _____ from the point.

9) Erick received _____ phone calls warning him not to report to the police.

7. Paraphrase the following sentences.

1) By focusing on the "evils of the Internet," politicians and legislators, parents and the media are all straying away from the more pressing issues.

2) Males gives incredible statistics which prove that deviance among adults towards children is greater than deviance attributed to the electronic media.

3) The biggest problem then concerning the Internet is the way the media and others are blowing the issue out of proportion.

4) Wilkins also gives the example of *Time* magazines article that according to her sparked the debate on Internet censorship.

Part IV. Writing

8. Quick writing: Before reading the article, try to brainstorm and write down the pros and cons of the Internet. Then discuss with your partner/group to get more ideas and inspirations.

9. Write an essay (about 300 words) on either of the following topics:

1) Suppose you are a reader of the newspaper article "Stop Blaming the Internet". Write a short essay to the editor to state your point of view: whether you agree with the author or not, and why. Try to combine the supporting evidence you have learned from this article or found from other sources.

2) It is a general phenomenon in China that parents ask their children to acquire various skills in different courses for the development of their intelligence, because they believe that achievements lie with Intelligence Quotient, whereas psychologists discover that Emotion Intelligence is the key to success. They think that while IQ tells you how smart you are, EQ tells you how well you use your smartness. What view do you hold? Write an essay on the following topic:

IQ Vs EQ: Who is likely to succeed in their future career, people with higher IQ, or people with higher EQ?

> **Use the following checklist to revise your draft and finalize your paper before it comes to your instructor.**
>
> 1) Does the title give the reader a clue to the subject of your essay?
> 2) Is the topic debatable?
> 3) Does the thesis statement assert one main, clearly focused idea?
> 4) Have you supported your assertions with enough detailed evidence? For example, are the points of the comparison and contrast well organized to support the main argument?
> 5) Are all the paragraphs smoothly linked in a logical order? Is your paper coherent with good transitions?
> 6) Is there a convincing ending for the essay in your concluding paragraph(s)?
> 7) Are sources introduced properly and cited correctly in the body of your essay?

Text C

We Should Not Permit Internet Censorship[1] (Abridged)

❶   The internet is the largest and most **diverse** source of information our planet has ever known. The internet is **integrating** our daily life **transactions**. This is possible because newspapers, television programs, movies, phone calls, computer data, commercial services such as banking and shopping, and a host of other sources of information and communication are all being reduced to the same digital format, and are all sent along fiber optic cables (光纤电缆).

❷   The libraries of the world, once online, will probably combine to form a larger base of information than anyone has ever imagined. This vast library of information will be **accessible** in an instant, with the click of a mouse, where internet technology is available. We can compare the internet to another technological advance—nuclear energy, which also changed the world. Like nuclear energy, knowledge is very powerful, and can be used for both good and evil deeds. Knowledge can indeed have the same **converse** negative side like nuclear energy does. Nuclear energy can be used to power entire cities, or it can be used to erase them. There is an important distinction to be made here. Knowledge is what we use to search for the truth in life, and this fact makes knowledge indispensable. Once we know the truth we can be free from manipulation. Because the internet is so unique in the way it allows access to information, we must protect the internet as a very precious resource. Censoring the internet may lead to a chain of related effects. The first is the upset of the natural balance of information on the internet. This happens when information is removed, thus narrowing the spectrum

---

1 This essay was taken and slightly adapted from http://www.123HelpMe.com/view.asp?id=10768.

of available information. From this spectrum of information we derive bits of knowledge. So the second effect of censoring the internet is reduced knowledge. If we allow censorship to weaken the material our searching tool, knowledge, is made of, then we might even lose the truth. The loss of the truth is the third effect of censoring the internet. The final effect of censoring the internet is manipulation made easy. Before we follow this causal chain through its effects, I think it is important to explain what I mean by the truth.

3   I think of the truth in two related forms. The first, I'll refer to as personal truth. Personal truth involves a process that starts with a question. The person asking the question **accumulates** as much knowledge as possible from information. As knowledge accumulates, information becomes easier to **navigate** because knowledge increases the persons' ability to think critically. So, knowledge is used to find more knowledge until a satisfactory answer has been reached. In this way I am equating knowledge with a smaller, personal truth.

4   The second form of truth that I envision is universal truth. This is the kind of truth that Plato is teaching in The Allegory of the Cave. This is the kind of truth that the inscription on the south face of the UT Tower refers to. I imagine this form of truth to **encompass** all smaller, personal truths. The way I see it, the insights we gain from our personal truths are used as new knowledge in our search for universal truth. As our level of knowledge reaches new **benchmarks**, it is more difficult to manipulate us with **inferior** levels of information. The internet's diverse information has the potential to free us from manipulation at any level, because we will know the truth.

5   Now that I have explained the two forms of truth, we can look at the effects censorship has on our search for truth. The first effect of censoring the internet is the upset of the natural balance of information on the internet. This happens when information is removed from the web, thus narrowing the spectrum of available information. Until the Supreme Court ruled broad internet **filters unconstitutional**, all public facilities would have soon been susceptible to information filters, which would effectively reduce the internet to the level of a child. For example, you could not access any information on the web dealing with reproduction, because it contains the word "sex". This even included plant reproduction. How problematic might this censorship have been for a biologist at UT, a public institution? A person couldn't have found information on breast cancer, because it has the word "breast" in it. If we allow the spectrum of information available on the internet to be narrowed, we are allowing the reduction of the food for our thought. Consider the light spectrum, ROYGBIV. We all learned in school that light is made up of many different wavelengths, with corresponding colors. How different would the world look if there were no green light? Things would look pretty different. Has anyone ever tried on a pair of those blue-blocker sunglasses, or any sunglasses with amber lenses? The world looks pretty different. This is what censorship does. Censorship can change the mix of things and ultimately effect the way we see the big picture, our knowledge. The second related effect of censoring the internet is reduced knowledge. This is a simple but very important concept to understand. Our knowledge is derived from the information we think through. If censorship changes the natural diversity of information on the WWW, the way we think with our minds is changed in the same way that our vision is altered when the light spectrum is narrowed. This might change our knowledge in such a way that our ability to see the truth would be altered. Maybe the truth would just look different and unrecognizable under different light. Either way, we may risk losing the truth.

6 If we lose the truth, what can we follow? The truth is what gives us **orientation** to what is right in life. If we lose the truth, our new truth would become the truth given to us by those in power. They would be able to filter the information we receive, however they want.

7 Censoring the largest, most diverse source of information our planet has ever known can make manipulation easy. If we allow the Internet to be censored, we may allow the essential diversity of information on the WWW to be altered. As the diversity of information on the web is reduced, so is the knowledge we might find to use in our search for the truth. If we lose the truth, we would be **at the mercy of** an artificial, filtered truth given to us by those in power. We would be at the mercy of whoever is synthesizing the truth, for whatever purpose they want to use us.

📖 Words and Phrases

accessible	[ək'sesəbl]	*a.*	可得到的；可进入的
accumulate	[ə'kju:mjuleit]	*vt. & vi.*	积累，增加，聚集
▲ benchmark	['bentʃmɑ:k]	*n.*	基准点，参照点
▲ converse	[kən'vɜ:s]	*a.*	相反的；逆向的；倒的
diverse	[dai'vɜ:s]	*a.*	不同的，多种多样的
▲ encompass	[in'kʌmpəs]	*vt. & vi.*	围绕；包含；包围；完成
filter	['filtə]	*n.*	过滤器；滤色镜；滤光器
		vt. & vi.	过滤；渗透
inferior	[in'fiəriə]	*n.*	低于他人者；次品；部下，属下
		a.	下等的；差的；下级的

integrate	['intigreit]	*vt. & vi.*	整合，结合，使成一体
★ navigate	['nævigeit]	*v.*	航行；驾驶；操纵
★ orientation	[ˌɔːriən'teiʃn]	*n.*	方向，目标；熟悉，适应；情况介绍
transaction	[træn'zækʃn]	*n.*	交易；执行，办理
▲ unconstitutional	[ˌʌnkɔnsti'tjuːʃənl]	*a.*	违反宪法的，非立宪的

| at the mercy of | | | 任凭……的摆布，完全受……支配 |

 **Exercises**

Part I. Understanding the text

1. **Pre-reading: The title of this essay has clearly shown the main argument. Suppose you are the author, what supporting ideas would you give to back up your main argument? Write down as many points as possible before reading the essay. Discuss your ideas with your partner/group, and try to expand your list to include more supporting ideas.**

2. **Summarize the main idea of each paragraph, and workout the outline of the essay with reference to the following:**
   - Thesis statement of the essay
   - Main idea of each paragraph

3. **Study the essay closely and try to complete the following table.**

Questions	Answers (Yes, No or Partly)	Improvement
Does the introduction and /or conclusion clearly present the overall argument?		
Are the supporting points clearly organized and presented (as topic sentences in the body paragraphs)?		
Are the topic sentences in the body paragraphs supported with adequate evidence?		
Are transitional words used appropriately to help the reader follow the author's flow of logic?		

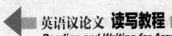
4. **Read through the essay again, and try to locate examples of the use of comparison and contrast in the author's argumentation. Analyze one example from the essay with reference to the following:**

1) Example: _____

2) Sentence structure or phrases that indicate the use of comparison and contrast:

_____

3) Similarities and differences between the things compared:

_____

Part II. Writing skills development

5. **Read Paragraphs 3 and 4 carefully and answer the following questions.**

1) What is the purpose of these two paragraphs? Do they contribute to the overall argument?

2) What evidence is used to support the idea(s) in these two paragraphs?

6. **Discuss with your partner how coherence within and across paragraphs is achieved within this essay.**

Part III. Language focus

7. **Try to match the words to their corresponding denotations in the two columns below.**

a. censor	1) the process of doing business
b. integrate	2) to include a wide range of ideas, subjects, etc.
c. transaction	3) to make someone think and behave exactly as you want them to, by skillfully deceiving or influencing them
d. susceptible	4) to examine, cut out, parts of (a book, internet information, etc.)
e. converse	5) opposite
f. encompass	6) likely to suffer from a particular illness or be affected by a particular problem
g. manipulate	7) to combine (parts) into a whole; complete (sth. that is imperfect or incomplete) by adding parts

8. **Paraphrase the following sentences.**

1) This vast library of information will be accessible in an instant, with the click of a mouse, where internet technology is available.

2) Until the Supreme Court ruled broad internet filters unconstitutional, all public facilities would have soon been susceptible to information filters, which would ef-

fectively reduce the internet to the level of a child.

3) If we lose the truth, we will be at the mercy of an artificial, filtered truth given to us by those in power.

Part IV. Writing

9. Writing is a method of inquiry (Richardson, 2000). It is not just a "mopping-up activity" at the end of an inquiry; rather, it is a way of "knowing"—"a method of discovery and analysis." By writing in different ways, we can discover different aspects of our topic and our relation to it; as a result, we can learn something new about the topic and ourselves.

Suggested Writing Steps:

1) Prewriting: Do a thorough review of the literature related to the writing topic.
2) Outlining: Work out an outline of the essay, including an overall argument, main supporting ideas, types of evidence, structure planning, etc.
3) Drafting: Write the first draft.
4) Revising: Rewrite the first draft according to the principles we have emphasized, proofread carefully to eliminate grammatical errors.
5) Peer/teacher review: Based on teacher/peer feedback, revise the essay and do more research about the topic to reinforce the argument.

Based on your findings in Exercise 5, try to re-write the article "We Should Not Permit Internet Censorship", omitting the irrelevant evidence and re-organize the structure to make it more coherent. You are encouraged to add new evidence to make your argument more effective and convincing.

Unit Summary

1. In this unit, you have practiced supporting arguments with comparison and contrast. While making comparison and contrast, you are supposed to:

1) Determine the purpose of the comparison and contrast. Will it contribute to your argumentative essay?
2) Keep the comparison and contrast short and to the point.
3) Organize the points of the comparison and contrast (subject-by-subject or point-by-point or a combination of both).
4) Use appropriate transitions to help reader follow your flow of logic.

For similarities: *similarly, likewise, in the same way, in the same manner, equally important, similar to, the same as...*

For differences: *by comparison, on the other hand, in contrast to, on the contrary, different from, conversely...*

2. Identify and analyze the use of comparison and contrast in the following extracts.

1) If children wanted to learn how to make a pipe bomb, they mail-ordered the book to get the answers just as easily as they would search for the subject on the web. There will be children who circumvent passwords, surfwatch software, and seemingly innocuous links to find the "adult" material. But these are the same kids who would visit every convenience store in a five mile radius to find the one stocking of Playboy.

2) The average American child will witness 200,000 acts of TV violence by the time that child graduates from high school. None of these varied interests note that during the eighteen years between a child's birth and graduation from high school, there will be fifteen million cases of real violence in American homes grave enough to require hospital emergency treatment.

3) The great advantage of this is that it speeds up the process of getting work completed. In the past when computers were not as developed as they are today researching through methods of books, magazines and other written material was tedious and took a longer time.

4) A computer can only provide information. A teacher actually takes the information and teaches his or her students how to integrate it into their lives.

3. Choose the right word to complete each of the following sentences. Change the form where necessary.

outweigh	recipe	synthesize	brainwash	navigate
comply with	filter	accessible	emit	accumulate

1) Remember, nothing here is offered as a blueprint or _____.

2) Because of the snow, many parts of the country are only _____ by helicopter.

3) A transponder is a device that _____ radar signals identifying and locating aircraft for air traffic controllers.

4) It is unjust that a privileged few should continue to _____ wealth.

5) The benefits to patients who are taking the drug far _____ the risks.

6) These firms know what the local law is, and could _____ some Internet content as demanded by it.

7) DDT is a pesticide that was first _____ in 1874.

8) Failure to _____ these requirements is a criminal offence.

9) The kids are _____ into seeing qualities like gentleness and shyness as negative and weak.

10) Pudding is currently trying to _____ through a whole stack of information on his PhD. project FPGA.

4. Read with a critical eye.

Critical Reading

Critical reading is more than accepting or remembering whatever we read. It means we remain alert and adopt a questioning, exploring and evaluating attitude throughout the reading process. So when reading an article, we should carefully deal with the ideas that the authors convey, which is especially true in argumentative essays—those that take a stand on a debatable topic. We cannot unquestionably believe the evidence used for argumentation because some authors attempt to convince readers by using emotionally charged language, by emphasizing certain facts over others (Kirszner & Mandell, 2010) (as presented in the last paragraph of "Stop Blaming the Internet"). Try to double check the evidence by conducting a comprehensive review of relevant literature, and analyze the credibility of the opinions on both sides of an issue.

Critical reading is an important part of the invention process. It gives us access to information, exposes us to different ideas, and provokes us to think, but it really takes time and effort to develop such abilities.

Now let's begin by conducting a review of the topic "Should the Internet Be Blamed and Why" (on the Internet and other sources) and check the evidence you find with that in the text. Can you find any flaw in the author's argumentation? How can you challenge his/her point of view?

5. Write an essay (about 300 words) on the topic "Internet Censorship VS Burning the Books".

Prewriting

Work out the outline of the essay and ask yourself:	**✔ or ✗**
What is the overall stance/argument of the essay?	☐
Is the overall stance/argument obvious in Introduction and/or Conclusion?	☐
Is the main idea clear in each supporting paragraph?	☐
How many paragraphs will the essay have?	☐
Does the outline follow a logical sequence of ideas?	☐

Writing

Write the first draft alone.

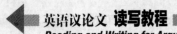
Revising

Once you have the first draft of your paper completed, (peer) review it with the following questions in mind: ✔ or ✗

Does the Introduction or Conclusion clearly present the overall argument?   ☐
Are the ideas clearly and logically organized?   ☐
Is the main argument in each supporting paragraph supported with adequate evidence?   ☐
Are the sentences grammatically correct and concise?   ☐
Is coherence within and across paragraphs adequately achieved?   ☐

Reference:

Kirszner, L. G. & Mandell, S. R. (2010). *The Wadsworth Handbook* (8ᵗʰ ed). Hong Kong: Cengage Learning Asia Pte.Ltd.

Writing Skill Development

Supporting Evidence and Effective Argumentation (4)

Deduction and Induction[1]

Deduction（演绎）

Deduction is the process of reasoning using general rules or principles to form a judgment about a particular fact or situation (*Longman Dictionary of Contemporary English*, 1998). A deductive argument is an argument in which it is thought that the premises provide a guarantee of the truth of the conclusion. In a deductive argument, the premises are intended to provide support for the conclusion that is so strong that, if the premises are true, it would be impossible for the conclusion to be false.

[*Major premise*]	All men are mortal.
[*Minor premise*]	Michael Collins was a man.
[*Conclusion*]	Therefore, Michael Collins was mortal.

Deduction is the process of reasoning ***from the general to the specific,*** in which ***a conclusion follows necessarily from the premises***; or a process in which ***general***

---

1 Abridged from the following websites:
http://philosophy.lander.edu/logic/index.html;
http://www.iep.utm.edu/ded-ind/;
http://www.citsoft.com/holmes/adventures/speckled.band.txt.

principles are applied to specific instances or details (Chesñevar, Maguitman & Loui, 2000).

Induction（归纳）

An inductive argument is an argument in which it is thought that the premises provide reasons supporting the probable truth of the conclusion. In an inductive argument, the premises are intended only to be so strong that, if they are true, then it is unlikely that the conclusion is false.

[*Premise 1*]	A red-eyed fruit fly has RNA.
[*Premise 2*]	A white-eyed fruit fly has RNA.
[*Premise 3*]	A Hawaiian fruit fly has RNA.
[*Conclusion*]	Therefore, all fruit flies have RNA.

Difference between deductive and inductive arguments

Deductive arguments are those in which the truth of the conclusion is thought to be completely guaranteed and not just made probable by the truth of the premises, if the argument is a sound one, the truth of the conclusion is "contained within" the truth of the premises; i.e., the conclusion does not go beyond what the truth of the premises implicitly requires. For this reason, deductive arguments are usually limited to inferences that follow from definitions, mathematics and rules of formal logic. For example, the following are deductive arguments:

> There are 32 books on the top-shelf of the bookcase, and 12 on the lower shelf of the bookcase. There are no books anywhere else in my bookcase. Therefore, there are 44 books in the bookcase.

> Bergen is either in Norway or Sweden. If Bergen is in Norway, then Bergen is in Scandinavia. If Bergen is in Sweden, then Bergen is in Scandinavia. Therefore, Bergen is in Scandinavia.

Inductive arguments, on the other hand, can appeal to any consideration that might be thought relevant to the probability of the truth of the conclusion. Inductive arguments, therefore, can take very wide ranging forms, including arguments dealing with statistical data, generalizations from past experiences, appeals to signs, evidence or authority, and causal relationships.

Because the difference between inductive and deductive arguments involves the strength of evidence which the author believes the premises provide for the conclusion, inductive and deductive arguments differ with regard to the standards of evaluation that are applicable to them. The difference does not have to do with the content or subject matter of the argument. Indeed, the same utterance may be used to present either a deductive or an inductive argument, depending on the intentions of the person advancing it. Consider the following example.

> Dom Perignon is a champagne, so it must be made in France.

It might be clear from context that the speaker believes that having been made in the Champagne area of France is part of the defining feature of "champagne" proper and that therefore, the conclusion follows from the premise by definition. If it is the intention of the speaker that the evidence is of this sort, then the argument is deductive. However, it may be that no such thought is in the speaker's mind. He or she may merely believe that most champagne is made in France, and may be reasoning probabilistically. If this is his or her intention, then the argument is inductive.

Different types of deductive arguments

In general deductive arguments fall into several types. The following are examples, not exhaustive categories:

a. Necessary analytic inferences: they follow from the truths of the meanings of words.

> Peter is Jon's brother, so Jon must be Peter's brother.

b. Mathematical inferences: they follow from the truths of mathematics.

> Since there are more people in the world than there are hairs on your and my head, the population of the world is greater than the hairs on your head.

c. Logical inferences: they follow from the truths of logic.

> If you work hard, then you will succeed, and if you succeed, then you will be happy; therefore, if you work hard, you will be happy.

Different types of inductive arguments

Some examples of inductive argument:

a. Extrapolations: To infer unknown information from known information.

> Increasing voltage leads to increasing rpm.

b. Predictions: Conclusions are drawn from known or assumed facts or statements (the stock market predictions, for example).

c. Part to whole: Since some things of a certain kind are this way, all things of that kind are this way.

d. Analogy: A conclusion is drawn by arguing that there are distinct similarities in a certain respect between two different events.

> Pupils are more like oysters than sausages. The job of teaching is not to stuff them and then seal them up, but to help them open and reveal the riches within. There are pearls in each of us, if only we knew how to cultivate them with ardor and persistence (Harris, 1994).

➡ **Now test yourself on the following examples. Can you tell from deductive and inductive argument?**

1. All throughout history people repeat the same mistakes, so we can conclude that mistakes will be made in the future.

2. The whale is a mammal, so all killer whales are mammals.

3. All killer whales are mammals, so the whale is a mammal.

4. Dumbbell training is inherently safe. I've never observed a torn muscle or any other serious injury resulting from the proper use of dumbbells (Philips & D'Orso, 1999).

5. All human beings have the ability to think rationally and realistically. We all can realize, "Even if I am probably correct, there is still room for questioning." Thus we can allow discussion, disconfirmation, and new evidence to change our minds (Prochaska et al., 1994).

6. When plants landscaped with crushed rock are watered, evaporation of soil moisture sometimes creates colorful crusts of salts on the surface of the ground. The minerals in these crusts contain concentrations of zinc, molybdenum, and copper, and the concentrations of these elements are sometimes deemed unsafe. Consequently, undesirable trace elements are getting into the environment (Perkins, 2005).

7. It is not recorded what part either Themistocles or Aristides took in the debate of the council of war at Marathon. But from the character of Themistocles, his boldness, and his intuitive genius for extemporizing the best measure in every emergency (a quality which the greatest of historians ascribe to him beyond all his contemporaries), we may well believe that the vote of Themistocles was for prompt and decisive action (Creasy, 1994).

References:

Chesñevar, C., Maguitman, A., & Loui, R. (2000). Logical Models of Argument. *ACM Computing Surveys*, 32(4), 337-383.

Creasy, E. S. (1994). *Fifteen Decisive Battles of the World 1851*. New York: DaCapo Press.

Harris, S. J. (1994). *What True Education Should Do*. In M. C. F. Orlando (ed.), *The*

Thoughtful Reader. Fla.: Harcourt Brace & Co.

Perkins, S. (2005). Landscaping Stones May Pose Risks to the Environment. *Science News*, 167(3).

Philips, B., & Michael D'Orso, M. (1999). *Body for Life*. New York: Harper Collins.

Prochaska, J. O. et al. (1994). *Changing for Good*. New York: William Morrow.

Reading for Ideas

Text A

Argument, Truth and the Social Side of Reasoning

By Gary Gutting[1]

❶ Philosophers rightly think of themselves as experts on reasoning. After all, it was a philosopher, Aristotle, who developed the science of logic. But psychologists have also had some interesting things to say about the subject. A fascinating paper by Dan Sperber and Hugo Mercier has recently generated a lot of discussion.

❷ Sperber and Mercier begin from well-established facts about our deep-rooted tendencies to make mistakes in our reasoning. We have a very hard time **sticking to** rules of deductive logic, and we constantly make basic errors in **statistical reasoning**. Most importantly, we **are** strongly **inclined to** "confirmation-bias": We systematically focus on data that support a view we hold and ignore data that **count against** it.

❸ These facts suggest that our **evolutionary** development has not done an especially good job of making us competent reasoners. Sperber and Mercier, however, point out that this is true only if the point of reasoning is to draw true conclusions. Fallacious (谬误的) reasoning, especially reasoning that focuses on what supports our views and ignores what counts against them, is very effective for the purpose of winning arguments with other people. So, they suggest, it makes sense to think that the evolutionary point of human reasoning is to win arguments, not to reach the truth.

❹ This **formulation** led critics to objections that **echo** traditional philosophical arguments against the **skeptical** rejection of truth. Do Sperber and Mercier think that the point of their own reasoning is not truth but winning an argument? If not, then their

---

1 Gary Gutting teaches philosophy at the University of Notre Dame and co-edits *Notre Dame Philosophical Reviews*, an on-line book review journal. His most recent book is *What Philosophers Know: Case Studies in Recent Analytic Philosophy*.

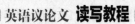

theory is **falsified** by their own reasoning. If so, they are merely trying to win an argument, and there's no reason why scientists—who are interested in truth, not just winning arguments—should pay any attention to what they say. Sperber and Mercier seem **caught in** a destructive **dilemma**, logically damned if they do and damned if they don't.

5 Philosophical thinking has led to this dilemma, but a bit more philosophy shows a way out. The root of the dilemma is the distinction between seeking the truth and winning an argument. The distinction makes sense for cases where someone does not care about knowing the truth and argues only to **convince** other people **of** something, whether or not it's true. But, suppose my goal is simply to know the truth, how do I go about achieving this knowledge? Plato long ago pointed out that it is not enough just to believe what is true. Suppose I believe that there are an **odd number** of **galaxies** in the universe and in fact there are. Still, unless I have adequate support for my belief, I cannot be said to *know* it. It's just an unsupported opinion. Knowing the truth requires not just true belief but also justification for the belief.

6 But how do I **justify** a belief and so come to know that it's true? There are competing philosophical answers to this question, but one fits particularly well with Sperber and Mercier's **approach**. This is the view that justification is a matter of being able to *convince other people* that a claim is correct, a view held in various ways by the classic American **pragmatists** and, in recent years, by Richard Rorty[1] and Jürgen Habermas[2].

7 The key point is that justification—and therefore knowledge of the truth—is a social process. This need not mean that claims are true *because* we come to **rational** agreement about them. But such agreement, properly arrived at, is the best possible justification of a claim to truth. For example, our best guarantee that stars are **gigantic** masses of hot gas is that scientists have developed arguments for this claim that almost anyone who **looks into** the matter will accept.

8 This pragmatic view understands seeking the truth as a *special case* of trying to win an argument: Not winning by forcing or tricking people into agreement, but by achieving agreement through honest arguments. The important practical conclusion is that finding the truth does require winning arguments, but not in the sense that my argument defeats yours. Rather, *we* find an argument that defeats all contrary arguments. Sperber and Mercier in fact approach this philosophical view when they argue that reasoning is most **problematic** when carried out by isolated individuals and is most effective when carried out in social groups.

9 The pragmatic philosophy of justification makes it clear why Sperber and Mercier's

---

1 Richard Rorty (1931—2007), American philosopher.
2 Jürgen Habermas (1929—   ), German philosopher, one of the most influential philosophers in the world.

psychological account of reasoning need not **fall victim to** the claim that it is a self-destructive **skepticism**. **Conversely**, the philosophical view gains **plausibility** from its **convergence** with the psychological account. This symbiosis（共生关系）is an instructive example of how philosophy and **empirical** psychology can **fruitfully interact**.

Words and Phrases

approach	[ə'prəutʃ]	*n.*	方法，方式	
		vt.	处理	
★ convergence	[kən'vɜːdʒəns]	*n.*	会聚，聚合	
conversely	['kɔnvɜːsli]	*adv.*	相反地	
dilemma	[di'lemə]	*n.*	困境，进退两难	
echo	['ekəu]	*vt.*	重复（他人的话等）	
★ empirical	[im'pirikl]	*a.*	经验的；实证的	
evolutionary	[ˌiːvə'luːʃnəri]	*a.*	进化的	
falsify	['fɔːlsifai]	*vt.*	证明……虚假	
★ formulation	[ˌfɔːmju'leiʃn]	*n.*	构想；系统的阐述	
fruitfully	['fruːtfəli]	*adv.*	富有成效地	
★ galaxy	['gæləksi]	*n.*	星系	
★ gigantic	[dʒai'gæntik]	*a.*	巨大的，庞大的	
interact	[ˌintər'ækt]	*vi.*	互相作用，互相影响	
justify	['dʒʌstifai]	*vt.*	证明……是正当的，为……辩护	
			justification *n.* 证实，理由	
plausibility	[ˌplɔːzə'biləti]	*n.*	可信性	
▲ pragmatist	['prægmətist]	*n.*	实用主义者	
★ problematic	[ˌprɔblə'mætik]	*a.*	不确定的，有疑问的	
rational	['ræʃnəl]	*a.*	理性的，合理的	
reasoning	['riːzəniŋ]	*n.*	推论，推理	
★ skeptical	['skeptikəl]	*a.*	怀疑论的，不可知论的	
★ skepticism	['skeptisizəm]	*n.*	怀疑论	

be caught in	遇到；陷入
be inclined to	倾向于，赞同
convince (sb.) of (sth.)	使……确信
count against	对……不利

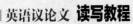
fall victim to	成为……的牺牲品
look into	研究，调查
odd number	奇数
statistical reasoning	统计推理
stick to	坚持；遵守

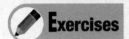 **Exercises**

Part I. Understanding the text

1. **Study the title of Text A.**
   - What are the key words in the essay title?
   - Why do you think they are the key words?

2. **Spend 5 minutes browsing the essay and answer the following questions.**
   - What's the view held by Sperber and Mercier?
   - What's the view of the critics mentioned in the essay?
   - What's the view of the author of the essay?

3. **Read this article carefully and analyze the arguments made by Sperber and Mercier and those by the critics of their theory.**

   Sperber and Mercier:
   - Starting from facts of fallacious reasoning:

     1) _____

     2) _____

     3) _____

   - Reason for the popularity of fallacious reasoning:

     _____

   - Conclusion reached by Sperber and Mercier:

     _____

   Critics of Sperber and Mercier:
   - Using the two researchers' own arguments to argue against their conclusion:

     _____

4. Read Paragraphs 5–9, and analyze how the author of the essay defends Sperber and Mercier.

	Argument made by the author
Paragraph 5	
Paragraph 6	
Paragraphs 7–8	
Paragraph 9	

Part II. Writing skills development

5. Inductive reasoning and deductive reasoning are employed in this essay. Read through Paragraphs 2, 3, and 9, and find out inductive and deductive arguments in each paragraph.

6. Can you sum up phrases and/or sentence structures indicating inductive or deductive reasoning? Discuss with your classmates.

Part III. Language focus

7. Choose the right word to complete each of the following sentences. Change the form where necessary.

converse	falsify	incline	echo	skeptical
justify	approach	convince	plausibility	interact

1) The results of the research have _____ the money and time spent on it.

2) Most politicians seem to be _____ to ignore the drug problem.

3) The company's environmental claims have been treated with _____ by conservationists.

4) The charges against him include fraud, bribery, and _____ business records.

5) Modern architects are building museums that can _____ with the visitors.

6) It's useless trying to _____ her that she doesn't need to lose any weight.

7) I need to tell the teacher that I cannot come to his class on Tuesday, but I don't quite know how to _____ the subject.

8) The design of this museum _____ that of Metropolitan Museum of Art.

9) In the US, you drive on the right hand side of the road, but in Britain the _____ applies.

10) In Chapter 2 of the book, the author goes on to test the _____ of these assumptions.

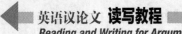

8. Paraphrase the following sentences.

1) This formulation led critics to objections that echo traditional philosophical arguments against the skeptical rejection of truth.

2) Sperber and Mercier's psychological account of reasoning need not fall victim to the claim that it is a self-destructive skepticism.

3) The symbiosis is an instructive example of how philosophy and empirical psychology can fruitfully interact.

Part IV. Writing

9. Write a paragraph on the topic of "Can we find the truth?" using deductive or inductive reasoning. You can refer to some of the examples in the essay.

Text B

Who Needs the Humanities?

By Steve Fuller[1]

❶   Nowadays, in country after country, policymakers have become **obsessed with** the need to strengthen science education. But what about the humanities—all those disciplines (literature, history, languages, and so forth) whose **relevance** to economic competitiveness is not so obvious?

❷   We need the humanities only if we **are committed to** the idea of humanity. If the humanities have become obsolete（过时的）, then it may be that humanity is losing its salience（特点）.

❸   I do not mean that we are becoming "less human" in the sense of "inhumane". If We live in a time when traditionally human-centered concerns like "rights" have been extended to animals, if not nature as a whole. Rather, the problem is whether there is anything **distinctive** about being human that makes special demands of higher education. I believe that the answer continues to be yes.

❹   Today, it sounds old-fashioned to describe the university's purpose as being to "**cultivate**" people, as if it were a glorified finishing school. However, once we **set aside** its elitist（杰出人物的，精英的）history, there remains a strong element of truth to this idea, especially when applied to the humanities. Although we now think of academic

---

1 Steve Fuller is Professor of Sociology at the University of Warwick, United Kingdom. He is the author of *The Knowledge Book: Key Concepts in Philosophy, Science and Culture.*

disciplines, including the humanities, as being "research-led", this understates（不充分地陈述）the university's historic role in **converting** the primate（灵长类的）**Homo sapiens** into a creature whose interests, **aspirations**, and achievements extend beyond successful **reproduction**.

5 What was originally called the "**liberal arts**" provided the skills necessary for this transformation. By **submitting** to a common **regime** of speaking, writing, reading, observing, and calculating, the "upright ape" acquired the capacity to reason in public. This enabled first him and then her to command authority regardless of birth, resulting in the **forging** of networks and even institutions whose benefits cut deeply across bloodlines. We too easily forget that our **heterogeneous** societies rely on at least a watered-down（冲淡的，无力的）version of this training to maintain political and economic order.

6 The university began with the humanities at its heart, but today it is playing catch-up with the natural sciences. This is largely because the natural sciences have most closely imitated the productivity measures associated with industry. The result is a "bigger is better" mentality that stresses ever more publications, **patents**, and **citations**. Yet, this **agenda** tends to be pursued without much concern for how—or if—these measures feed into something of greater social, cultural, and even economic relevance.

7 The Science Citation Index, originally designed to help researchers **discern** aggregate trends in increasingly complex subject domains in sciences, has helped measure productivity. But now these trends are **routinely** converted into **norms** against which the performance of particular universities, departments, and even individual researchers is judged. What is most easily measured has become confused with what is most worth measuring.

8 But, more profoundly, this entire line of thinking neglects the distinctly transformative capacity of the knowledge in which the humanities **specializes**. An adequate assessment of this capacity requires looking at its effects. As with John Maynard Keynes's notion that **returns** on public investment must be measured as the long-term consequence of other investments that it stimulates across the economy and society, the knowledge generated by the humanities should be evaluated in the same way.

9 This idea is lost in today's **cost accounting** for universities, which treats what transpires（发生）between teacher and student in the classroom as similar to what happens between producer and consumer in the market. In both cases, it is assumed that the value of the exchanged good is decided shortly after its delivery according to how it satisfies an immediate need. Not surprisingly, students value their degree by the first job it gets them rather than the life it prepares them for over the next half-century.

❿ Today, it is hard to believe that in the heyday（全盛期）of the **welfare state**, universities were both more **elite** and more publicly funded than they are today. Back then, it was assumed that the benefits of academic training extended not only, or even primarily, to those who experienced it but also, and more importantly, to the rest of the population, whose lives were variously **enriched** by the application of the arts and sciences.

⓫ Of course, this enrichment included such practical benefits as medical breakthroughs and labor-saving technologies. But the enrichment provided by the humanities was no less enduring, though its subtler nature makes it harder to track. Nevertheless, to paraphrase Keynes, every time we turn on the radio or television, read a newspaper, pick up a novel, or watch a movie, we are in the thrall（束缚）of one or more dead humanists who set the terms of reference through which we see the world.

⓬ In its long history as the **premier** form of academic knowledge, the humanities were frequently criticized for their **subversive** character. That some would now question whether the humanities have any impact at all merely reflects the crude and shortsighted way in which the value of academic knowledge is measured and judged today. Perhaps that befits creatures whose lives are "solitary, poor, nasty, brutish, and short", to recall Thomas Hobbes' description of the state of nature. But it does a grave injustice to those of us who still **aspire to** full-fledged（成熟的）humanity.

Words and Phrases

agenda	[ə'dʒendə]	*n.*	议程
aspiration	[ˌæspə'reiʃn]	*n.*	志向，抱负
citation	[sai'teiʃn]	*n.*	引用
convert	[kən'vɜːt]	*vt.*	转变，变换
cultivate	['kʌltiveit]	*vt.*	培养，陶冶
★ discern	[di'sɜːn]	*vt.*	辨明，分清
distinctive	[di'stiŋktiv]	*a.*	有特色的，特殊的
★ elite	[ei'liːt]	*a.*	杰出的；名牌的
enrich	[in'ritʃ]	*vt.*	使丰富
forging	['fɔːdʒiŋ]	*n.*	锻造
▲ heterogeneous	[ˌhetərə'dʒiːniəs]	*a.*	多样化的
norm	[nɔːm]	*n.*	基准；规范
★ patent	['peitnt]	*n.*	专利

★ premier	['premiə]	*a.*	首位的；首要的
★ regime	[rei'ʒi:m]	*n.*	机制；社会制度
relevance	['reləvəns]	*n.*	关联，相关性
reproduction	[ˌri:prə'dʌkʃn]	*n.*	生殖；繁育
returns	[ri'tɜ:nz]	*n.*	收益，利润
★ routinely	[ru:'ti:nli]	*adv.*	惯常地；令人厌烦地
specialize	['speʃəlaiz]	*vi.*	专攻；专门从事
submit	[səb'mit]	*vi.*	屈从；忍受
▲ subversive	[səb'vɜ:siv]	*a.*	破坏性的，颠覆性的

aspire to	渴求
be committed to	致力于
be obsessed with	沉迷于……
cost accounting	成本核算
Homo sapiens	人类
liberal arts	人文科学
set aside	不顾；不理会
welfare state	福利国家

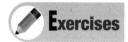 **Exercises**

Part I. Understanding the text

1. Study the title of Text B.

- What are the key words in the essay title?
- Why do you think they are the key words?

2. Discuss the following questions with your partner.

- What's your major?
- What do you think of the humanities?
- Is it necessary to enhance the study of the humanities in universities?

3. Read Paragraphs 4–11, and discuss with your partner: How does the author argue for the necessity of the humanities?

4. Fill in the following chart to see how the author establishes the importance of the humanities step by step.

Paragraph 4
_____

⇩

Paragraph 5

How does a university cultivate people?

By _____

⇩

Paragraph 6

Why is the humanities ignored today?

1. _____

_____

2. _____

_____

⇩

Paragraph 7	Paragraph 8	Paragraph 9
_____	What should be measured?	What's wrong with cost accounting for universities?
_____	_____	
_____	_____	

⇩

Paragraph 10

Recalling past glory:
_____

⇩

Paragraph 11

The value of the humanities:
_____

Paragraph 12
Conclusion:
_____
_____

Part II. Writing skills development

5. Identify deductive reasoning in Paragraph 8 and discuss it with your partner.

Part III. Language focus

6. **Choose the right word to complete each of the following sentences. Change the form where necessary.**

obsess	aspiration	citation	cultivate	submit
relevance	commit	convert	enrich	specialize

1) All applicants should _____ their application before September 2nd.

2) The villagers _____ mostly maize and beans.

3) She's always wanted to find out the truth of the accident, but recently it's become a(n)_____.

4) Big companies were accused of _____ themselves at the expense of their customers.

5) Few people who _____ to fame ever achieve it.

6) She is known chiefly for her _____ to the cause of feminism.

7) The hospital is unable to provide the highly _____ care needed by very sick babies.

8) For further information, please refer to the _____ leaflet.

9) All _____ are taken from the 1973 edition of the book.

10) He used not to like exercise, but his wife has _____ him to it.

7. **Paraphrase the following sentences.**

1) Once we set aside its elitist history, there remains a strong element of truth to this idea, especially when applied to the humanities.

2) Although we now think of academic disciplines, including the humanities, as being "research-led", this understates the university's historic role in converting the primate Homo sapiens into a creature whose interests, aspirations, and achievements extend beyond successful reproduction.

3) As with Maynard Keynes's notion that returns on public investment must be measured as the long-term consequence of other investments that it stimulates across the economy and society, the knowledge generated by the humanities should be evaluated in the same way.

Part IV. Writing

8. **Charles Murray, author of *Bell Curve*, in his controversial article titled "For most people, college is a waste of time", called for "getting rid of the BA and replacing it with evidence of competence"—the CPA exam model. What do you think of his claim? Write an essay supporting or refuting his notion, using deduction/induction techniques learned in this unit.**

Text C

Experiments in Philosophy (Adapted)

By Joshua Knobe[1]

❶   Aristotle once wrote that philosophy begins in wonder, but one might equally well say that philosophy begins with inner conflict. The cases in which we **are** most **drawn to** philosophy are precisely the cases in which we feel as though there is something pulling us toward one side of a question but also something pulling us, perhaps equally powerfully, toward the other.

❷   But how exactly can philosophy help us in cases like these? If we feel something within ourselves drawing us in one direction but also something drawing us the other way, what exactly can philosophy do to offer us **illumination**?

❸   One traditional answer is that philosophy can help us out by offering us some insight into human nature. Suppose we feel a sense of puzzlement about whether God exists, or whether there are objective moral truths, or whether human beings have free will.

❹   The traditional view was that philosophers could help us get to the bottom of this puzzlement by exploring the sources of the conflict within our own minds. If you look back to the work of some of the greatest thinkers of the 19th century—Mill, Marx, Nietzsche—you can find extraordinary intellectual achievements along these basic lines.

---

1 Joshua Knobe is an assistant professor at Yale University, where he is appointed both in Cognitive Science and in Philosophy. He is a co-editor, with Shaun Nichols, of the volume *Experimental Philosophy*.

5   This traditional approach is now back **with a vengeance**. Philosophers today are once again looking for the roots of philosophical conflicts in our human nature, and they are once again suggesting that we can make progress on philosophical questions by reaching a better understanding of our own minds. But these days, philosophers are **going after** these issues using a new set of **methodologies**. They are **pursuing** the traditional questions using all the tools of modern **cognitive science**. They are **teaming up with** researchers in other **disciplines**, conducting experimental studies, publishing in some of the top journals of psychology. Work in this new vein has come to be known as experimental philosophy.

6   Here's an important question that is worth pursuing further. The study of human nature, whether in Nietzsche or in a contemporary psychology journal, **is** obviously **relevant to** certain purely scientific questions, but how could this sort of work ever help us to answer the distinctive questions of *philosophy*? It may be of some interest just to **figure out** how people ordinarily think, but how could facts about how people ordinarily think ever tell us which views were actually right or wrong?

7   Instead of just considering this question in the abstract, let's focus on one particular example. Take the age-old problem of free will. If all of our actions are determined by prior events—just one thing causing the next, which causes the next—then is it ever possible for human beings to be morally responsible for the things we do? Faced with this question, many people feel themselves pulled in competing directions—it is as though there is something compelling them to say yes, but also something that makes them want to say no.

8   What is it that draws us in these two conflicting directions?

9   We conducted a simple experiment. All participants in the study were told about a deterministic（决定论的）universe (which we called "Universe A"), and all participants received exactly the same information about how this universe worked. The question then was whether people would think that it was possible in such a universe to be fully morally responsible.

10   But now comes the trick. Some participants were asked in a way designed to **trigger** abstract, theoretical reasoning, while others were asked in a way designed to trigger a more **immediate** emotional response. Specifically, participants in one condition were given the abstract question:

11   In Universe A, is it possible for a person to be fully morally responsible for their actions?

12   Meanwhile, participants in the other condition were given a more concrete and emotionally **fraught** example:

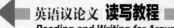
⑬   In Universe A, a man named Bill has become attracted to his secretary, and he decides that the only way to be with her is to kill his wife and three children. He knows that it is impossible to escape from his house in the event of a fire. Before he leaves on a business trip, he sets up a device in his basement that burns down the house and kills his family.

⑭   Is Bill fully morally responsible for killing his wife and children?

⑮   The results showed a striking difference between conditions. Of the participants who received the abstract question, the vast majority (86%) said that it was not possible for anyone to be morally responsible in the deterministic universe. But then, in the more concrete case, we found exactly the opposite results. There, most participants (72%) said that Bill actually *was* responsible for what he had done.

⑯   The results indicated that people might be drawn toward one view by their capacity for abstract, theoretical reasoning, while **simultaneously** being drawn in the opposite direction by their more immediate emotional reactions. It is as though their capacity for abstract reasoning tells them, "This person was completely determined and therefore cannot be held responsible," while their capacity for immediate emotional reaction keeps screaming, "But he did such a horrible thing! Surely, he is responsible for it."

⑰   What we have in this example is just one very simple **initial** experiment. Needless to say, the actual body of research on this topic involves numerous different studies, and the scientific issues arising here can be quite complex. But let us put all those issues to the side for the moment. Instead, we can just return to our original question. How can experiments like these possibly help us to answer the more traditional questions of philosophy?

⑱   The simple study I have been discussing here can offer at least a rough sense of how such an **inquiry** works. The idea is not that we **subject** philosophical questions **to** some kind of Gallup poll. ("Well, the vote came out 65% to 35%, so I guess the answer is…human beings do have free will!") Rather, the aim is to get a better understanding of the psychological **mechanisms** at the root of our sense of conflict and then to begin thinking about which of these mechanisms are worthy of our trust and which might simply be **leading** us **astray**.

⑲   So, what is the answer in the specific case of the conflict we feel about free will? Should we be putting our faith in our capacity for abstract theoretical reasoning, or should we be relying on our more immediate emotional responses? At the moment, there is no **consensus** on this question within the experimental philosophy community. What all experimental philosophers do agree on, however, is that we will be able to do a better job of addressing these fundamental philosophical questions if we can arrive at a better understanding of the way our own minds work.

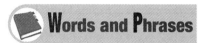 **Words and Phrases**

consensus	[kən'sensəs]	*n.*	共识，一致意见
discipline	['disəplin]	*n.*	学科
▲ fraught	[frɔ:t]	*a.*	充满……的
★ illumination	[iˌlu:mi'neiʃn]	*n.*	解释；启发
immediate	[i'mi:diət]	*a.*	直接的
initial	[i'niʃəl]	*a.*	初步的
inquiry	[in'kwaiəri]	*n.*	探究，探索
mechanism	['mekənizəm]	*n.*	机制
★ methodology	[ˌmeθə'dɔlədʒi]	*n.*	方法论
pursue	[pə'sju:]	*vt.*	从事；继续
★ simultaneously	[ˌsiməl'teiniəsli]	*adv.*	同时发生地，同时进行地
★ trigger	['trigə]	*vt.*	触发，引起

be drawn to	被……所吸引
be relevant to	与……有关的
cognitive science	认知科学
figure out	想出，搞清楚
go after	追逐，追求
lead astray	把……引入歧途
subject... to...,	提供……呈交
team up with	与……合作
with a vengeance	猛烈地，极度地

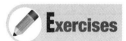 **Exercises**

Part I. Understanding the text

1. Study the title of Text C.

- What are the key words in the essay title?
- Why do you think they are the key words?

2. Spend 8 minutes reading the essay, and fill in the following chart.

Paragraphs 1–2
The question: _____

⇩

Paragraphs 3–4
The answer: _____
Example: _____

⇩

Paragraphs 5–6
New development in Philosophy:
_____
The question: What's the merit of doing so?

⇩

Paragraphs 7–16
Analysis by scientific experiments:
Paragraphs 7-8: _____
Paragraphs 9-14: _____
Paragraphs 15-16: _____

⇩

Paragraph 17
Repetition of the question: _____

⇩

Paragraph 18
The answer: _____

⇩

Paragraph 19
Conclusion: _____

Part II. Writing skills development

3. The author mainly uses inductive argument to prove the advantages of experimental philosophy. Can you find out where and how the author does it?

Part III. Language focus

4. Choose the right word to complete each of the following sentences. Change the form where necessary.

immediate	consensus	discipline	initial	inquiry
pursue	trigger	astray	illuminate	draw

1) The dogs were running in the woods in _____ of a rabbit.

2) _____ reports say that seven people have died in the accident, though this has not yet been confirmed.

3) The government promised that there would be no tax increases in the _____ future.

4) Citizens have demanded a full _____ into the government's handling of the crisis.

5) His parents worried that she might be led _____ by his unsuitable friends.

6) The general _____ was that technology was a double-edged sword.

7) Is it wise to _____ conclusions from the results of a single survey?

8) At night the city is beautifully _____ .

9) The racial killings at the weekend have _____ off a wave of protests through the country.

10) I don't have enough self-_____ to save money.

5. Paraphrase the following sentences.

1) The cases in which we are most drawn to philosophy are precisely the cases in which we feel as though there is something pulling us toward one side of a question but also something pulling us, perhaps equally powerfully, toward the other.

2) This tradition is now back with a vengeance.

3) Let us put all those issues to the side for the moment.

Part IV. Writing

6. Rewrite the essay in 200-250 words.

Unit Summary

In this unit, you have learned induction and deduction. The three articles in this unit all employ the use of inductive and deductive reasoning. Now, do the following exercises to consolidate your knowledge.

1. **What is inductive and deductive reasoning?**

2. **Can you give some examples of inductive and deductive arguments?**

3. **Can you determine whether the following are inductive or deductive arguments?**

   1) There is a common substance among the arts because there are general conditions without which an experience is not possible.

   2) In investigating hereditary characteristics, we find that vast amounts of literature in the last few years point toward two types of fiber in human muscle tissue: Type 1, slow twitch, or red; and Type 2, fast twitch or white muscle fiber. It is believed that the number of white and red muscle fibers is genetically predetermined and remains unchanged during a lifetime. Consequently, in accordance with the distribution that prevails, some people appear to be quicker than others.

   3) Given the view that species evolve into one another, then members of one species must somehow give rise to members of another species. It follows that members of the second species must somehow derive as variants of members of the first.

   4) Chick embryos inoculated with human fibrosarcoma (纤维组织) cells derived from a type of bone cancer were dosed for nine days with an amount of alcohol corresponding to about two glasses of wine a day in people. Those embryos developed an extensive network of blood vessels and doubled in size. The cancer in the alcohol-dosed embryos secreted a protein called vascular endothelial growth factor. These data suggest that alcohol is an important mechanism for cancer growth.

   5) There is no relation between "sincerity" and value as art. The volumes of agonizingly felt love poetry perpetrated by adolescents and the dreary (however fervently felt) religious verse which fills libraries, are sufficient proof of this.

4. **Write your essay: Use what you have learned in this unit to write an argumentative essay on any topic related to philosophy (e.g. religion, literature, language, ethics, philosophy, etc.). At this stage, you shall be able to write an essay of 200 to 250 words.**

Prewriting

Work out the outline of the essay and ask yourself: ✔ or ✘

What is the overall stance/argument of the essay?   ☐

Is the overall stance/argument obvious in Introduction and/or Conclusion?   ☐

Is the main idea clear in each supporting paragraph?   ☐

How many paragraphs will the essay have?   ☐

Does the outline follow a logical sequence of ideas?   ☐

Writing

Write the first draft alone.

Revising

Once you have the first draft of your paper completed, (peer) review it with the following questions in mind:

Does the Introduction and/or Conclusion clearly present the overall argument?

Are the ideas clearly and logically organized?

Is the main argument in each supporting paragraph supported with adequate evidence?

Are the sentences grammatical and concise?

Is coherence within and across paragraphs adequately achieved?

---

5. One crucial aspect of understanding essays and essay questions is the meaning of key words used in them. Match the words (a–t) to their definitions (1–20) in the following two boxes, and make sure you have fully understood them.

Words/Phrases	Definitions
a. reasoning	1. to be reasonable, logical or comprehensible
b. develop	2. to continue doing an activity or trying to achieve something over a long period of time
c. generate	3. a situation in which it is very difficult to decide what to do, because all the choices seem equally good or equally bad
d. be inclined to	4. to give an acceptable explanation for something that other people think is unreasonable
e. falsify	5. a sudden clear understanding of something or part of something, especially a complicated situation or idea
f. dilemma	6. consisting of many different parts and often difficult to understand
g. make sense	7. to develop and improve
h. justify	8. to be likely to do something or behave in a particular way

(continued)

Words/Phrases	Definitions
i. approach	9. to change something into a different form of thing, or to change something so that it can be used for a different purpose or in a different way
j. insight	10. a process of thinking carefully about something in order to make a judgment
k. pursue	11. directly relating to the subject or problem being discussed or considered
l. trigger	12. to express in a shorter, clearer, or different way what someone has said or written
m. complex	13. to design or make a new idea, product, system, etc. over a period of time
n. conflict	14. to make something happen very quickly, especially a series of events
o. address	15. to desire and work towards achieving something important
p. relevant	16. a state of disagreement or argument between people, groups, countries, etc.
q. cultivate	17. to prove or declare false
r. convert	18. to give attention to or deal with (a matter or problem)
s. aspire	19. a method of doing something or dealing with a problem
t. paraphrase	20. to produce or cause something

Social Science

Writing Skill Development

Supporting Evidence and Effective Argumentation (5)

Clear Flow of Reasoning and Avoidance of False Arguments

A clear flow of logical reasoning

In argumentative essay writing, it is best to assume that you are writing for educated skeptical neutral readers. They may not be hostile to your claim(s) but they need to be convinced. So you should be attempting to control the type of evidence selected and the form of argument to persuade them (Chesñevar et al., 2000). In addition, you should keep in mind that the readers trust your opinions because they trust not only your evidence but your interpretation of it in a clear flow of logical reasoning.

A clear flow of logical reasoning in writing an argumentation should respect the following four criteria (Chesñevar et al., 2000):

➡ **Consistency in meaning between the main idea (topic sentence) and the supporting ideas (supporting sentences)**

Every essay should have a main argument/thesis that is supported by supporting arguments/ideas (see more details in Unit 1). Similarly, every paragraph should have a point, or main idea, represented in the topic sentence (usually located at the beginning of the paragraph). Supporting sentences further divide the main idea of the paragraph, often into several specific, supporting ideas/sentences, in order to explain and prove the main idea of the paragraph (Willard, 1989). When necessary, the paragraph ends with a concluding/closing sentence which restates the main point of the paragraph.

[*Topic sentence*]	The American Revolution ended the power of a sovereign central government over the colonies.
[*Supporting sentences*]	Britain had had the power to appoint and remove governors, members of upper houses of legislatures, judges, and other officials. It had had the power to veto colonial legislation, to review cases appealed from colonial supreme courts, and to use armed force.
[*Concluding/closing sentence*]	All of this superintending power was wiped out by independence.

Source: Jensen, 1957, 39.

Effective supporting sentences aim for unity (consistency in meaning between the main idea and the supporting ideas). Unity means that all the sentences in a paragraph stick to the same topic. Any supporting sentences that stray off-topic do not belong in the paragraph and any irrelevant information that does not directly relate to the topic sentence should be removed or relocated to a different paragraph (Willard, 1989).

[*Topic sentence*]	Food is an integral part of the human's life.
[*Supporting sentence*]	The key issue of the competition in the food industry is the quality of products or many products are usually not healthy for the consumers.

Source: http://www.ehow.com/info_8383552_factors-unify-paragraph.html.

The supporting sentences do not "support" the topic sentence in any way. They just drift aimlessly to a new, unrelated subject area and should belong to another paragraph.

➡ **Adequacy/Sufficiency of evidence**

There should be enough evidence to support a claim/argument. The amount of evidence required depends upon the length of your essay, the readers and the nature of the thesis.

● **Determining the sufficiency of evidence**

As you look at the evidence supporting an argument, ask yourself if you make use of enough evidence to convince a reasonable reader. For example, to prove the statement that "many writing assignments at the university level are in some way related to argument," an example of one Engineering assignment would most likely be insufficient, whereas several examples from different disciplines would probably make it hold true.

➡ Substantiality of evidence (credible and accurate evidence)

Evidence shouldn't be used unless it is accurate and up-to-date and it is not persuasive unless the readers believe in the writer's credibility.

● **Determining the credibility of evidence**

It is important to decide how credible (believable and authoritative) a piece of evidence is within an argument. For example, to illustrate a view on university administration, evidence (e.g., facts and statistics) cited from *The Journal of Higher Education* will be much more credible than that taken from *The National Inquirer*.

● **Determining the accuracy of evidence**

The premises should provide enough evidence for the conclusion, trying to satisfy the criteria of truth and congruence with the important beliefs, which in our mind, means adapting to socially accepted ideas, and also to scientific rules (Chesñevar et al., 2000).

As you look at the evidence supporting an argument, ask yourself if this evidence "tells the truth." Are statistics gathered in verifiable ways from good sources? Are the quotations complete and fair (not out of context)? Are the facts verifiable from other sources?

For example, to support the argument "College students are very enthusiastic about learning argumentation skills," a writer uses the following piece of evidence:

> In a survey conducted in my residence hall, 92% of the respondents asserted that they enjoyed writing arguments more than any other activities listed on the questionnaire.

Readers might ask questions like "Who conducted the survey?" "Who were the respondents?" and "What were the other activities listed on the questionnaire?" Thus the evidence might be questionable and fails to support the argument strongly.

➡ Coherence

Coherence means having internal elements or parts connected, especially a logical, orderly, and aesthetically consistent relationship of parts (Halliday & Hasan, 1976). As proposed by Halliday and Hasan (1976), such grammatical and lexical devices as *reference, ellipsis*（省略）, *substitution*（替代）, *conjunction* and *lexical cohesion* create "texture"—the property of being a text. These devices form cohesive relations between

sentences and elements in sentences, thus contributing to the coherence of the text.

Reference covers the use of pronouns, definite article, demonstratives（指示词）and the comparatives. *Conjunction/transition* refers to the use of additive（附加）, causal（因果）, temporal（时间）, adversative（反义语）, and continuative words and phrases. *Lexical cohesions* include repetition of the same word, synonyms, antonyms, superordinates（上义词）and collocations（词的搭配）(Halliday & Hasan, 1976).

A persuasive argumentative essay must be written with a strong sense of coherence. Please study the following rules of how coherence can be achieved (Chesñevar et al., 2000):

* *Make sure that the grammatical subject of your sentences reflects the real subject of your paragraph.* Do these subjects match your paragraph's subject in most cases? (*Reference*)

* *Make sure that your grammatical subjects are consistent.* Again, look at the grammatical subjects of all your sentences. (*Reference*)

* *Make sure that your sentences look backward as well as forward.* In order for a paragraph to be coherent, each sentence should begin by linking itself firmly to the sentence that came before. (*Conjunction*)

* *Follow the principle of moving from old to new.* Put the old information at the beginning of the sentence and the new information at the end. (*Conjunction*)

* *Use repetition to create a sense of unity.* Repeating key words and phrases at appropriate moments will give your reader a sense of coherence in your work. (*Lexical cohesion*)

* *Use transition/conjunction markers wisely.* Effective paragraphs use transitional words and phrases to create coherence, or flow, between sentences. Table 6.1 lists some common and useful transitional markers.

Table 6.1: Transitional Markers (Willard, 1989)

Transition	Transitional markers
Addition	again, also, and, and then, besides, equally important, finally, first, further, furthermore, in addition, in the first place, last, moreover, next, second, still, too
Comparison	also, in the same way, likewise, similarly
Concession	granted, naturally, of course
Contrast	although, and yet, at the same time, despite that, even so, even though, however, in contrast, in spite of, instead, nevertheless, on the contrary, on the other hand, otherwise, regardless, still, though, yet, while

(continued)

Transition	Transitional markers
Emphasis	certainly, indeed, in fact, of course
Example or illustration	after all, as an illustration, even, for example, for instance, indeed, in fact, in other words, in short, of course, namely, specifically, that is, to illustrate, thus
Summary	all in all, altogether, as has been said, finally, in brief, in conclusion, in other words, in particular, in short, in summary, on the whole, therefore, to summarize
Time sequence	after a while, afterward, again, also, as long as, at last, at length, at that time, before, earlier, eventually, finally, formerly, further, furthermore, in addition, in the first place, in the past, last, lately, meanwhile, moreover, next, presently, shortly, simultaneously, since, so far, subsequently, then, thereafter, until, until now, when

Avoiding logical fallacies

Fallacies are statements that might sound reasonable or superficially true but are actually flawed or dishonest (Edward, 2009). Therefore, being familiar with a few types of fallacies will reduce the chances that you will be fooled by the fallacious arguments, and you will be less likely to engage in fallacious reasoning yourself (Edward, 2009).

➡ **Fallacy of hasty generalization** (HG)（草率结论）(fallacy of insufficient statistics): A generalization based on too little evidence, or on evidence that is biased.

   Example: After being in New York for a week, I can tell you: All New Yorkers are rude.

➡ **Fallacy of false alternatives** (FA)/(Either/Or Fallacy): Only two possibilities are presented when in fact several exist.

   Example 1   America: love it or leave it.
   Example 2   Shut down all nuclear power plants or watch your children and grandchildren die from radiation poisoning.

➡ **Non sequitur**（非根据前提的推理）: The conclusion does not follow logically from the premise.

   Example: My teacher is pretty; I'll learn a lot from her.

➡ **Personal attack** (*Argumentum Ad Hominem*, literally, "argument toward the man." Also called "Poisoning the Well"): Attacking or praising the people who make an argu-

ment, rather than discussing the argument itself. This practice is fallacious because the personal character of an individual is logically irrelevant to the truth or falseness of the argument itself.

Example 1 We can't elect him mayor. He cheats on his wife!

➡ **Red herring**（不相干的事实/红鲱鱼谬论）: Distracting the audience by drawing attention to an irrelevant issue.

Example: Why worry about nuclear war when we're all going to die anyway?

➡ **Circular reasoning/Begging the question**（循环论证）: Asserting a point that has just been made.

Example 1 She is ignorant because she was never educated.
Example 2 We sin because we're sinners.

This sort of "reasoning" is fallacious because simply assuming that the conclusion is true (directly or indirectly) in the premises does not constitute evidence for that conclusion.

➡ **Fallacy of false cause** (FC): Fallacy of false cause occurs when a causal conclusion is reached on the basis of very inadequate reasons (Edward, 2009).

Example 1 The farm bankruptcy rate reached 20% just two years after Reagan became President. Thus, this high bankruptcy rate among farmers was due to Reagan being President.
Example 2 All the really prosperous countries in the world are democratic. So, their prosperity results from democracy.

➡ **Fallacy of equivocation** (EQ)（含糊其辞）: Falsely equates two meanings of the same word.

Example: The end of a thing is its perfection; hence, death is the perfection of life.

The argument is fallacious because there are two different definitions of the word "end" involved in the argument.

➡ **Fallacy of argument from ignorance** (IG): An argument based on lack of knowledge.

Example: No one has proved that metal amalgam dental fillings（汞合金牙齿填充物）are dangerous to your health; therefore, they are safe.

References:

Chesñevar, C., Maguitman, A. & Loui, R. (2000). Logical Models of Argument. *ACM Computing Surveys*, 32(4), 337–383.

Edward, D. T. (2009). *Attacking Faulty Reasoning: A Practical Guide to Fallacy-free Arguments* (6th ed.). Belmont, California: Wadsworth.

Halliday, M. A. K. & Hasan, R. (1976). *Cohesion in English*. London: Longman.

Jensen, M. (1957). Democracy and the American Revolution. *Huntington Library Quarterly*, 20, 312–341.

Willard, C. A. (1989). *A Theory of Argumentation*. Retrieved from wikipedia.org/wiki /www.logicalfallacies.info.

Reading for Ideas

Text A

The Many Career Opportunities for Recipients of Degrees in Mathematics[1]

❶　It is **asserted** that once a person decides to study **mathematics** they are bound to a narrow career sphere that is available to them. According to this assertion the only possible jobs are teaching jobs at middle school, high school, college, and university levels.

❷　I am **in total opposition of** this assertion. I believe that if a person studies mathematics, they will have a world of options.

❸　First of all, the teaching profession alone offers an **assortment** of different levels of teaching. One could teach at the **elementary**, middle school, high school, college, and university levels. There are also teacher's aids, research assistants, and student teachers, as well as **substitute** teachers. The demand for teachers is elevating at an **alarming** rate. This goes for teachers in general, but especially for teachers interested in teaching in the mathematics or science fields.

❹　**By no means** does studying mathematics limit a person to the teaching profession alone. Besides being a teacher, who technically is a mathematician, there is also the obvious profession of being a mathematician without being a teacher. There are also opportunities such as becoming an engineer, a research scientist, or a manager of a business. Mathematics **majors** work for such companies as IBM[2], AT&T[3] Bell Labs（美国

---

1 This essay was retrieved from 123HelpMe.com.
2 IBM: 全球最大的信息技术和业务解决方案公司，目前拥有全球雇员 30 多万人，业务遍及 160 多个国家和地区。
3 AT&T 公司（AT&T Inc.，为 American Telephone & Telegraph 的缩写）美国电话电报公司

137

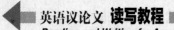
AT&T 贝尔实验室）, American Airlines[1], FedEx[2], L.L.Bean[3], and Perdue Farms Inc[4]., to name a few (Madison, 1990). There are also mathematicians employed in such government agencies as the Bureau of the Census, Department of Agriculture, and NASA[5] Goddard Space Center（美国哥达德航天中心）(Valerie, 1993). Mathematicians are needed in the fields of law and medicine as well as in the arts, such as **sculpting,** music, and television. The possibilities are seemingly endless. When you think about it, almost every job involves mathematics.

❺ This can be further supported by the statistics from the fields of employment of mathematics degree **recipients**. The year before last, only about 30% of mathematics degree recipients actually became teachers. The other 70% of that year chose to take on various work activities such as reporting, statistics, computing activities, research and development, management and **administration,** production and **inspection**, as well as a few other activities.

❻ For people receiving their **bachelors'** degree in mathematics only 42% went into the field of mathematics and statistics. The other recipients of bachelors' degree in mathematics took jobs in other fields. 40% were employed in the field of computer science, 14% the field of engineering, and 2% in the field of **psychology**.

❼ Similar statistics were found for people receiving their masters' degree in mathematics, except for a rather large 50% increase in those entering the field of mathematics and statistics. Of those receiving their masters' degree in mathematics, 62% found jobs related to mathematics or statistics; only 15% went into the field of computer science compared to the 40% of those who received only their bachelors' degrees in mathematics, 17% the field of engineering and 6% the field of psychology.

❽ At the time of these statistics three quarters of people with mathematical science degrees were not classified as working as mathematical scientists. Also, one quarter of people with bachelors' degrees in mathematics, one third of people with masters' degrees in mathematics, and three quarters of people with **doctorates** in mathematics were employed at educational institutions. These percentages show that not even a majority of people who received any level of degree in mathematics were employed as teachers.

---

1 American Airlines：美国航空公司（常被译为美利坚航空公司，通常简称美航）

2 Fedex（FedEx Corp.）：联邦快递，隶属于美国联邦快递集团。

3 L.L.Bean：创始人 Leon Leonwood Bean 名字的缩写。L.L.Bean 是美国著名的户外用品品牌，创建于 1912 年，至今已有 100 年的悠久历史。

4 Perdue Farms Inc.: 普渡农场有限公司，美国著名产销农副产品的公司。

5 NASA（National Aeronautics and Space Administration）美国宇航局

❾ Simultaneously, it is true that not every job opening could be properly satisfied by a person who majored in mathematics, but for the most part that person would have an advantage over other applicants because of their knowledge in mathematics.

❿ On the whole, there are many fields of employment open to people who have received their degrees in mathematics. The jobs are out there if the **prospective** workers have good search skills for jobs, which are essential. Along with that there are seven easy steps to finding the right job: (1) know yourself, (2) set your goals, (3) prepare a powerful resume, (4) establish a network, (5) apply for positions, (6) prepare yourself for the job interview, and (7) **evaluate** the job offers you receive. These seven steps will greatly increase a mathematics major's chances of finding the right job. Therefore it is a sensible option to take mathematics as one's major, especially for a person who cherishes strong interest in it.

References:

Madison, B. (1990). *A Challenge of Andrew Sterrett, 101 Careers in Mathematics.* Washington D. C: National Academic Press.

Valerie, T. L. (1993). Career Opportunities in Mathematics. *The Black Collegian, the Mathematical Association of America (IV)*, 23, 144-151.

Words and Phrases

administration	[ədˌminiˈstreiʃn]	*n.*	管理；行政；实施；行政机构
alarming	[əˈlɑːmiŋ]	*a.*	令人担忧的；使人惊恐的
			alarm *n.* 警报；惊慌；警告器
			vt. 恐吓；警告
assert	[əˈsɜːt]	*vt.*	断言，主张
▲ assortment	[əˈsɔːtmənt]	*n.*	分类；混合物
			▲ assorted *a.* 多样混合的
bachelor	[ˈbætʃələ]	*n.*	学士；单身汉；（尚未交配的）小雄兽
▲ doctorate	[ˈdɔktərit]	*n.*	博士学位；博士头衔
elementary	[ˌeliˈmentri]	*a.*	初级的；基本的；[化学]元素的
evaluate	[iˈvæljueit]	*vt. & vi.*	评价；估价；求……的值
inspection	[inˈspekʃn]	*n.*	检验；视察，检查

major	['meidʒə]	*vi.*	主修
		n.	[人类]成年人；主修科目；陆军少校
		a.	主要的；重要的；主修的；较多的
mathematics	[ˌmæθə'mætiks]	*n.*	数学；数学运算；数学专业
opposition	[ˌɔpə'ziʃn]	*n.*	反对；反对派；在野党；敌对
★ prospective	[prə'spektiv]	*a.*	预期的
psychology	[sai'kɔlədʒi]	*n.*	心理学；心理状态
★ recipient	[ri'sipiənt]	*n.*	接受者，受领者
★ sculpt	[skʌlpt]	*n.*	雕刻品
		vt. & vi.	造型；雕刻
			★ sculpture *n.* 雕刻，雕刻品，雕塑；[地理]刻蚀
			vt. 雕刻，雕塑；刻蚀
substitute	['sʌbstitjuːt, -tuːt]	*n.*	代用品；代替者
		vt. & vi.	替代；代替

| by no means | | 绝不 |
| in total opposition of | | 坚决反对 |

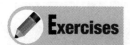 **Exercises**

Part I. Understanding the text

1. Study the title of Text A.
- What are the key words in the essay title?
- Why do you think they are the key words?

2. Spend 10 minutes browsing the essay and work out the outline of the essay, with reference to the following:
- Thesis statement/main argument
- Supporting ideas

After you have finished, discuss your outline with your partner.

3. In the author's opinion, there is a false statement about career opportunities for recipients of degrees in mathematics. What is it?

Part II. Writing skills development

4. **Read the following paragraph written by a student and identify the topic sentence and the sentence that should be omitted because it strays off the topic.**

   For both examiners and examinees, the examination can show what and how much the examinees have mastered. When the result of an examination is announced, more can be obtained than merely the scores. Results are just like mirrors for both the examinees and examiners. From the "reflections" of the exams, the examinee becomes aware of which aspects he or she has not done well and need remedial work. As far as the examiner is concerned, the exams do reveal to him or her how much of the teaching goal has been achieved and what should be improved in the teaching. Of course there is no denying that too many examinations will become heavy burdens to both examiners and examinees.

   The topic sentence: _____

   The sentence that strays off-topic: _____

5. **Read the following paragraphs of Text A and decide the argument and the type of evidence used therein (e.g. facts, statistics, research results, examples, reliable authority/sources, illustrative incidents or definition etc.).**

   1) Read Paragraph 3 and decide its argument and the type of evidence used to support the argument.

      Argument: _____

      Type of evidence: _____

   2) Read Paragraphs 4–8 and decide its argument and the type of evidence used to support the argument.

      Argument: _____

      Type of evidence: _____

6. **Now read the statements below and discuss with your partner the questions about the clear flow of reasoning in Paragraphs 4–9 of the essay:**

   The premises

   a. The teaching profession alone offers an assortment of different levels of teaching to recipients of degrees in mathematics.

b. Here is also the obvious profession of being a mathematician, an engineer, a research scientist, or a manager of a business.

The conclusion

There are many career opportunities for recipients of degrees in mathematics.

Do the premises provide enough evidence for the conclusion?

Are the premises true, probable and/or reliable?

Is there an adequate relation between the premises and the conclusion?

7. **Read the text again and discuss with your partner how coherence within and across paragraphs is achieved.**

Part III. Language focus

8. **Choose the right word to complete each of the following sentences. Change the form where necessary.**

assert	psychology	evaluate	opposition	substitute
major	elementary	prospective	administration	inspection

1) Managers are required to _____ all proposals by the same competent techniques.

2) She was taken aback by her son's strong _____ to her remarriage.

3) Mr. Helm plans to _____ that the bill violates the First Amendment.

4) On closer_____, it was found to be false.

5) The new dam is a _____ construction project, funded by the government.

6) The special mix of experience and skills are required of the _____ candidate.

7) In the case of a highly intelligent animal, _____ training is easy.

8) These biases help to show exactly why we need _____ experiments and why we can't rely on our intuitions about the behaviour of others.

9) She is seeking a _____ for the very man whose departure made her cry.

10) The teaching management system is used by educational administrators to _____ teaching.

9. **Paraphrase the following sentences.**

1) By no means does studying mathematics limit a person to the teaching profession alone.

2) These percentages show that not even a majority of people who received any level of degree in mathematics were employed as teachers.

3) It is true that not every job opening could be properly satisfied by a person who majored in mathematics, but for the most part that person would have an advantage over other applicants because of this knowledge in mathematics.

Part IV. Writing

10. Discuss with your partner on what information you might expect to follow each of the following sentences:

- If a person studies mathematics they have a world of options open to them.
- Maybe most people who study mathematics won't become millionaires, but they do have the opportunity to.

11. Read the text again and study the following phrases and sentence structures used to support the arguments.

Statistics	• Last year, only about 30% of mathematics degree recipients actually became teachers. • …further supported by the statistics from…
Comparison & Contrast	• …that person would have an advantage over other applicants.
Examples	• One could teach at the elementary, middle school, … • …as well as in the arts, such as sculpting, music, and television. • …chose to take on various work activities such as reporting, statistics, …
Illustrative incidents	• This directly applies to me because I'm majoring in Secondary Education in mathematics and I plan on being a high school mathematics teacher.

12. Now suppose you are going to write a short essay in support of *Taking Part-time Jobs*, which following sentence would best serve as the topic sentence and what type of evidence would you use to develop/support it?

- Students can promote their study through part-time jobs.
- There are many advantages for a student to have a part-time job.
- Part-time jobs can partly relieve students' financial burden.
- Students can accumulate work experiences through part-time jobs.

What kind of logical fallacy should you avoid?

Type/types of logical fallacy you should avoid _____ when you

_____

A. express the comparison & contrast between the students who have part-time job experiences and those who have not…

B. present the reasons why students can promote their study through part-time jobs.

Now discuss your ideas with your partner and give your reasons.

13. **Write out the essay discussed above, with reference to the following phrases and sentence structures.**

Examples	• If a law student finds a part-time job in a law firm, his practice will enable him to better understand what he has learned from books. • …taking part-time jobs becomes a way for poor students to meet their great expenses in campus lives.
Cause & Effect	• More and more college students abandon study because of their taking part-time jobs, so quite a few people are opposed to part-time jobs.
Comparison & Contrast	• …It's easier to find jobs for those who have accumulated experiences in part-time jobs.
Illustrative incidents	• …the part-time job can offer him opportunities to go beyond what he has been taught in class, and he will learn something that doesn't exist in books but in practice.

Suggested writing steps:
- Take a few minutes to plan and make outlines before you begin writing the essay.
- Make sure that your argument and evidence are adequate, reasonable and effective.
- Write the first draft alone.
- Peer review each other's writing.
- Revise your first draft.

Text B

Hidden Tigers: Why Do Chinese Children Do So Well at School?[1]

By Warwick Mansell[2]

❶ Children of Chinese **origin,** whether rich or poor, do incredibly well in school—but hardly any studies have been done to find out why.

❷ It seems a hugely under-researched **phenomenon** within English education. But Jessie Tang thinks she has the answer.

❸ "It's mostly the parents. Chinese parents tend to push their children a lot, and have really high **expectations.** I think it's maybe because they did not have the opportunities that we have these days. They want us to **take advantage of** them." Jessie, 18, an A-level[3] student at Watford grammar school for girls, whose father arrived in England from Hong Kong, was being asked about what seems an amazing success story buried and barely commented upon within English schools' results.

❹ The **statistics** relate to the achievement of pupils of Chinese **ethnicity,** revealed last autumn in a report by the Equality and Human Rights **Commission** on Inequality in Britain. This showed not only that British Chinese youngsters are the highest performing ethnic group in England at GCSE[4], which has been known for years. It also showed that this group seemed to be **singularly** successful in achieving that goal of educational policy-makers everywhere: a narrow performance gap between those from the poorest homes, and the rest.

❺ Further evidence of the success of pupils of Chinese **heritage** came through the world's most well-known international testing study, Pisa.[5] This found 15-year-olds from Shanghai, China, easily **outperforming** those of all other nationalities.

❻ The **domestic** statistics show that, at GCSE, children of Chinese ethnicity— classed simply as "Chinese" in the data—who are **eligible** for free school meals (FSM) perform better than the national average for all pupils, rich and poor.

---

1 This essay was retrieved from guardian.co.uk.

2 Warwick Mansell: The former TES journalist writes for NAHT on current education issues. TES: The leading UK website for teachers and education professionals. NAHT: The National Association for All School Leaders (UK).

3 A Level:〈英〉英语学校里某一课程结束时举行的高深考试

4 GCSE: General Certificate of Secondary Education 普通中学教育证书

5 Pisa: The Programme for International Student Assessment (PISA), a worldwide evaluation of 15-year-old school pupils' scholastic performance.

7   Not only that, but FSM Chinese pupils do better than those of most other ethnic backgrounds, even when compared with children from **better-off** homes (those not eligible for free school meals).

8   A detailed look at the figures makes this clearer. Some 71% of Chinese FSM pupils achieved five good GCSEs, including English and math, in 2009. For non-FSM Chinese pupils, the figure was 72%.

9   Every other ethnic group had a gap of at least 10 percentage points between children who do not count as eligible for free meals, and those who do. The gap for white pupils stood at 32 percentage points.

10   In primary schools, the picture is similar. Remarkably, in 2009, in English key stage 2 tests, Chinese FSM pupils outperformed not just their counterparts from other ethnic groups—easily outstripping（胜过）white children—but even Chinese pupils not eligible for free meals.

11   Michael Gove, the education secretary, told his party conference last autumn that the performance of FSM pupils **as a whole** was a "**reproach** to our **conscience.**" So what do Chinese pupils have going for them that other children do not?

12   Anyone investigating this subject will be struck by the limited research available. Only one academic team seems to have looked into British Chinese pupils' experience in detail in recent years.

13   The team, who interviewed 80 Chinese pupils, 30 Chinese parents and 30 teachers in 2005, identified several factors behind the success, although they stress that not all British Chinese pupils achieve. One explanation, though, shines through their findings.

14   Becky Francis, a visiting professor at King's College London, director of education at the Royal Society of Arts and one of the researchers, says: "Our main argument is that families of Chinese heritage see taking education seriously as a **fundamental pillar** of their Chinese **identity,** and a way of differentiating themselves not just within their own group, but from other ethnic groups as well."

15   Recent coverage of Amy Chua's book on "tiger parenting", Battle **Hymn** of The Tiger Mother, has also focused attention on parenting styles promoting achievement in children of Chinese ethnicity.

16   The argument that Chinese families put special value on education is sensitive **territory**, of course, as most parents would profess a **commitment** to helping their child do well. Academics also stress that the numbers of pupils classed as "Chinese" are small—only 2,236 took GCSEs last year, from a total cohort of nearly 600,000—and results should be **interpreted cautiously**. However, there is tentative evidence, both from interviews with parents and from analyses of background values existing in Chinese culture, that family commitment to education is particularly strong.

17 Some 13 of the 30 British Chinese parents interviewed said their children were also being educated at Chinese "supplementary schools". These offer **tuition** in Chinese language and culture on the weekends.

18 Several of the parents also said they paid for tutoring outside school hours. Researchers found that among British Chinese families this was not related to social class: a number of working-class parents paid for this, too. Asked to respond to the question "Is education important?", all 80 pupils agreed. High parental expectations also seem to have been a factor in many—though not all—children's experiences.

19 One pupil is **quoted** saying: "My parents expect me to get the best grades. And if I don't, then they'll continuously nag at me to do better... Like if I get a B, they'll be like, 'Why didn't you get an A?' "

20 A paper presented at last year's British Educational Research Association conference, covering performance across all ethnic groups, found no link between the occupation of Chinese pupils' parents and their GCSE scores, unlike for children from all other ethnicities.

21 Ramesh Kapadia, a visiting professor at London University's Institute of Education, who presented the paper, says: "I think within Chinese society, there is an emphasis on practice. Children are told: 'If you want to learn something, practice, practice and practice it again and you will get better.' It may be that this helps to motivate pupils when the rewards can seem a long way away."

22 There is a mixed picture overall, though, as to how far this school success is being translated into employment prospects. The Equality and Human Rights Commission report found that British Chinese men and women were twice as likely to be in professional jobs as their white British counterparts. But average earnings remained around 11% lower throughout the population than for those classed as "white Christian".

23 Whether the Chinese experience can be replicated（复制）among other pupils is debatable. Some might see evidence that Chinese families **emphasize** hard work, and the results that follow, as simple proof that all can succeed, given the right attitude.

㉔ However, Francis says such a view should be treated cautiously, the team's 2005 paper arguing that "Chinese constructions of ethnic identity and education are very specific." Much research has shown links, generally, between poverty and underachievement（学习成绩不良）.

㉕ Jessie, whose father works in a takeaway restaurant and whose mother, originally from Malaysia, works at Heathrow airport, has 12 GCSEs including six As and an offer to read music at Royal Holloway[1], London. She attended a Chinese supplementary school from the age of five. She says many Chinese families are **keen** on their children pursuing careers in medicine, so she is "rebelling a bit", but wanted to pursue a subject she enjoys.

㉖ The Department for Education was unable to point to any particular study it has commissioned to look at British Chinese pupils' success. Given the scale of that success, it seems surprising that the phenomenon has not been **investigated** further.

Words and Phrases

better-off	['betəˌɔf]	a.	较富裕的；境况较好的
cautiously	['kɔːʃəsli]	adv.	慎重地，谨慎地
commission	[kə'miʃn]	n.	委员会；佣金；委任状
		vt.	委任；使服役；委托制作
commitment	[kə'mitmənt]	n.	承诺，保证；委托；承担义务；献身
conscience	['kɔnʃəns]	n.	道德心，良心
domestic	[də'mestik]	a.	家庭的；国内的；驯养的
		n.	国货；佣人
★ eligible	['elidʒəbl]	a.	符合条件的；有资格当选的；合格的
		n.	合格者；适任者；有资格者
emphasize	['emfəsaiz]	vt.	强调；加强
ethnicity	[eθ'nisəti]	n.	种族划分；种族性
			ethnic a. 人种的；种族的；异教徒的
expectation	[ˌekspek'teiʃn]	n.	期待；预期；指望
fundamental	[ˌfʌndə'mentl]	a.	基本的，根本的
		n.	基本原理；基本原则
★ heritage	['heritidʒ]	n.	传统；遗产；继承物；继承权

1 Royal Holloway, University of London (RHUL): A constituent college of the University of London. The college has three faculties, 18 academic departments. 伦敦大学皇家霍洛威学院

▲ hymn	[him]	*n.*	赞美诗；圣歌；欢乐的歌
		vt. & vi.	唱赞美歌
identity	[ai'dentəti]	*n.*	身份；同一性，一致；特性；恒等式
investigate	[in'vestigeit]	*vt. & vi.*	调查；研究
interpret	[in'tɜ:prit]	*vi.*	解释；翻译
		vt.	说明；口译
keen	[ki:n]	*a.*	敏锐的，敏捷的；渴望的
		n.	痛哭，挽歌
origin	['ɔridʒin]	*n.*	起源；原点；出身；开端
▲ outperform	[ˌautpə'fɔ:m]	*vt.*	胜过；做得比……好；跑赢大盘
phenomenon	[fə'nɔminən]	*n.*	现象；奇迹；杰出的人才
pillar	['pilə]	*n.*	柱子，柱形物；栋梁；墩
quote	[kwəut, kəut]	*vt. & vi.*	引述；举证用；报价
		n.	引用
★ reproach	[ri'prəutʃ]	*vt.*	责备；申斥
		n.	责备；耻辱
singularly	['siŋgjuləli]	*adv.*	异常地；非常地；令人无法理解地
			singular *n.* 单数
			a. 单一的；非凡的，异常的；持异议的
statistics	[stə'tistiks]	*n.*	统计；统计学；[统计] 统计资料
territory	['teritəri]	*n.*	领域；领土，地域；范围；版图
★ tuition	[tju'iʃn]	*n.*	学费；讲授

| as a whole | | 总体上 |
| take advantage of | | 利用 |

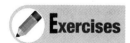

Part I. Understanding the text

1. **Study the title of Text B.**

   ● What are the key words in the essay title?

   ● Why do you think they are the key words?

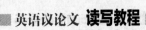
2. **Spend 10 minutes browsing the essay and work out the outline of the essay, with reference to the following:**

- Thesis statement/main argument
- Supporting ideas

After you have finished, discuss your outline with another student.

Part II. Writing skills development

3. **Read the following paragraphs of Text A and decide the arguments and the types of evidence used therein (e.g., facts, statistics, research results, examples, reliable authority/sources, illustrative incidents, etc.).**

1) Read Paragraphs 6–8 and decide its argument and the types of evidence used to support the argument.

   Argument: _____.

   Type of evidence: _____.

2) Read Paragraphs 14–16 and decide its argument and the type of evidence used to support the argument.

   Argument: _____.

   Type of evidence: _____.

4. **Now discuss with your partner the clear flow of reasoning in Paragraphs 3, 15, 16, 19 of the essay.**

> The premises:
>
> a. An outstanding student thinks that her success and that of other Chinese students is mostly because of the parents (Paragraph 3).
>
> b. Chinese focus attention on parenting styles promoting achievement in children (Paragraph 15).
>
> c. Most Chinese parents would profess a commitment to helping their child do well (Paragraphs 16–19).
>
> The conclusion:
>
> Chinese parents tend to push their children a lot, and have really high expectations.

Do the premises provide enough evidence for the conclusion?

Are the premises true, probable and/or reliable?

Is there an adequate relation between the premises and the conclusion?

5. Read the following statement and identify the type of fallacy (e.g., FC, HG, FA, IG and EQ) used in it.

> Person A and Person B walk past a pawn shop（典当行）. Person A remarks that a watch in a window display looks like the one his grandfather used to wear. On the basis of this remark, Person B concludes that:
>
> Person A's grandfather pawned his watch; or
>
> Person A's grandfather had expensive tastes in jewelry; or
>
> Person A's grandfather was ostentatious（虚荣的）; or
>
> Person A's grandfather cannot tell the time any more.

6. Read the text again and discuss with your partner how coherence within and across paragraphs is achieved.

Part III. Language focus

7. Choose the right word to complete each of the following sentences. Change the form where necessary.

commitment	conscience	investigate	outperform	quote
emphasize	domestic	cautiously	singularly	reveal

1) The slowdown in _____ demand was offset by an increase in exports.

2) The government reaffirmed its _____ to the peace process.

3) He _____ the importance of careful driving/that careful driving was important.

4) Kindness and understanding will often draw a boy to unburden his _____.

5) However, as evidence began to accumulate, experts felt obliged to _____.

6) We take off our shoes and creep _____ along the passage.

7) In recent years the Austrian economy has _____ most other industrial economies.

8) The poem is too long to _____ in its entirety.

9) It was a _____ inopportune moment to stage an anti-British demonstration.

10) We tried our best to head Henry off the topic, because we knew he'd _____ confidential information.

8. Paraphrase the following sentences.

1) It also showed that this group seemed to be singularly successful in achieving that goal of educational policy-makers everywhere: a narrow performance gap between those from the poorest homes, and the rest.

2) Not only that, but FSM Chinese pupils do better than those of most other ethnic backgrounds, even when compared with children from better-off homes (those not eligible for free school meals).

3) The argument that Chinese families put special value on education is sensitive territory, of course, as most parents would profess a commitment to helping their child do well.

Part IV. Writing

9. Discuss with your partner on what information you might expect to follow each of the following sentences:

- Further evidence of the success of pupils of Chinese heritage came through the world's most well-known international testing study, Pisa.

- Anyone investigating this subject will be struck by the limited research available.

10. Read the text again and study the following phrases and sentence structures used to support arguments.

Research results	• This showed not only that British Chinese youngsters are the highest performing ethnic group in England at GCSE, which has been known for years. It also showed that…
Statistics	• …, a detailed look at the figures makes this clearer. Some 71% of Chinese FSM pupils achieved five good GCSEs, including English and maths, in 2009. For non-FSM Chinese pupils, the figure was 72%.
Quotes	• "It's mostly the parents. Chinese parents tend to push their children a lot, and have really high expectations. …" Jessie, 18, an A-level student, …
	• One pupil is quoted saying: "My parents expect me to get the best grades. And if I don't, then they'll continuously nag at me to do better…"
Comparison & Contrast	• 15-year-olds from Shanghai, China, easily outperforming those of all other nationalities.
	• Chinese FSM pupils outperformed not just their counterparts from other ethnic groups—easily outstripping white children—but even Chinese pupils not eligible for free meals.

11. Use the following clues to write an essay which develops the following topic sentence: *Practice Makes Perfect.*

❖ The more one practices, the more skillful he/she will be.

❖ In English study, … In our daily life, …

❖ Take a few minutes to plan before you jump into writing the essay.
❖ Discuss with your partner about:
  a. Whether your argument and evidence are adequate, reasonable and effective?
  b. Is there an adequate relation between the premises and the conclusion in your argument?
❖ Write the first draft alone.
❖ Peer review each other's writing.
❖ Revise your first draft.

Text ❻

Why I Want a Wife[1]

By Judy Syfers[2]

❶ I belong to that classification of people known as wives. I am A Wife.

❷ And, not altogether **incidentally**, I am a mother. Not too long ago a male friend of mine appeared on the scene fresh from a recent **divorce.** He had one child, who is, of course, with his ex-wife. He is looking for another wife. As I thought about him while I was ironing one evening, it suddenly occurred to me that I too, would like to have a wife. Why do I want a wife?

❸ I would like to go back to school so that I can become **economically independent**, support myself, and if need be, support those dependent upon me. I want a wife who will work and send me to school. And while I am going to school I want a wife to take care of my children. I want a wife to **keep track of** the children's doctor and **dentist appointments.** And to keep track of mine, too, I want a wife to make sure my children eat properly and are kept clean. I want a wife who will wash the children's clothes and keep them mended. I want a wife who is a good **nurturing attendant** to my children, who arranges for their schooling, makes sure that they have an **adequate** social life with their **peers**, takes them to the park, the zoo, etc. I want a wife who takes care of the children when they are sick, a wife who arranges to be around when the children need special care, because, of course, I cannot miss classes at school. My wife must arrange to lose time at work and not lose the job. It may mean a small cut in my

---

1 This essay was retrieved from cwluherstory/CWLUArchive/wantawife.html.
  Editor's Note: This classic piece of feminist humor appeared in the premier issue of *Ms. Magazine* and was widely circulated in the women's movement.
2 Judy Syfers (1937—), born in San Francisco, USA, wrote the classic feminist essay, in 1971. Being a wife, and mother of two children, she argues against the inequality between the sexes in this essay. The essay, published on *Ms. Magazine*, 1971, is a wickedly humorous introduction to the sex roles defined by conventional marriage.

wife's income from time to time, but I guess I can **tolerate** that. **Needless to say,** my wife will arrange and pay for the care of the children while she is working.

❹   I want a wife who will take care of my physical needs. I want a wife who will keep my house clean; a wife who will pick up after my children, a wife who will pick up after me. I want a wife who will keep my clothes clean, ironed, mended, replaced when need be, and who will see to it that my personal things are kept in their proper place so that I can find what I need the minute I need it. I want a wife who cooks the meals a wife who is a good cook. I want a wife who will plan the menus, do the necessary grocery shopping, prepare the meals, serve them pleasantly, and then do the cleaning up while I do my studying. I want a wife who will care for me when I am sick and sympathize with my pain and loss of time from school. I want a wife to go along when our family takes a vacation so that someone can continue care for me and my kids when I need a rest and change of scene. I want a wife who will not bother me with **rambling complaints about** a wife's duties. I want a wife who will listen to me when I feel the need to explain a rather difficult point I have **come across** in my course of studies. And I want a wife who will type my papers for me when I have written them.

❺   I want a wife who will take care of the details of my social life. When my wife and I are invited out by my friends, I want a wife who takes care of the **baby-sitting** arrangements. When I meet people at school that I like and want to **entertain,** I want a wife who will have the house clean, will prepare a special meal, serve it to me and my friends, and not **interrupt** when I talk about things that interest me and my friends. I want a wife who will have arranged that the children are fed and ready for bed before my guests arrive so that the children do not bother us. I want a wife who takes care of the needs of my quests so that they feel comfortable, who makes sure that they have an **ashtray,** that they are passed the hors d'oeuvres（开胃食品）, that they are offered a second helping of the food, that their wine glasses are replenished（再装满）when necessary, that their coffee is served to them as they like it. And I want a wife who knows that sometimes I need a night out by myself.

❻   I want a wife who is **sensitive** to my sexual needs, a wife who makes love **passionately** and eagerly when I feel like it, a wife who makes sure that I am satisfied. And, of course, I want a wife who will not demand sexual attention when I am not in the mood for it. I want a wife who **assumes** the complete responsibility for **birth control,** because I do not want more children. I want a wife who will remain sexually faithful to me so that I do not have to **clutter up** my intellectual life with **jealousies.** And I want a wife who understands that my sexual needs may **entail** more than strict **adherence** to monogamy（一夫一妻制）. I must, after all, be able to relate to people as fully as possible.

❼ If, **by chance**, I find another person more suitable as a wife than the wife I already have, I want the **liberty** to replace my present wife with another one. Naturally, I will expect a fresh, new life; my wife will take the children and be solely responsible for them so that I am left free.

❽ When I **am through with** school and have a job, I want my wife to **quit** working and remain at home so that my wife can more fully and completely take care of a wife's duties.

❾ My God, who wouldn't want this kind of wife?

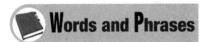 **Words and Phrases**

adequate	['ædikwət]	a.	充足的；适当的；胜任的
★ adherence	[əd'hiərəns]	n.	坚持；依附；忠诚
appointment	[ə'pointmənt]	n.	约会；任命；约定；任命的职位
ashtray	['æʃtrei]	n.	烟灰缸
assume	[ə'sju:m]	vt.	假定，设想；采取，呈现
★ attendant	[ə'tendənt]	n.	服务员，侍者；随员
		a.	伴随的；侍候的
baby-sitting	['beibisitiŋ]	n.	托婴服务
complaint	[kəm'pleint]	n.	抱怨；诉苦；委屈
dentist	['dentist]	n.	牙科医生
divorce	[di'vo:s]	n.	离婚；分离
		vt. & vi.	（使）离婚，（使）分离；与……离婚
economically	[i:kə'nomikli]	adv.	在经济上地；节俭地；经济地
★ entail	[in'teil]	vt.	使必需；使蒙受；使承担；遗传给
		n.	[法] 限定继承权
entertain	[entə'tein]	vt. & vi.	招待；怀抱；容纳
★ incidentally	[insi'dentli]	adv.	顺便；偶然地；附带地
independent	[indi'pendənt]	a.	独立的；单独的；不受约束的
		n.	独立自主者；无党派者
interrupt	[intə'rʌpt]	n.	中断
		vt. & vi.	中断；打断；插嘴；妨碍
★ jealousy	['dʒeləsi]	n.	嫉妒；猜忌；戒备
liberty	['libəti]	n.	自由；许可；冒失

★ nurture	['nɜːtʃə]	n.	养育；教养；营养物
		vt.	养育；鼓励；培植
▲ passionately	['pæʃənətli]	adv.	热情地；强烈地；激昂地
			▲ passionate a. 充满热情的
peer	[piə]	n.	贵族；同等的人
		vi.	凝视，盯着看；窥视
quit	[kwit]	vt.& vi.	辞职；离开；放弃
		n.	离开；[计] 退出
sensitive	['sensətiv]	a.	敏感的；[仪] 灵敏的；易受伤害的
tolerate	['tɔləreit]	vt.	忍受；默许；宽恕

be through with	完成，抛弃
birth control	避孕；[医] 节育
by chance	碰巧，偶然
clutter up	使散乱
come across	来到；偶遇，不期而遇
keep track of	保持与……的联系
needless to say	不必说
ramble about	闲逛，漫步于；漫谈

 **Exercises**

Part I. Understanding the text

1. **Study the title of Text C.**
   - What are the key words in the essay title?
   - Why do you think they are the key words?

2. **Spend 10 minutes browsing the essay and work out the outline of the essay, with reference to the following:**
   - Thesis statement/main argument
   - Supporting ideas

   After you have finished, discuss your outline with your partner.

3. The author describes all the responsibilities she and other women should assume in both deductive reasoning and inductive reasoning.

1) Fill in the blank:

Deductive reasoning

Major premise: All wives are supposed to be perfect.

Minor premise: I am a wife and mother.

Conclusion: _____.

2) Fill in the blank:

Inductive reasoning

Premise 1:   A perfect wife should take care of her husband's physical needs.

Premise 2:   A perfect wife should take care of the details of her husband's social life.

Premise 3:   A perfect wife should work while taking care of the children and doing the housework.

Conclusion: _____.

3) Read the following paragraph and identify the type of reasoning in it.

I want a wife who will take care of the details of my social life. When my wife and I are invited out by my friends, I want a wife who takes care of the baby-sitting arrangements. When I meet people at school that I like and want to entertain, I want a wife who will have the house clean, will prepare a special meal, serve it to me and my friends, and not interrupt when I talk about things that interest me and my friends.

Type of reasoning: _____.

4. Read the text and answer the following questions.

1) The tone of the passage is _____.

   a. formal   b. informal   c. playful   d. ironic

2) According to this passage, a wife should, above all, _____.

   a. pay more attention to keeping the house rather than keeping up her appearance

   b. accept the fact that a woman's place is in the home

   c. try her best to please her husband and friends

   d. respect her husband's wishes in most cases

3) With which of the following statements would the author most likely disagree?

a. A wife should take a more active part both at home and at work.

b. A wife's career and interests are as important as those of her husband's.

c. A wife should be equal in all things to her husband.

d. A wife's main task is to complement, not compete with her husband.

4) In this passage, the author chose to repeat "I want a wife who…" rather than "she" or "her" to refer to a wife in the family. It probably suggests that _____.

a. it mainly deals with women's issues

b. a wife is defined as a voiceless and formless servant

c. a person of either sex should be able to do a wife's job

d. anyone would like to have this type of ideal wife

5) The purpose of the author seems to be _____.

a. to make clear some misunderstanding concerning a wife's duty

b. to complain about all the responsibilities she and other women assume

c. to explain why she herself would like to have a wife

d. to define a wife's economic, physical, social responsibilities

Part II. Writing skills development

5. Read the text again and discuss with your partner how coherence within and across paragraphs is achieved.

Part III. Language focus

6. Choose the right word to complete each of the following sentences. Change the form where necessary.

appointment	assume	complaint	divorce	entertain
interrupt	adequate	peer	sensitive	tolerate

1) Some organizations outlaw this sort of thing but most _____ it, more or less.

2) A(n) _____ water supply for city people is already a problem no government can take lightly.

3) We are expecting many guests today; would you please help me _____ them?

4) Furthermore, there is a marked absence of _____ pressure here, which would make itself palpably felt when such anti-social conduct occurs.

5) The coldness soon broke out into open _____.

6) He secured the _____ of professor of English literature in the university.

7) Her husband's involvement with another woman led to their _____.

8) Infant mortality is a highly _____ barometer of socio-economic conditions.

9) The telephone rang and _____ my train of thought.

10) I was mistakenly _____ to be a Welshman because of my surname.

7. Paraphrase the following sentences.

1) Not too long ago a male friend of mine appeared on the scene fresh from a recent divorce.

2) I want a wife who is a good nurturing attendant to my children, who arranges for their schooling, makes sure that they have an adequate social life with their peers, takes them to the park, the zoo, etc.

3) I want a wife who will remain sexually faithful to me so that I do not have to clutter up my intellectual life with jealousies.

Part IV. Writing

8. Now discuss with your partner on what information you might expect to follow each of the following sentences:

- I want a wife who will take care of my physical needs (Paragraph 4).
- I want a wife who will take care of the details of my social life (Paragraph 5).

9. Now imagine you are going to write a short opinion essay on *Women's Role in China*, which following sentence would serve best as the topic sentence?
What type of evidence would you use to develop/support it?

- There was clearly a double standard for men and women in the old days.
- Traditionally, Chinese women were limited to a relatively small role in society.
- Women inferiority to men was heavily stressed since the feudal days of China.

In what type/types of reasoning do you write?

Type/types of reasoning _____ if _____

A. the topic sentence appears at the very beginning

B. the topic sentence appears at the end.

What kind of *logical fallacy* should you avoid?

Type/types of *logical fallacy* you should avoid _____ when _____

A. you express the comparison & contrast between women and men

B. you present the reasons why women…

10. Write out the essay discussed above, with reference to the following phrases and sentence structures.

Examples	• As stated by Confucian philosophy, women were to remain ignorant and to obey men throughout their lives. • Various old proverbs, such as "The absence of talent in a woman is a virtue" induced Chinese families to keep their daughters ignorant and uneducated…
Cause & Effect	• … This was also a cause of the high illiteracy rate for women… • In fact, men tended to marry multiple wives to show that he was wealthy enough to support a large family.
Comparison & Contrast	• The wife, on the other hand, has to be tolerant of her husband's polygamist behavior.

Suggested writing steps:

- Take a few minutes to plan and make an outline before you begin writing the essay.
- Make sure that your arguments and evidence are adequate, reasonable and effective.
- Write the first draft alone.
- Peer review each other's writing.
- Revise your first draft.

Unit Summary

In this unit, you have reviewed and practiced learning how to write in a clear flow of reasoning and avoid false arguments. Now, do the following exercises to consolidate your knowledge.

1. How could you explain the following terms?

1) The *four criteria* of a clear flow of reasoning.

2) Different types of fallacies (*HG; FA; FC; IG; EQ*).

2. Identify the type of reasoning the author may conduct and the function of the underlined sentences in each extract below.

1) In whatever situation men can be placed, they may find conveniences and inconveniences. In whatever company, they may find people and conversations more or less pleasing. At whatever table, they may find meat and drink of better and worse taste, dishes better or worse prepared. In whatever climate, they may find good

and bad weather. <u>Under whatever government, they may find good and bad laws, and good and bad administration of these laws</u>. In every poem or work of genius, they may see beauties and faults. In almost every face and every person, they may discover fine features and defects, good and bad qualities. Therefore, we may say that there is something good and something bad in everything/everybody.

2) It is true that not every job opening can be properly satisfied by a person who majored in mathematics, but <u>for the most part that person would have an advantage over other applicants because of their knowledge in mathematics</u>. I believe that a strong background in mathematics is an asset to a person looking into just about any field of work.

3) The teaching profession alone offers an assortment of different levels of teaching. One could teach at the elementary, middle school, high school, college, and university levels. <u>There are also teacher's aids, research assistants, and student teachers, as well as substitute teachers</u>. The demand for teachers is elevating at an alarming rate. This goes for teachers in general, but especially for teachers interested in teaching in the mathematics or science fields.

Now discuss with your partner the following questions about a clear flow of reasoning in each extract above.

- Do the premises provide enough evidence for the conclusion?
- Are the premises true, probable and/or reliable?
- Is there an adequate relation between the premises and the conclusion?

3. The following paragraph is a typical one that follows the rule "one idea (topic) dominates one paragraph." Identify the topic sentence, the supporting sentences and the concluding sentence of it.

I am against smoking marijuana（大麻）because it causes paranoia（妄想狂）, laziness, and lung cancer. I first believe that people should not smoke marijuana because reaching a state of paranoia can cause a person to act irrational, which can lead to a huge mistake and regret. For example, one day my friend smoked some weed, and he started complaining about his heart racing, and he was sweating excessively. Out of panic, he ran down the street crying, and the cops arrested him. Second, marijuana causes laziness, which prevents people from living up to their potential. For instance, I watched a movie about a guy who smoked marijuana regularly. He became so lazy that he failed out of school, and he was also fired from his job because he always called in sick when he was really stoned and lazy. I am finally against smoking marijuana because it causes lung cancer, which shortens the life of a person. An example of a shortened life due to marijuana is my neighbor who smoked weed every day. At the age of forty-five, he was diagnosed

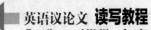
with lung cancer. If he did not smoke marijuana every day, then he probably would have lived a lot longer and raised his family. In conclusion, marijuana may make some people feel good, but the long term affects for such a short period of pleasure can be devastating; therefore, I am fully against the smoking of this drug.

Topic sentence _____

Supporting sentences _____

Concluding sentence _____

4. **Write your essay: Use the skills you have learned in this unit and write an argumentative essay on any topic related to social science. At this stage, you shall be able to write an essay of 200 to 250 words.**

> **Prewriting**
>
> **Work out the outline of the essay and ask yourself:**
> What is the overall stance/argument of the essay?
> Is the overall stance/argument obvious in Introduction and/or Conclusion?
> Is the main idea clear in each supporting paragraph?
> How many paragraphs will the essay have?
> Does the outline follow a logical sequence of ideas/ a clear flow of reasoning?

> **Writing**
>
> Write the first draft alone.

> **Revising**
>
> **Once you have the first draft of your paper completed, (peer) review it with the following questions in mind:**
> Does the Introduction and/or Conclusion clearly present the overall argument?
> Are the ideas clearly and logically organized?
> Is the main argument in each supporting paragraph supported with adequate evidence?
> Are the sentences grammatical and concise?
> Is coherence within and across paragraphs adequately achieved?
> After that, please revise your first draft.

5. Match the following words (a–v) to their definitions (1–22). Make sure you have fully understood them.

Words	Definitions
a. adequate	1. sufficient to satisfy a requirement or meet a need
b. complaint	2. the process or condition of adhering
c. involve	3. to undertake the duties of (an office); to take for granted; suppose
d. entail	4. an expression of pain, dissatisfaction, or resentment
e. eligible	5. to have, impose, or require as a necessary accompaniment or consequence
f. heritage	6. to extend hospitality toward
g. administration	7. to hinder or stop the action or discourse of (someone) by breaking in on
h. major	8. to engage as a participant
i. pursue	9. official examination or review, as of troops
j. adherence	10. to allow without prohibiting or opposing; permit
k. entertain	11. a source of moral or ethical judgment or pronouncement
l. inspection	12. one that has the same functions and characteristics as another; an opposite number
m. counterpart	13. qualified or entitled to be chosen
n. outperform	14. something that is passed down from preceding generations; a tradition
o. reproach	15. to surpass (another) in performance
p. evaluate	16. one that takes the place of another; a replacement
q. substitute	17. to express disapproval of, criticism of, or disappointment in (someone)
r. doctorate	18. management of an institution, public or private
s. conscience	19. the degree or status of a doctor as conferred by a university
t. interrupt	20. to examine and judge carefully; appraise
u. assume	21. of or relating to the field of academic study in which a student specializes
v. tolerate	22. to follow in an effort to overtake or capture; chase; to be engaged in (a vocation or hobby)

Unit
7

Life Science / Health

Writing Skill Development

The Whole Essay (1)

Characteristics of argumentative essays

In developing an argumentative essay, you need to take a position on a narrowed issue, make a clear and specific claim about the issue, analyze your audience, and give reasons and evidence to support the claim. In addition, you should follow a logical line of reasoning, use emotional appeals appropriately, and acknowledge, accommodate, and/or refute opposing views (McWhorter, 2000).

➡ An argument focuses on a narrowed issue

An issue is a controversy, problem, or idea about which people disagree. In choosing an issue, therefore, be sure it is *arguable*. Depending on the issue you choose and the audience you write for, *a clear definition* of the issue may be required (McWhorter, 2000). For less familiar issues, readers may need *background information*. In addition, the issue you choose should be *narrow enough* to deal with adequately in an essay-length argument. For an essay on organ transplants, for instance, you could limit your argument to transplants of a particular organ or to one aspect of the issue, such as who does and does not receive them.

Look at the following two issues and see how to limit the topic and list the background information readers might need to understand the issues.

Computer networks and the right of privacy	
[*Limited topics*]	Privacy in the workplace or on the Internet; security of Internet transactions and accounts; corporate information without individuals' knowledge, etc.
[*Background*]	Define the networks to be discussed; examples of privacy violation; relevant court cases, etc.

Mandatory drug testing	
[*Limited topics*]	Compulsory drug testing for members of particular professions (e.g. hospital workers, train engineers, police officers); compulsory drug testing of athletes for the use of stimulants, etc.
[*Background*]	Laws and company policies giving official command to drug testing; effects of drugs on job performance; relevant constitutional issues, etc.

➡ An argument states a specific claim in a thesis

To build a convincing argument, you need to make a clear and specific claim. If writing arguments is new to you, it is best to state your claim early in the essay. Doing so will help you keep your argument on track. As you gain experience in writing arguments, you can experiment with placing your thesis later in the essay.

Here are a few examples of how general claims can be narrowed into clear and specific thesis statements.

[*General*]	More standards are needed to protect children in day-care centers.
[*Specific*]	Statewide standards are needed to regulate the child-caregiver ratio and the qualifications of workers in day-care centers.

[*General*]	The use of animals in testing should be prohibited.
[*Specific*]	The testing of cosmetics and skin-care products on animals should be prohibited.

While all arguments make and support a claim, some also call for a specific action to be taken. An essay opposing human cloning, for example, might argue for a ban on that practice as well as urge readers to take action against it, such as by voicing their opinions in letters to congressional representatives. Claims of policy often include a call for action.

➡ An argument depends on careful audience analysis

To build a convincing argument, it is essential to know your audience. You could begin by deciding whether your audience agrees or disagrees with your claim, or whether the audience is neutral about or wavering on the claim (McWhorter, 2000). You should also determine how familiar your audience is with the issue.

Agreeing Audiences. When you write for an audience that agrees with your claim, the focus is usually on urging readers to take a specific action. So instead of presenting numerous facts and statistics as evidence, you can center on stressing your shared viewpoint and building emotional ties with your audience in order to encourage your readers to act on their beliefs (McWhorter, 2000).

Neutral or Wavering Audiences. Audiences are neutral or wavering when they have not made up their minds about or given much thought to an issue. In writing to a neutral or wavering audience, be straightforward, emphasize importance of the issue and offer explanations why readers may have misunderstandings about it.

Disagreeing Audiences. Such an audience holds viewpoints in opposition to yours and may also be hostile to your claim. In writing to a disagreeing audience, be sure to follow a logical line of reasoning. First establish a common ground with your readers by mentioning shared interests, concerns, experiences and points in your argument (McWhorter, 2000). Then, when you state your claim, the audience may be more open to consider your argument.

For each of the following claims, see how you would argue in support of it for an agreeing audience, a neutral or wavering audience, and a disagreeing audience.

Portraying the effects of violent crime realistically on television may help to reduce crime rate.

a) Urge readers to write to companies that advertise during shows that portray violence unrealistically, arguing the need for action. (to agreeing audiences)

b) Provide examples of victims who die of real violence; contrast with unrealistic examples from TV shows. (to neutral or wavering audiences)

c) Establish a common ground (the desire to reduce violent crime); present same examples as for b), and the results of studies that show an increase in violence related with increased television viewing. (to disagreeing audiences)

Children who spend too much time interacting with a computer may fail to learn how to interact with people.

a) Give advice on ways to get computerized children involved with social activities. (to agreeing audiences)

b) Provide examples of children who involve themselves too much with computers along with expert opinions. (to neutral or wavering audiences)

c) Acknowledge that children will need to be comfortable using computers, but argue that there are more other social skills they need to command as well. (to disagreeing audiences)

➡ An argument presents reasons supported by convincing evidence

The major support for your position consists of the *reasons* that you offer for that position. These reasons must be backed up with *evidence,* such as facts, examples, and expert opinions, whose quality that you present to support your position determines the success of your argument (Anker, 2012).

As described in Anker (2012), *facts* are statements or observations that can be proved true; *statistics*—numerical facts based on research—can be persuasive evidence to back up your position; *examples* are specific experiences or pieces of information that support your position; and *expert opinion* is the opinion of someone who is considered an expert in the area you are writing about (For more, see Unit 2).

➡ An argument follows a logical line of reasoning

The reasons and evidence in an argument should follow a logical line of reasoning. The most common types of reasoning—induction and deduction—use evidence in different ways to arrive at a conclusion (see Diagrams 1 & 2). Whereas inductive reasoning begins with evidence and moves to a conclusion, deductive reasoning begins with a commonly accepted statement or premise and shows how conclusion follows from it (McWhorter, 2000). You can use one or both types of reasoning in an argument essay to help keep your argument on a logical path.

Diagram 1: Inductive Reasoning

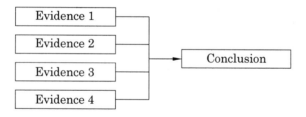

Diagram 2: Deductive Reasoning

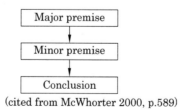

(cited from McWhorter 2000, p.589)

When you use *inductive reasoning* in an argumentative essay, the conclusion becomes the claim and the specific pieces of evidence support your reasons making the claim. For example, suppose you make a claim that "Pat's Used Car is unreliable." As support you might offer the following reasons and evidence:

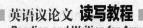

[*Reason*]	Pat's Used Car does not provide accurate information about products.
[*Evidence*]	My sister's car had its odometer reading damaged. My best friend bought a car whose chassis（底盘）had been damaged, yet the sales person claimed the car had never been in an accident.
[*Reason*]	Pat's Used Car doesn't honor its commitments to customers.
[*Evidence*]	The dealership refused to honor the ninety-day guarantee for a car I purchased there. A local newspaper recently featured Pat's in a report on businesses that fail to honor guarantees.

When you use *deductive reasoning*, it may be helpful to put your argument in the form of a syllogism. The syllogism will help you write your claim and organize and evaluate your reasons and evidence. Suppose you want to support the claim that "State funding for Kids First, an early childhood program, should remain intact." You might use the following syllogism to build your argument.

[*Major premise*]	State-funded early childhood programs have increased at-risk children's readiness to attend school.
[*Minor premise*]	Kids First is a popular early childhood program in our state.
[*Conclusion*]	Kids First is likely to increase at-risk children's readiness to attend school.

➡ An argument appeals to readers' needs and values

Although an effective argument relies mainly on credible evidence and logical reasoning, emotional appeals can help support and enhance a sound argument. *Emotional appeals* are directed toward readers' needs and values. *Needs* can be biological or psychological (food and drink, sex, a sense of belonging, and esteem, for example); and *values* are principles or qualities that readers consider important, worthwhile, or desirable (Anker, 2012).

➡ An argument recognizes opposing views

Recognizing or countering opposing arguments forces you to think hard about your own claims. Considering readers' objections, you may adjust your own reasoning and end up with a stronger argument. There are three methods of recognizing opposing views in an argumentative essay: *acknowledgement*, *accommodation*, and *refutation* (Anker, 2012).

(a) When you *acknowledge* an opposing viewpoint, you admit that it exists and that you have given it serious consideration.

(b) When you *accommodate* an opposing viewpoint, you acknowledge readers' concerns, accept some of them, and incorporate them into your own argument.

(c) When you *refute* an opposing viewpoint, you demonstrate the weakness of the opponent's argument.

For the two claims listed on page 166, see how to identify opposing viewpoints and consider how to *acknowledge, accommodate,* or *refute* them in the following examples.

Portraying the effects of violent crime realistically on television may help to reduce crime rate.

Possible opposing arguments:

a) Portraying violence more realistically on television will reduce people's sensitivity to it, not stop them from it.

Response: Refute by noting that portraying the effects of actual violence has prevented crimes and changed people's minds, citing such examples as the television images of wars and civil rights movement.

b) Violence images have no effect on people who commit violent crimes.

Response: Refute by citing studies that show a high crime rate among heavy television viewers.

Children who spend too much time interacting with a computer may fail to learn how to interact with people.

Possible opposing arguments:

a) There are many opportunities to interact with people on the Internet.

Response: Accommodate by pointing out that interactions with strangers on the Internet can be valuable but limited, or refute by noting that the uncertainty and potential danger of interacting with strangers on the Internet.

b) Children who take advantage of all the computer offers learn more than children with a more active social life.

Response: Acknowledge; admit that there is much to learn from educational computer programs and the Internet as well as from playing with children.

Main components of an argumentative essay: A graphic organizer

The graphic organizer below will help you analyze arguments as well as plan those that you write. Some arguments, for example, may begin with a claim, whereas others may start with evidence or opposing viewpoints. Whatever your argument's sequence, you can adapt this organizer to fit your essay. Note, however, that not every element will appear in every argument. Some arguments, such as those written for an agreeing audience, may not deal with opposing viewpoints.

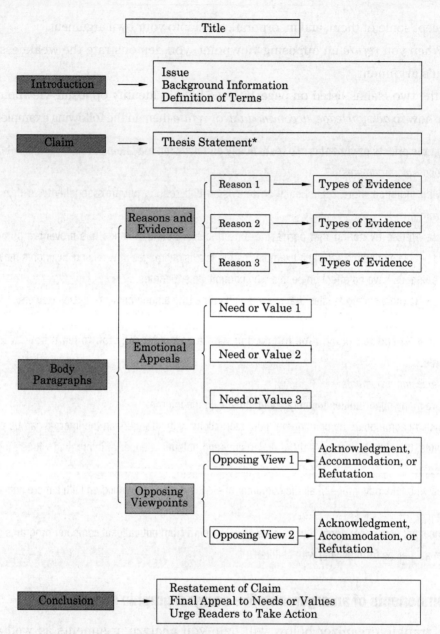

* The thesis statement may appear anywhere within the argument.

(cited from McWhorter 2000, p. 593)

References:

Anker, S. (2012). *Real Essays with Readings*. Boston, NY: Bedford/St. Martin's.

McWhorter, K. T. (2000). *Successful College Writing*. Boston, NY: Bedford/St. Martin's.

Reading for Ideas

Text A

A Scientist: "I Am the Enemy"

By Ronald M. Kline, MD[1]

❶ I am the enemy! One of those vilified（被诽谤的）, inhumane physician scientists involved in animal research. How strange, for I have never thought of myself as an evil person. I became a **pediatrician** because of my love for children and my desire to keep them healthy. During medical school and **residency**, however, I saw many children die of leukemia（白血病）, **prematurity** and traumatic（外伤）injury—circumstances against which medicine has made tremendous progress, but still has far to go. More important, I also saw children, alive and healthy, thanks to advances in medical science such as infant **respirators**, **potent antibiotics**, new surgical techniques and the entire field of organ **transplantation**. My desire to **tip the scales** in favor of the healthy, happy children drew me to medical research.

❷ My accusers claim that I **inflict** torture on animals for the sole purpose of career **advancement**. My experiments supposedly have no relevance to medicine and are easily replaced by computer **simulation**. Meanwhile, an apathetic（冷漠的）public barely watches, convinced that the issue has no significance, and publicity-**conscious** politicians increasingly **give way to** the demands of the activists.

❸ We in medical research have also been unconscionably apathetic. We have allowed the most extreme animal-rights protesters to seize the **initiative** and frame the issue as one of "animal **fraud**". We have been **complacent** in our belief that a knowledgeable public would sense the importance of animal research to the public health. Perhaps we have been mistaken in not responding to the emotional tone of the argument created by those sad **posters** of animals by waving equally sad posters of children dying of leukemia or cystic fibrosis（囊肿性纤维化）.

❹ **Much is made of** the pain inflicted on these animals **in the name of** medical science. The animal-rights activists **contend** that this is evidence of our malevolent （恶毒的）and sadistic（虐待狂的）nature. A more reasonable argument, however, can be advanced in our defense. Life is often cruel, both to animals and human beings.

---

1 The article was originally published in *Newsweek*, December 18, 1989. Dr. Kline is the Director of Pediatric Bone Marrow Transplantation.

Teenagers get thrown from the back of a pickup truck and suffer severe head injuries. Toddlers（学步的儿童）barely able to walk, find themselves at the bottom of a swimming pool while a parent checks the mail. Physicians hoping to alleviate（减轻）the pain and suffering these tragedies cause have but three choices: create an animal model of the injury or disease and use that model to understand the process and test new therapies; experiment on human beings—some experiments will succeed, most will fail—or finally, leave medical knowledge **static**, hoping that accidental discoveries will lead us to the advances.

5 Some animal-rights activists would suggest a fourth choice, claiming that computer models can simulate animal experiments, thus making the actual experiments unnecessary. Computers can simulate, reasonably well, the effects of well-understood principles on complex systems, as in the application of the laws of physics to airplane and automobile design. However, when the principles themselves are **in question**, as is the case with the complex biological systems under study, computer modeling alone is of little value.

6 One of the terrifying effects of the effort to restrict the use of animals in medical research is that the impact will not be felt for years and decades: drugs that might have been discovered will not be; surgical techniques that might have been developed will not be, and fundamental biological processes that might have been understood will remain mysteries. There is the danger that politically expedient（权益的）solutions will be found to placate（平息）a **vocal** minority, while the consequences of those decisions will not be apparent until long after the decisions are made and the decision makers forgotten.

7 Fortunately, most of us enjoy good health, and the trauma of watching one's child die has become a rare experience. Yet our good fortune should not make us **unappreciative** of the health we enjoy or the advances that make it possible. **Vaccines**, antibiotics, insulin（胰岛素）and drugs to treat heart disease, hypertension（高血压）and stroke are all based on animal research. Most complex surgical procedures, such as coronary（冠状的）-**artery bypass** and organ transplantation, are initially developed in animals. Presently undergoing animal studies are techniques to insert genes in humans in order to replace the defective ones found to be the cause of so much disease. These studies will effectively end if animal research is severely restricted.

8 In America today, death has become an event isolated from our daily existence—out of the sight and thoughts of most of us. As a doctor who has watched many children die, and their parents **grieve**, I am particularly angered by people capable of so much **compassion** for a dog or a cat, but with seemingly so little for a dying human being.

These people seem so **insulated** from the reality of human life and death and what it means.

❾ Make no mistake, however: I am not advocating the needlessly cruel treatment of animals. To the extent that the animal-rights movement has made us more aware of the needs of these animals, and made us search harder for suitable alternatives, they have made a significant contribution. But if the more **radical** members of this movement are successful in limiting further research, their efforts will bring about a tragedy that will cost many lives. The real question is whether an apathetic majority can be aroused to protect its future against a vocal, but misdirected, minority.

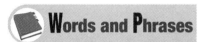 **Words and Phrases**

★ advancement	[əd'vɑːnsmənt]	n.	前进，进步；提升
★ antibiotic	[ˌæntibai'ɔtik]	n.	抗生素，抗菌素
		a.	抗生的；抗菌的
★ artery	['ɑːtəri]	n.	动脉；干道；主流
★ bypass	['baipɑːs]	n.	旁路；[公路] 支路
		vt.	绕开；忽视；设旁路；迂回
▲ compassion	[kəm'pæʃn]	n.	同情；怜悯；怜悯之心
▲ complacent	[kəm'pleisnt]	a.	自满的；得意的；满足的
conscious	['kɔnʃəs]	a.	意识到的；故意的；神志清醒的
★ contend	[kən'tend]	vt. & vi.	争论，争辩；（坚决）主张
		n.	争论，争辩；竞争；战斗
fraud	[frɔːd]	n.	欺骗，欺诈
★ grieve	[griːv]	vi.	悲痛，哀悼
		vt.	使悲伤，使苦恼
★ inflict	[in'flikt]	vt.	使遭受（损伤、痛苦等）；使……承受；给予（打击等）
★ initiative	[i'niʃətiv]	n.	主动性；首创精神；主动权；主动的行动，倡议
★ insulated	['insjuleitid]	a.	隔绝的，隔离的
			★ insulate vt. 使隔离，使孤立；使绝缘，使隔热
▲ pediatrician	[ˌpiːdiə'triʃn]	n.	儿科医师（= pediatrist）
poster	['pəustə]	n.	海报，广告；招贴
▲ potent	['pəutnt]	a.	有效的；强有力的；有说服力的

★	prematurity	[pri:mə'tjurəti]	n.	早熟；过早；未成熟；早开花
	radical	['rædikl]	a.	激进的；根本的；彻底的
			n.	基础；激进分子
	residency	['rezidənsi]	n.	住院医生实习期；住处
▲	respirator	['respəreitə]	n.	[医]呼吸器；防毒面具
★	simulation	[ˌsimju'leiʃn]	n.	模仿；假装；冒充
				simulate *vt.* 模仿；假装；冒充
	static	['stætik]	a.	静态的；静电的；静力的
			n.	静力学；静态
	tip	[tip]	vt.	使倾斜；倾倒；给小费
			n.	小费
	transplantation	[ˌtrænsplɑ:n'teiʃn]	n.	移植（器官等）；移栽（植物等）
				transplant *vt.* 移植；移栽
	unappreciative	[ˌʌnəp'ri:ʃətiv]	a.	不赏识的；不识抬举的
★	vaccine	['væksi:n]	n.	疫苗；预防疫苗
★	vocal	['vəukl]	a.	激烈表达意见的；常言无忌的

give way to	让步，屈服
in question	讨论中；考虑中的；有疑问的
in the name of...	以……名义，凭……
make much of	渲染，强调
tip the scales	起决定作用，扭转局面

Exercises

Part I. Understanding the text

1. Study the title of Text A.

- What are the key words in the essay title?

- Why do you think they are the key words?

2. Spend 5 minutes browsing the essay and answer the following questions.

- What's the thesis statement/main argument in this essay?

- What are the supporting points/arguments?

After you have finished, discuss your answers with your partner.

Part II. Writing skills development

3. **Read the following paragraphs of Text A and decide the argument and the type of evidence used therein: facts, research results, examples/cases, reliable authority/sources, or illustrative incidents, etc.**

   1) Read Paragraphs 4–5 and decide its argument and the type of evidence used to support the argument.

      Argument: _____

      Type of evidence: _____

   2) Read Paragraph 6 and decide its argument, and the type of evidence used to support the argument.

      Argument: _____

      Type of evidence: _____

   3) Read Paragraph 7 and decide its argument and type of evidence used to support the argument.

      Argument: _____

      Type of evidence: _____

   4) Read Paragraph 8 and decide its argument and the type of evidence used to support the argument.

      Argument: _____

      Type of evidence: _____

4. **Read the text again and discuss with your partner how coherence across paragraphs is achieved.**

Part III. Language focus

5. **Choose the right word to complete each of the following sentences. Change the form where necessary.**

respiration	inflict	prematurity	radical	simulate
initiative	reside	transplant	vaccine	appreciative

   1) Researchers found no evidence of a link between _____, birth weight and the amount of caffeine consumed by mothers-to-be.

   2) The fire fighters wore _____ to help them breathe in the smoke-filled house.

   3) He _____ a great deal of suffering on his wife and children.

   4) I would _____ it if you could send me some relevant information at your earliest convenience.

   5) A machine that _____ conditions in space has been installed in our laboratory.

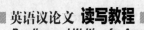

6) Early results show that the _____ not only failed to protect us, it appeared to put some people at high risk of infection.

7) Most people who have been diagnosed with serious illnesses need _____ operations within a year otherwise they would die.

8) With a strong sense of responsibility for the children, she took the _____ in organizing the Children's Foundation.

9) To qualify for a permanent _____, applicants must hold a Shanghai Residency Card and have lived in the city for at least seven years.

10) What he expressed at the conference represented the _____ views of the left wing of the party.

6. Paraphrase the following sentences.

1) My desire to tip the scales in favor of the healthy, happy children drew me to medical research.

2) Perhaps we have been mistaken in not responding to the emotional tone of the argument created by those sad posters of animals by waving equally sad posters of children dying of leukemia or cystic fibrosis.

3) Yet our good fortune should not make us unappreciative of the health we enjoy or the advances that make it possible.

Part IV. Writing

7. Write a paragraph to argue for or against one of the following two claims, applying one or two of the supporting techniques that have been learned.

● The result of animal experiments is not applicable to humans.

● Computer models can simulate animal experiments.

Text B

An Argument in Support of Euthanasia or Physician-Assisted Suicide[1]

By Nicole Smith

❶   In recent years, a great deal of public debate has **swelled** over the issue of euthanasia（安乐死）, also known as physician assisted **suicide**. Although the argument on both sides offer valid points, it is absolutely crucial that all human beings be entitled the

---

1 This essay was retrieved from http://www.articlemyriad.com/argument-euthanasia-physician-assisted-suicide.

essential right to be painlessly and safely relieved of suffering caused by diseases and other painful terminal conditions. Persons experiencing constant pain and misery as a result of health issues must be allowed the right to die with dignity if they so choose. In a society such as ours that is very concerned with issues of **autonomy** and personal rights and **guarantees** and is quick to make heated argument on both sides, there is no reason why our freedom to choose should end at the right to die a peaceful death if a medical situation is hopeless and causing unending pain and suffering.

❷   While those who oppose euthanasia or assisted suicide make the argument that allowing such freedoms will lead to **wholesale slaughter** of persons society **deems** "**unwanted**" and offers other more **speculative** and ethereal（缥缈的）reasons to prevent this right from being **granted**, persons with painful terminal conditions are being kept alive against their will. As this argument in favor of euthanasia suggests the **speculation** should be overlooked in favor of those who are suffering and do not have recourse（求助）. In other words, by making the argument of not allowing the right for a person to have access to this solution of a much safer **humane** suicide, the state is effectively making it impossible for a person to die with dignity and thus they are doing a great disservice（伤害）to those suffering with no other recourse to end the great pain of their condition without **undue** suffering on the part of family members or themselves.

❸   Cancer, advanced cases of AIDS, and other terminal conditions are often incredibly painful and **enduring**. Patients suffering from such illnesses can often survive for long periods of time because of advanced treatments but often, the treatments themselves are **crippling**. Some who suffer from such terminal conditions have the right to make the argument that they should be able to choose assisted suicide so as not to put themselves through such pain and instead cope with their illness at home. No matter what the case, the point remains that these are people who are suffering and who do not see a light at the end of the tunnel—they know that death is **imminent** and they often are reasonably certain that until that moment comes, the **remainder** of their time will be spent being in pain and putting their families through pain as well.

❹   According to one study that poses a similar argument about assisted suicide or euthanasia, "About two-thirds of oncology（肿瘤）patients and the public found euthanasia and physician-assisted suicide acceptable for patients with unremitting（不断的）pain. More than a quarter of oncology patients had seriously thought about euthanasia or physician-assisted suicide and nearly 12% seriously discussed these interventions with physicians and others" (Emanuel et al., 2006). Given such results, it is clear that the people who matter the most in this debate, those who are in great unending pain

seeking relief, should have their needs addressed. Given the fact that many of them see a need for a right to die with dignity and not **prolong agony** for themselves and their family members, there should be no reason why these wishes should not be respected.

5   As suggested by this argument in favor of euthanasia or physician assisted suicide, the right to die, although it should be a natural right granted to all wishing to die with dignity, is hotly **contested**. Although 75% see that such an act would be acceptable, the fact that only 12% discussed it with their doctors is not because they are not considering it as a **viable** option to end their pain, but because of the **stigmas** attached to euthanasia (legally, socially, politically, and spiritually speaking). In short, it is time to **shed** the negative **connotations** the word "euthanasia" carries, get rid of the stigmas, and allow people the only relief they can truly have from terminal and incredibly painful conditions.

6   **Aside from** offering freedom from pain and an undignified death, the other serious issue is a factor of freedom. In the United States, we **pride ourselves on** the wide range of freedoms that impact our daily lives, but what is happiness for someone with a terminal condition who is being forced to live through the pain because the same government that allows other freedoms denies this one? For some reason the ability to make a valid argument about euthanasia or physician assisted suicide is **stunted** when the right to die is involved. Given the results of the study about the right to die mentioned previously, the fact remains that it is the beliefs of a minority of the population that prevent the majority from having access to the good death that assisted suicide provides, access which it is clear from opinion polls that they want and to which they should be entitled on the grounds of respect and compassion. This right to die a dignified death should be at the **forefront** of concerns and debates rather than issues that do not have any direct **bearing** on the lives of those suffering at this very moment with no recourse. In order to preserve our rights as human beings, it is necessary to **stand up for** this one because it is a matter of the **preservation** of someone's right to choose his or her own course, happiness, and **ultimate** fate.

7   Although they are present the minority viewpoint in the United States among cancer patients and some members of the general public in terms of the argument over the right to die when it is physician assisted euthanasia, the opposition contends that allowing euthanasia will lead us down a dangerous road. "The moment we begin to **define** who can and cannot die, we are ultimately leading ourselves to new questions of who should and should not die. This is the same reasoning behind the eugenics（优生学） movements and argument that spawned（酿成） such horrors as the Holocaust（大屠 杀）" (Emanuel, 2006). This is a classic example of a **slippery** slope（骑虎难下的局面）

argument, which is not the most sound basis for an argument yet nonetheless has **to date** had an impact on policy decisions regarding the right to die.

8   It is difficult to think that allowing people who are in serious pain will eventually lead to mass slaughter, but this argument **sways** many because of the **inherent** fear we have of repeating history, particularly history from some of mankind's darkest moments. While this argument on assisted suicide or human euthanasia presented here is certainly not concerning deciding on **legality** who lives and who dies and instead argues in favor of a patient's right to choose, it is nonetheless useful to examine the opposition to see if there are any potential **drawbacks** to allowing euthanasia.

9   In sum, the arguments against the legality of euthanasia or physician-assisted suicide are often based on speculative theories that do not have the **weight** of scientific, statistical, or other data to back them up. On the other hand, there is **a wealth of** material that indicates that there are a great many people who are suffering from pain caused from terminal conditions yet are forced to **live out the rest of their lives in** an undignified and unwanted way. The only way to **live up to** our constant promises of freedom in this country and the only way to offer those dying in ways that many of us cannot fathom（领会）unless we have seen it firsthand（直接地）is to offer this one hope. Not to do so would in itself be inhumane and it is not worth the **sacrifice** of forcing these people to live against their will for the sake of speculative theories that rely on logical fallacies（谬论）that are common to begin with, especially in a debate that is so heated and is so **reliant** on issues of personal feeling and **sentiment** as opposed to **hard and fast** scientific or statistical data.

Reference:

Emanuel, E. J., Daniels, E. R., Fairclough, D. L. & Clarridge, B. R. (2006). Euthanasia and Physician-Assisted Suicide: Attitudes and Experiences of Oncology Patients, Oncologists, and the Public. *Lancet*, 347, 1805–1810.

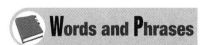 **Words and Phrases**

agony	['ægəni]	*n.*	极大的痛苦；临死的挣扎；苦恼
★ autonomy	[ɔː'tɒnəmi]	*n.*	自主权；自主性；自治；自治权
bearing	['beəriŋ]	*n.*	关系；方位；举止；[机]轴承
▲ connotation	[ˌkɒnə'teiʃn]	*n.*	内涵；含蓄；暗示，隐含意义
contest	[kən'test]	*vt.*	争辩；提出质疑
	['kɒntest]	*n.*	竞赛；争夺；争论

	crippling	['kripliŋ]	a.	严重损害身体的，有严重后果的
★	deem	[di:m]	vi.	认为，持某种看法；作某种评价
	define	[di'fain]	vt. & vi.	阐明，说明；给……下定义；解释
★	drawback	['drɔ:bæk]	n.	缺点；不利条件；后退；远离；退缩
	enduring	[in'djuəriŋ]	a.	能忍受的；持久的
▲	forefront	['fɔ:frʌnt]	n.	位于最前列；处于领先地位；最前部
	grant	['grɑ:nt]	vt.	授予；允许；承认；批准
			n.	拨款；[法] 授予物
	guarantee	[,gærən'ti:]	n.	保证；担保；保证人；保证书；抵押品
★	humane	[hju:'mein]	a.	仁慈的，人道的；高尚的
▲	imminent	['iminənt]	a.	即将来临的；迫近的；危机的
	inherent	[in'hiərənt]	a.	固有的；内在的；生来的
	legality	[li:'gæləti]	n.	合法；合法性；墨守法规
★	preservation	[,prezə'veiʃn]	n.	保存；保护；防腐
★	prolong	[prə'lɔŋ]	vt.	延长；拖延
★	remainder	[ri'meində]	n.	剩余；[数] 余数；残余；剩余物
★	reliant	[ri'laiənt]	a.	依赖的，依靠的
	sacrifice	['sækrifais]	n.	牺牲；祭品；供奉
★	sentiment	['sentimənt]	n.	感情，情绪；情操；多愁善感
	shed	[ʃed]	vt.	摆脱；流出；散发；倾吐
★	slaughter	['slɔ:tə]	n.	屠宰，屠杀；杀戮；消灭
	slippery	['slipəri]	a.	滑的；狡猾的；不稳定的
★	speculation	[,spekju'leiʃn]	n.	推测；思索；投机；投机买卖
★	speculative	['spekjulətiv]	a.	推测的；投机的；冒险的
▲	stigma	['stigmə]	n.	耻辱；污名；烙印；特征
▲	stunt	[stʌnt]	vt.	阻碍……的正常发展或生长
			n.	噱头；手腕；绝技
	suicide	['su:isaid]	n.	自杀；自杀行为；自杀者
	sway	[swei]	vt. & vi.	影响；动摇
	swell	[swel]	vt. & vi.	使（数量）逐渐增加；膨胀；肿胀
			n.	肿胀；隆起
	ultimate	['ʌltimət]	a.	最终的；极限的；根本的
	undue	[ʌn'dju:]	a.	过度的，过分的；不适当的
	unwanted	[,ʌn'wɔntid]	a.	有害的；不需要的；讨厌的
▲	viable	['vaiəbl]	a.	可行的；能养活的；能生育的

weight	[weit]	*n.*	重要性；影响
★ wholesale	['həulseil]	*a.*	大规模的；批发的
		n.	批发

aside from	除了……之外
a wealth of	很多的；大量的
hard and fast	一成不变的
live out one's life in/on/along etc.	以（某种方式或在某地方）终老
live up to	不辜负；做到；实践
pride oneself on	以……为自豪
stand up for	支持，坚持；拥护
to date	至今；迄今为止

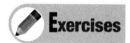

Exercises

Part I. Understanding the text.

1. Study the title of Text B.

- What are the key words in the essay title?
- Why do you think they are the key words?

2. Spend 5 minutes browsing the essay and answer the following questions.

- What's the thesis statement/main argument in this essay?
- What are the supporting points/arguments?

After you have finished, discuss your answers with your partner.

3. Read Paragraphs 6–8 and list the sub-arguments used to support the bigger argument—Euthanasia or physician assisted suicide is a factor of freedom.

Sub-argument in Paragraph 6: _____

Sub-argument in Paragraph 7: _____

Sub-argument in Paragraph 8: _____

Part II. Writing skills development

4. Complete the flowchart, which illustrates the *cause/effect* chain presented in Paragraphs 2–5.

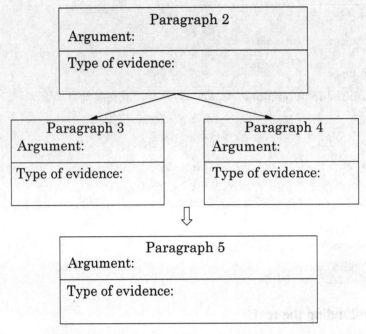

```
┌─────────────────────────────────────────┐
│              Paragraph 2                 │
│  Argument:                               │
├─────────────────────────────────────────┤
│  Type of evidence:                       │
└─────────────────────────────────────────┘

┌───────────────────────┐   ┌───────────────────────┐
│      Paragraph 3       │   │      Paragraph 4       │
│  Argument:             │   │  Argument:             │
├───────────────────────┤   ├───────────────────────┤
│  Type of evidence:     │   │  Type of evidence:     │
└───────────────────────┘   └───────────────────────┘

┌─────────────────────────────────────────┐
│              Paragraph 5                 │
│  Argument:                               │
├─────────────────────────────────────────┤
│  Type of evidence:                       │
└─────────────────────────────────────────┘
```

5. Read the text again and discuss with your partner how coherence across paragraphs is achieved.

Part III. Language focus

6. Choose the right word to complete each of the following sentences. Change the form where necessary.

connotation	grant	legal	reliant	sway
contest	dignify	speculate	swell	imminent

1) The Norton consortium（集团）has been _____ to build a shopping mall in this district.

2) In my opinion, she is far too _____ on her parents for financial support.

3) Watching just one romantic comedy is enough to _____ people's attitudes to romantic love, they found.

4) Under network circumstances, the _____ of copyright has changed from "printing copyright" to "digital copyright".

5) As he's got the first place in the English _____, he can't wait to tell his mother the good news.

6) Residents expressed different opinions on the _____ of the transition of power, but most expressed hope for peace and stability.

7) Nevertheless, the fear of _____ defaults（违约）has led some politicians to call for a federal law allowing states to declare bankruptcy.

8) There is some _____ that the president was aware of the situation.

9) Even in the prison camp we tried to remain some human _____.

10) Britain will see its population _____ from today's 62.2 million to 77 million, an increase of 24%.

7. Paraphrase the following sentences.

1) In a society such as ours that is very concerned with issues of autonomy and personal rights and guarantees and is quick to make heated argument on both sides, there is no reason why our freedom to choose should end at the right to die a peaceful death if a medical situation is hopeless and causing unending pain and suffering.

2) In other words, by making the argument that not allowing the right for a person to have access to this solution of a much safer humane suicide, the state is effectively making it impossible for a person to die with dignity and thus they are doing a great disservice to those suffering with no other recourse to end the great pain of their condition without undue suffering on the part of family members.

3) In the United States, we pride ourselves on the wide range of freedoms that impact our daily lives, but what is happiness for someone with a terminal condition who is being forced to live through the pain because the same government that allows other freedoms denies this one?

Part IV. Writing

8. Write a paragraph to argue for or against one of the following two claims, applying one or two of the supporting techniques that have been learned.

- People with painful terminal conditions should not be forced to stay alive.
- Allowing euthanasia will discourage the search for new cures and treatments for the terminally ill.

Text C

The Case Against Physician-Assisted
Suicide: For the Right to End-of-Life Care[1]

by Herbert Hendin

❶ Euthanasia is a word **coined** from Greek in the seventeenth century to refer to an easy, painless, happy death. In modern times, however, it has come to mean a physician's causing a patient's death by injection of a lethal（致命的）dose of **medication**. In physician-assisted suicide, the physician **prescribes** the lethal dose, knowing the patient intends to end his or her life.

❷ Compassion for suffering patients and respect for patient autonomy serve as the basis for the strongest arguments in favor of **legalizing** physician-assisted suicide. Compassion, however, is no guarantee against doing harm. A physician who does not know how to relieve a patient's suffering may compassionately, but inappropriately, agree to end the patient's life.

❸ Patient autonomy is an **illusion** when physicians are not trained to assess and treat patient suffering. The choice for patients then becomes continued agony or a **hastened** death. Most physicians do not have such training. We have only recently recognized the need to train general physicians in palliative care（姑息治疗）, training that teaches them how to relieve the suffering of patients with serious, life-threatening illnesses. Studies show that the less physicians know about palliative care, the more they favor assisted suicide or euthanasia; the more they know, the less they favor it.

❹ What happens to autonomy and compassion when assisted suicide and euthanasia are legally practiced? The Netherlands（荷兰）, the only country in which assisted suicide and euthanasia have had legal **sanction** for two decades, provides the best laboratory to help us evaluate what they mean in **actuality**. The Dutch（荷兰人）experience served as a **stimulus** for an assisted-suicide law in Oregon（俄勒冈）— the one U.S. state to sanction it.

❺ I was one of a few foreign researchers who had the opportunity to extensively study the situation in the Netherlands, discuss specific cases with leading Dutch **practitioners**, and interview Dutch government **sponsored** euthanasia researchers about their work. We all independently concluded that guidelines established

---

1 *The Case Against Physician-Assisted Suicide: For the Right to End-of-Life Care* by Herbert Hendin was originally published in *Psychiatric Times*. Hendin uses his access to studies of physician–assisted suicide in the Netherlands, where it has been practiced in some form since 1984, to make a case against its legalization elsewhere.

by the Dutch for the practice of assisted suicide and euthanasia were **consistently** violated and could not be enforced. In the guidelines, a competent patient who has unrelievable suffering makes a voluntary request to a physician. The physician, before going forward, must **consult with** another physician and must report the case to the authorities.

6　Concern over **charges** of **abuse** led the Dutch government to undertake studies of the practice in 1990, 1995, and in 2001 in which physicians' **anonymity** was protected, and they were given **immunity** for anything they revealed. Violations of the guidelines then became evident. Half of Dutch doctors feel free to suggest euthanasia to their patients, which **compromises** the voluntariness of the process. Fifty percent of cases were not reported, which made regulation impossible. The most alarming concern has been the **documentation** of several thousand cases a year in which patients who have not given their **consent** have their lives ended by physicians. A quarter of physicians stated that they "**terminated** the lives of patients without an **explicit** request" from the patient. Another third of the physicians could **conceive of** doing so.

7　An **illustration** of a case presented to me as requiring euthanasia without consent involved a Dutch **nun** who was dying painfully of cancer. Her physician felt her religion prevented her from agreeing to euthanasia so he felt both justified and compassionate in ending her life without telling her he was doing so. Practicing assisted suicide and euthanasia appears to encourage physicians to think they know best who should live and who should die, an attitude that leads them to make such decisions without consulting patients—a practice that has no legal sanction in the Netherlands or anywhere else.

8　Compassion is not always involved. In one documented case, a patient with dissemi-nated（扩散的）breast cancer who had rejected the possibility of euthanasia had her life ended because, in the physician's words: "It could have taken another week before she died. I just needed this bed."

9　The government-sanctioned studies suggest an **erosion** of medical standards in the care of terminally ill patients in the Netherlands when 50% of Dutch cases of assisted suicide and euthanasia are not reported, more than 50% of Dutch doctors feel free to suggest euthanasia to their patients, and 25% admit to ending patients' lives without their consent.

10　Euthanasia, intended originally for the exceptional case, became an accepted way of dealing with serious or terminal illness in the Netherlands. In the process palliative care became one of the casualties, while hospices care has **lagged behind** that of other countries. In **testimony** given before the British House of Lords, Zbigniew Zylicz, one of the few palliative care experts in the Netherlands, **attributed** Dutch deficiencies in palliative care **to** the easier alternative of euthanasia.

⓫ The World Health Organization has recommended that governments not consider assisted suicide and euthanasia until they have **demonstrated** the availability and practice of palliative care for their citizens. All states and all countries have a long way to go to achieve this goal.

⓬ People are only beginning to learn that, with well-trained doctors and nurses and good end-of-life care, it is possible to avoid the pain of the past experiences of many of their loved ones and to achieve a good death. The right to such care is the right that patients should demand and the challenge that every country needs to meet.

📖 Words and Phrases

abuse	[ə'bjus]	*n.*	滥用（职权等）；虐待；凌辱；〈古〉欺骗
★ actuality	[ˌæktʃu'æləti]	*n.*	现实；现存；现实性；现状
▲ anonymity	[ˌænə'niməti]	*n.*	匿名，笔者不明
charge	[tʃɑːdʒ]	*n.*	控告；收费；负荷；充电
coin	[kɔin]	*vt. & vi.*	创造；杜撰（新词等）；铸造；制造
compromise	['kɔmprəmaiz]	*vt. & vi.*	对……妥协；和解；让步
		n.	妥协；调和；和解；妥协方案，折中方案
consent	[kən'sent]	*vt. & vi. & n.*	同意；赞成；应允；答应
consistently	[kən'sistəntli]	*adv.*	一致地，始终如一地；协调地
demonstrate	['demənstreit]	*vt. & vi.*	（用实例，实验）说明，示范，表演
documentation	[ˌdɔkjumen'teiʃn]	*n.*	文件证据；证明文件
erosion	[i'rəuʒn]	*n.*	腐蚀；侵蚀（作用）；[医]糜烂，齿质腐损
explicit	[ik'splisit]	*a.*	明白的；明确的；直爽的；不隐讳的
hasten	['heisn]	*vt. & vi.*	赶紧，赶快；使加紧，催促；促进
illusion	[i'luːʒn]	*n.*	幻影；幻觉；妄想，幻想；错觉
illustration	[ˌilə'streiʃn]	*n.*	说明，例证，实例；图解，插画
★ immunity	[i'mjuːnəti]	*n.*	豁免；免疫力；免疫性；（税等的）免除
legalize	['liːgəlaiz]	*vt. & vi.*	法律认可，使合法，合法化

medication	[ˌmediˈkeiʃn]	n.	药物；药剂；物疗法；药物处理
▲ nun	[nʌn]	n.	修女；尼姑
▲ practitioner	[prækˈtiʃnə]	n.	从事者；实践者；实习者；练习者
prescribe	[priˈskraib]	vt. & vi.	开药；开处方
sanction	[ˈsæŋkʃn]	n.	批准；约束力；处罚
		vt. & vi.	批准；准许；制裁
sponsored	[ˈspɔnsəːd]	a.	赞助的；发起的
★ stimulus	[ˈstimjuləs]	n.	刺激；刺激物；促进因素
★ terminate	[ˈtɜːmineit]	vt. & vi.	结束；终止；满期；达到终点
★ testimony	[ˈtestiməni]	n.	证明；证据

attribute to...	把……归因于……
conceive of	构想出
consult with	与……商量（商议）
lag behind	落后；拖后

 **Exercises**

Part I. Understanding the text

1. **Study the title of Text C.**
   - What are the key words in the essay title?
   - Why do you think they are the key words?

2. **Spend 5 minutes browsing the essay and answer the following questions.**
   - What is the claim or argument Hendin makes in this essay?
   - Why does Hendin use information obtained from the Netherlands regarding physician-assisted suicide?

   After you have finished reading, discuss your answers with your partner.

Part II. Writing skills development

3. **Read the whole essay a second time. As you read the essay, mark the background information, reason, key supporting evidence, appeals to needs and values, opposing viewpoints and the conclusion, and then complete the following graphic organizer with the information you find in the essay.**

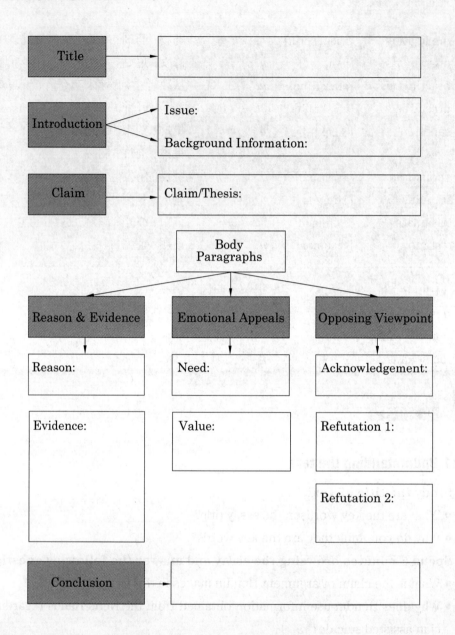

4. Read critically and answer the following questions.

1) In the opening paragraph, why does Hendin contrast the original definition of euthanasia with how the word is currently used?

2) In Paragraph 7, Hendin writes that practicing assisted suicide "appears to encourage physicians to think they know best who should live and who should die." Why do physicians have such authority in most circumstances? Is it good? Why?

3) In the next-to-last paragraph, Hendin summarizes recommendations that were made by the World Health Organization. Why does he do it? Do you think that this essay serves its intended purpose?

Part III. Language focus

5. Choose the right word to complete each of the following sentences. Change the form where necessary.

request	prescribe	sanction	illustration	explicit
deficiency	documentation	abuse	coin	medication

1) The doctor said if these medicines don't work he may have to _____ you something stronger.

2) He ignored the neighbor's _____ that he should make less noise.

3) As far as I know the church would not _____ the King's second marriage.

4) If you already have one of these libraries present on your computer, you do not need to install this _____ update.

5) It was obvious to see by looking at the needle marks on her arms that the young girl was a victim of drug _____.

6) Corn is one of the best indicators for nitrogen _____ among the field-crop plants.

7) The term "Information Highway" was _____ a few years ago.

8) _____ is often more useful than definition for giving the meaning of words.

9) But up to half of those people might not feel any better after they start taking the _____.

10) The point of this section is to make _____ the hard core assumptions that underlie strategic thinking and research.

6. Paraphrase the following sentences.

1) Compassion for suffering patients and respect for patient autonomy serve as the basis for the strongest arguments in favor of legalizing physician-assisted suicide.

2) Half of Dutch doctors feel free to suggest euthanasia to their patients, which compromises the voluntariness of the process.

3) An illustration of a case presented to me as requiring euthanasia without consent involved a Dutch nun who was dying painfully of cancer.

Part IV. Writing

7. Write a paragraph to argue for or against one of the following two claims, applying one or two of the supporting techniques that have been learned.

- Studies show that the less physicians know how to relieve a patient's suffering, the more they favor assisted suicide or euthanasia.

• An expert claims that Dutch deficiencies in palliative care are attributed to the easier alternative of euthanasia.

Unit Summary

In this unit, you have learned one possible structure of an argumentative essay "Main Issue + Support + Conclusion/Confirmation" and particularly the techniques you may use in writing an issue, a specific claim, a paragraph and an essay through identifying the characteristics and main components of an argumentative essay. Now, do the following exercises to consolidate your knowledge.

1. How could you explain the following items?

1) Thesis statement/claim

2) Reasons supported by convincing evidence

3) Countering or refuting opposing arguments

4) A logical line of reasoning

2. Identify the argument in each of the following short articles, and analyze the techniques of supporting the argument and types of evidence used.

1)   This is South Philadelphia—a microcosm（微观世界）of America, a place where people have gone to work, raised children, and then retired. Their daughters are our secretaries, clerks, and teachers. Their sons are our policemen, longshore-men（码头工人）, bankers, doctors, and lawyers. Economically these retired people once represented America's middle class. Yet in this typical urban neighborhood with its tap dance school, businessmen's association, American Cancer Society chapter, and local fire station, a two-year survey conducted by the Albert Einstein Medical Center's Social Service Division concluded that "very few if any of the elderly were without need."

These are men and women who have worked all their lives. These are our uncles, our aunts, our grandparents, our mothers, and our fathers. They live in a world of old newspaper clippings（简报）, pictures, and photographs of relatives who never visit.

— Loretta Schwartz-Nobel, *Starving in the Shadow of Plenty*

2)   The homeless, it seems, can be roughly divided into two groups: those who have had marginality and homelessness forced upon them and want nothing more to escape them, and a smaller number who have at least in part

chosen marginality, and now accept, or, in a few cases, embrace（接受）it.

I understand how dangerous it can be to introduce the idea of choice into a discussion of homelessness. It can all too easily be used for all the wrong reasons by all the wrong people to justify indifference or brutality toward the homeless, or to argue that they are getting only what they deserve.

And I understand, too, how complicated the notion can become: Many of the veterans on the street, or battered（受虐待的）women, or abused and runaway children, have chosen this life only as the lesser of evils, and because, in this society, there is often no place else to go.

And finally, I understand how much that happens on the street can combine to create an apparent acceptance of homelessness that is nothing more than the absolute absence of hope.

Nonetheless we must learn to accept that there may indeed be people on the street who have seen so much of our world, or have seen it so clearly, that to live in it becomes impossible.

— Peter Marin, *Go Ask Alice*

3) The case for a more restrictive immigration policy is based on three assumptions: that illegal aliens compete effectively with, and replace, large numbers of American workers; that the benefits to American society resulting from the aliens' contribution of low-cost labor are exceeded by the "social costs" resulting from their presence here; and that most illegal aliens entering the United States eventually settle here permanently, thus imposing an increasingly heavy, long-term burden upon the society.

There is as yet no direct evidence to support any of these assumptions: at least with respect to illegal aliens from Mexico, who still constitute at least 60 to 65 percent of the total flow and more than 90% of the illegal aliens apprehended each year.

Where careful independent studies of the impact of illegal immigration on labor markets have been made, they have found no evidence of large-scale displacement of legal resident workers by illegal aliens. Studies have also shown that Mexican illegals make amazingly little use of tax-supported social services while they are in the United States, and that the cost of the services they do outweighed by their contributions to Social Security and income tax revenues.

There is also abundant evidence indicating that the vast majority of illegal aliens from Mexico continue to maintain a pattern of "shuttle" migration, most of them returning to Mexico after six months or less of employment in the States. In fact, studies have shown that only a small minority of Mexican illegals even aspire（渴望）to settle permanently in the United States.

While illegal aliens from countries other than Mexico do seem to stay longer and make more use of social services, there is still no reliable evidence that they compete effectively with American workers for desirable jobs. The typical job held by the illegal alien, regardless of nationality, would not provide the average American family with more than a subsistence standard of living. In most states, it would provide less income than welfare payments.

Certainly in some geographic areas, types of enterprises, and job categories, illegal aliens may depress levels or "take jobs away" from American workers. But there is simply no hard evidence that these effects are as widespread or as serious as most policy-makers and the general public seem to believe.

— Wayne A. Cornelius, *Where the Door Is Closed in Illegal Aliens, Who Pays?*

3. **Write your essay: Use what you have learned in this unit and write an argumentative essay for a position of a debatable issue to which you can bring personal expertise and authority either through your own research like Hendin or through reading the essays by experts related to the issue—euthanasia. At this stage, you shall be able to write an essay of 200 to 250 words.**

Prewriting

Work out the outline of the essay and ask yourself:	✔ or ✗
What is the overall stance/argument of the essay?	☐
Is the overall stance/argument obvious in Introduction and/or Conclusion?	☐
Is the main idea clear in each supporting paragraph?	☐
How many paragraphs will the essay have?	☐
Does the outline follow a logical sequence of ideas?	☐

Writing

Write the first draft alone.

Revising

Once you have the first draft of your paper completed, (peer) review it with the following questions in mind:

Does the Introduction and/or Conclusion clearly present the overall argument?

Are the ideas clearly and logically organized?

Is the main argument in each supporting paragraph supported with adequate evidence?

Are the sentences grammatical and concise?

Is coherence within and across paragraphs adequately achieved?

4. Match the words (a–v) to their definitions (1–22). Make sure you have fully understood them.

Words	Definitions
a. compassion	1. protesting or complaining strongly and loudly about something
b. initiative	2. a piece of equipment that you wear over your nose and mouth to help you breathe in a place where there is gas, smoke etc.
c. pediatrician	3. a substance which contains the virus that causes a disease and used to protect people from that disease
d. potent	4. having a powerful effect or influence on your body or mind
e. respirator	5. a doctor who looks after children and treats their illnesses
f. vocal	6. the ability to make decisions and take action without waiting for someone to tell you what to do
g. vaccine	7. a strong feeling of sympathy for someone who is suffering, and a desire to help them
h. agony	8. a feeling or an idea that a word makes you think of that is not its actual meaning
i. connotation	9. if something entitles you to something, it gives you the official right to have or do it
j. contest	10. formal to give someone something that they have asked for, especially official permission to do something
k. entitle	11. an event that is imminent will happen very soon
l. grant	12. very severe pain
m. imminent	13. a competition
n. prolong	14. to say that a situation or event is caused by something
o. swell	15. an idea or opinion that is wrong, especially about yourself
p. wholesale	16. to deliberately make something such as a feeling or activity last longer
q. assess	17. to say what medicine or treatment a sick person should have
r. compromise	18. the fact of not being affected by a disease or harmed by something unpleasant
s. immunity	19. to gradually increase in amount or number; to gradually increase in size
t. prescribe	20. to reach an agreement with someone by both of you accepting less than you accepted at first
u. illusion	21. to make a judgment about a person or situation after thinking carefully about it
v. attribute... to	22. connected with the business of selling goods in large quantities, usually at low prices

Unit

8

Environment

Learning Objectives

1. To know the four steps in writing refutation paragraphs or essays;
2. To learn and identify ten refutation techniques;
3. To apply refutation techniques in paragraph or essay writing.

Writing Skill Development

The Whole Essay (2)

Main Issue + Refutation + Support
Main Issue + Support + Refutation

Definition of refutation

Refutation is the process of communication in which an individual directly attacks the arguments of others in order to reduce the effectiveness and influence of those arguments upon readers or audiences (Huber & Snider, 2005).

Refutation format: A four step process

Refutation is designed to introduce arguments, undermine opponents' arguments, rebuild arguments, and clarify own arguments. One way to do this is through a process called "four step refutation", often referred to as the "Four Ss" of signaling, stating, supporting, and summarizing, which is used regularly by individuals in day-to-day interactions (www.speaking.pitt.edu/student/argument/argumentfourstep.html).

Step 1: Signal ("They say...")

First clearly identify the claim you are going to refute along with the support for that argument. For instance:

> The other side said that Dr. Smith's study clearly shows that video games do not lead to violence.

You might introduce the opposing argument using a phrase which presents it as unsure or problematic. Some of such phrases include:

It	is may be could be might be has been	argued asserted contended maintained claimed said alleged true	that...

Step 2: State ("But I disagree...")

Next state what your main objection to the argument is. For instance:

> But Dr. Smith is biased.

Step 3: Support ("Because...")

Then offer your own reasons to support your disagreement. For instance:

> His research is entirely funded by the video game industry. That's what the 2001 investigation by the Parent's Defense League demonstrates.

Step 4: Summarize ("Therefore...")

Finally make a brief summary of your argument or conclude by showing how your refutation weakens or defeats your opponents' argument. For instance:

> So you can see that the other side has no credible evidence linking video games to violence, and they haven't established any need for their proposal.

Various techniques of refutation

Refutation will be in the air whenever differences of opinion arise and individuals become strong advocates of their own points of view (Huber & Snider, 2005). According to Huber and Snider (2005), there are various techniques of refutation.

➡ Refutation by demonstrating the opposite

Demonstrating the opposite is one of the most powerful tools of refutation by which the writer deliberately shows that the opposite conclusion should be drawn (Huber & Snider, 2005). For instance, to refute the counter-argument the writer might try to point out that other studies do not verify the conclusion or that negative instances show the contrary. If the opponent maintains the dangers or disadvantages of a new policy, the writer could insist on the benefits and advantages of it. For example (Hegyesi & Yeoman, 2002):

[*Counter-argument*]

Electric transportation represents an exciting technological option to improving the environment.

[*Refutation*]

While electric cars themselves are clean, generating the electricity to charge vehicle batteries produces air pollution and solid waste. Coal is the number one source of the total U.S. electricity production (54%). Out of the entire U.S. electric industry, coal-fired power plants contribute 96% of sulfur dioxide（二氧化硫）emissions, 93% nitrogen oxide（二氧化氮）emissions, 88% of carbon dioxide（二氧化碳）emissions, and 99% of mercury（汞）emissions. Coal-fired power plants are the single largest source of mercury pollution in the United States. According to the National Wildlife Federation, just one drop of mercury—1/70th of a teaspoon—can contaminate a 25-acre lake to the point where fish are unsafe to eat …

➡ Refutation by denying the evidence

This method of refutation is one in which the writer denies or damages the evidence of the opponent. Denying the evidence in refutation is like extracting the firewood from under the cauldron. The following weaknesses might make it possible for the evidence to be denied (Huber & Snider, 2005):

(a) The evidence comes from less authoritative sources;

(b) The evidence comes from less reliable sources;

(c) The evidence is just created or not valid/true;

(d) The evidence is not relevant;

(e) The opponent has not made a scientific study;

(f) The opponent has misinterpreted the statistics;

(g) The statistics are not comparable;

(h) The opponent is biased.

For instance, a discussion of whether a teacher is a charming middle-aged man has little relevancy to whether or not he is an excellent teacher. At least one can point out that it is irrelevant. For example (Singer, 2007):

[*Counter-argument*]

Global warming is man-made which is a scientific consensus（科学共识）among scientists.

[*Refutation*]

In identifying the burning of fossil fuels as the chief cause of warming today, many politicians and environmental activists simply appeal to a so-called "scientific consensus". There are two things wrong with this. First, there is no such consensus: An increasing number of climate scientists are raising serious questions about the political rush to judgment on this issue. For example, the widely touted（吹嘘）"consensus" of 2,500 scientists on the United Nations Intergovernmental Panel on Climate Change（IPCC, 政府间气候变化专门委员会）is an illusion: Most of the panelists have no scientific qualifications, and many of the others object to some part of the IPCC's report...

➡ Refutation through minimizing

In minimizing arguments the writer demonstrates quantitatively that the worth of the arguments or evidence is not so great as the opponent claims (Huber & Snider, 2005). The writer may try to point out the worst and least typical examples or cases, instead of the average ones, that have been presented. For example, if the opponent uses one extreme example to support corruption is widespread in education system, you may readily admit that there are problems existing in our education system of today but affirm that these problems aren't really very great. Please read the following passage:

Children in single-parent families usually have serious psychological problems. It was reported at the Tianjin TV Station that on 16th Sept. 2011, a 12-year-old boy committed suicide and wrote a letter before his death complaining about his parents' divorce.

The writer might well refute the argument by pointing out the example provided in this passage is not typical and average, thus minimizing the power of that evidence.

➡ Refutation by reducing the argument to an absurdity

To refute the counter-argument by reducing it to an absurdity, the writer might first present the general principle upon which the counter-argument is based and then he/she applies it to specific cases and make it sound ridiculous (Huber & Snider, 2005).

Benjamin Franklin used this very effectively in refuting the argument that a person should own property to be able to vote (Huber & Snider, 2005). He first stated the principle and then applied it: You say I should own property in order to vote; suppose I own a jackass（驴子）, I then own property and thus I can vote. But suppose I lose the jackass; I no longer own property, and therefore I can't vote. Thus, the vote represents not me but the jackass.

➡ Refutation by adopting the opposing argument

Adopting opposing arguments is also one useful technique by which you can influence readers. In certain situations you might "utilize the evidence, the premises, or other statements of opponents to support your own case" (Huber & Snider, 2005). This method

is also called turning the tables.

For example, in debating "We should close down nuclear generators because of potential for accidents," opponents often use evidence that the danger is not significant enough to worry about. The evidence in itself contains the implication that, if the danger were greater, it would be a grave concern. When people opposing it go even further and suggest means of preventing nuclear accidents, those favoring the ban can use that as additional evidence that the danger is so great that something ought to be done about it (Huber & Snider, 2005).

➡ Refutation by pointing out a dilemma

Pointing out a dilemma is another powerful tool for refutation. To refute the counter-argument the writer might show this counter-argument can lead to only two results or two solutions both of which are unfavorable to the opponent (Huber & Snider, 2005). The following is a typical example (Huber & Snider, 2005).

> A young woman made a contract with a teacher to learn law. The stipulations were that the young woman, who was without funds, would pay for her lessons after winning her first case in court. Unfortunately for the teacher, after the lessons were through and the young woman had learned the law completely, she decided not to practice. So the teacher sued her for payment. He expected to catch the students in the following dilemma: "If the court decides in my favor, the young woman will have to pay because the court has decided that she must pay. Therefore, I will get my money. On the other hand, if the court decides against me, then the young woman will have won her first case in court and by the terms of the contract will have to pay. Thus I will get my money." This was the case put before the court. The young woman, however, was a true student of the teacher. She built her refutation around this dilemma: "Should the court decide in my favor that I don't have to pay, I won't have to pay, and therefore I won't. On the other hand, if the court decides in favor of my teacher, the terms of the contract will hold, for I still will not have won my first case in court and thus, according to contract, I won't have to pay."

➡ Refutation by exposing fallacies in reasoning

One of the more effective and more frequently used methods of refutation is exposing fallacies in reasoning of the advocate: inductive, deductive, causal reasoning, and reasoning from analogy. Please have a detailed reading of Unit 6.

References:

Hegyesi, M. M. & Yeoman, B. K. (2002). *Is There Such a Thing as a Zero-emissions Vehicle?* Retrieved from http://www2.aashe.org/heasc/resources/pdf/2002%20Fall20Is%20 there%20a%20 20zero%20emission%20vehicle.pdf.

Huber, R. B. & Snider, A. C. (2005). *Influencing Through Argument*. New York: International Debate Education Association.

Singer, S. F. (2007). *Global Warming: Man-made or Natural?* Retrieved from http://www.hillsdale.edu/news/imprimis/archive/issue.asp?year=2007&month.

Reading for Ideas

Text Ⓐ

The Food Miles Mistake

By Ronald Bailey [1]

❶ I stopped by my favorite grocery store to pick up a red **onion** today. The young clerk running the cash register wore a t-shirt with the **slogan** "Eat Local". Oddly, the shop's shelves and coolers were **stuffed** with cheeses, **sausages**, **olives**, jams, cookies, and crackers from California, France, Italy, Spain, Belgium, Germany, and many other **exotic** locales（场所，地点）. As I walked home, I mused（沉思，默想）over the fact that I needed the onion to go with the organic Irish salmon（鲑鱼，大马哈鱼）and the Spanish capers [（腌制的）刺山果花蕾] my wife and I were having for dinner. The salmon was a gift from a visiting friend from Dublin. Now, I enjoy seeking out and eating locally produced foods. My wife and I make it a habit to shop at our town's weekly farmers market for fresh fruits and vegetables.

❷ But for some activists, eating local foods is no longer just a pleasure—it is a moral **obligation**. Why? Because locally produced foods are supposed to be better for the planet than foods shipped thousands of miles across oceans and continents. According to these activists, shipping foods over long distances results in the unnecessary emission of the greenhouse gases that are warming the planet. This concern has **given rise to** the concept of "food miles", that is, the distance food travels from farm to plate. Activists particularly dislike air freighting foods because it uses **relatively** more energy than other forms of transportation. Food miles are supposed to be a simple way to **gauge** food's impact on climate change.

---

1 Ronald Bailey is the award-winning science correspondent for *Reason* magazine and Reason.com, where he writes a weekly science and technology column. In 2006, Bailey was shortlisted by the editors of *Nature Biotechnology* as one of the personalities who have made the "most significant contributions" to biotechnology（生物技术）in the last 10 years. He is a member of the Society of Environmental Journalists（环境新闻记者协会）and the American Society for Bioethics and Humanities（美国生物伦理学和人道协会）.

❸   In their recent policy primer（初级读本，入门书）for the Mercatus Center at George University, however, economic **geographer** Pierre Desrochers and economic consultant Hiroko Shimizu challenge the **notion** that food miles are a good **sustainability indicator**. As Desrochers and Shimizu point out, the food trade has been historically driven by urbanization. As agriculture became more efficient, people were liberated from farms and able to develop other skills that helped raise general living standards. People freed from having to scrabble（努力，尽力）for food, for instance, could work in factories, write software, or become physicians. Modernization is a process in which people get further and further away from the farm.

❹   Modern technologies like canning and **refrigeration** made it possible to extend the food trade from **staple** grains and spices to fruits, vegetables, and meats. As a result, world trade in fruits and vegetables—fresh and processed—doubled in the 1980s and increased by 30% between 1990 and 2001. Fruits and vegetables **accounted for** 22% of the exports of developing economies in 2001. If farmers, processors, shippers, and retailers did not profit from providing distant consumers with these foods, the foods wouldn't be on store shelves. And consumers, of course, benefit from being able to buy fresh foods year around.

❺   So just how much carbon dioxide is emitted by transporting food from farm to fork? Desrochers and Shimizu cite a **comprehensive** study done by the United Kingdom's Department of Environment, Food and Rural Affairs（DEFRA，英国环境食品农村事务处）which reported that 82% of food miles were generated within the U.K. Consumer shopping trips accounted for 48% and trucking for 31% of British food miles. Air freight **amounted to** less than 1% of food miles. In total, food transportation accounted for only 1.8% of Britain's carbon dioxide emissions.

❻   In the United States, a 2007 analysis found that transporting food from producers to retailers accounted for only 4% of greenhouse emissions related to food. According to a 2000 study, agriculture was responsible for 7.7% of total U.S. greenhouse gas emissions. In that study, food transport accounted for 14% of the greenhouse gas emissions associated with agriculture, which means that food transport is responsible for about 1% of total U.S. greenhouse gas emissions.

❼   Food miles **advocates** fail to grasp the simple idea that food should be grown where it is most economically advantageous to do so. Relevant advantages consist of various combinations of soil, climate, labor, capital, and other factors. It is possible to grow bananas in Iceland, but Costa Rica really has the better climate for that activity. Transporting food is just one relatively small cost of providing modern consumers with their daily bread, meat, cheese, and vegetables. Desrochers and Shimizu argue that concentrating agricultural production in the most favorable regions is the best way to minimize human impacts on the environment.

8   Local food production does not always produce fewer greenhouse gas emissions. For example, the 2005 DEFRA study found that British tomato growers emit 2.4 metric tons of carbon dioxide for each ton of tomatoes grown compared to 0.6 tons of carbon dioxide for each ton of Spanish tomatoes. The difference is British tomatoes are produced in heated greenhouses. Another study found that cold storage of British apples produced more carbon dioxide than shipping New Zealand apples by sea to London. In addition, U.K. dairy farmers use twice as much energy to produce a metric ton of milk solids than do New Zealand farmers.

9   A die-hard（顽固的，死硬的）response to the above studies would be: Don't eat either British or Spanish tomatoes out of season; don't cold store apples, dry them in the sun instead; don't ever eat dairy products; and give your true love a bouquet of in season root vegetables（块根类蔬菜）for Valentine's Day. In order to reduce your food miles, the National Sustainable Agriculture Information Service（美国国家可持续农业信息服务处）makes these recommendations: Eat foods that are in season; eat minimally processed, packaged, and **marketed** food; use public transportation when grocery shopping; can and dry fruits and vegetables yourself; and plant a garden and grow as much of your own food as possible. In other words, spend more time and effort finding, growing, and preparing food at the expense of other productive or leisure activities.

10   Desrochers and Shimizu demonstrate that the debate over food miles is a **distraction** from the real issues that confront global food production. For instance, rich country **subsidies** amounting to more than $300 billion per year are severely **distorting** global agricultural production and trade. If the subsidies were removed, far more agricultural goods would be produced in and imported from developing countries, helping lift millions of people out of poverty. They warn that the food miles campaign is "providing a new set of **rhetorical** tools to **bolster** protectionist interests that are fundamentally **detrimental** to most of humankind." Ultimately, Desrochers and Shimizu's analysis shows that "the concept of food miles is... a **profoundly** flawed sustainability indicator."

📖 Words and Phrases

advocate	['ædvəkeit]	*n.*	倡导者，拥护者
		vt.	提倡，主张
▲ bolster	['bəulstə]	*vt.*	支持，鼓励（某人）；改善，加强（某事物）

comprehensive	[ˌkɔmpriˈhensiv]	*a.*	全面的，综合的，广泛的；有理解力的；容易了解的
▲ detrimental	[ˌdetriˈmentl]	*a.*	有害的，不利的
★ distort	[diˈstɔ:t]	*vt. & vi.*	扭曲，（使）变形；歪曲，曲解
distraction	[diˈstrækʃn]	*n.*	分散注意力；使人分心的事（人）；娱乐，消遣；心烦意乱
			distract *vt.* 分散注意力；使分心
★ exotic	[igˈzɔtik]	*a.*	非本国的，外（国）来的
★ gauge	[geidʒ]	*vt.*	计量，度量；估计，判断
		n.	厚度，直径；测量仪表；规格，尺度
geographer	[dʒiˈɔgrəfə]	*n.*	地理学家
indicator	[ˈindikeitə]	*n.*	标志，指示
			indicate *vt.* 指示，指出；标志，表明
marketed	[ˈmɑ:kitid]	*a.*	推销的；在市场上出售的
notion	[ˈnəuʃən]	*n.*	概念，观念；奇想；意图，打算
obligation	[ˌɔbliˈgeiʃn]	*n.*	义务，责任；承诺；恩惠
★ olive	[ˈɔliv]	*n.*	橄榄；橄榄树；橄榄色
onion	[ˈʌnjən]	*n.*	洋葱
★ profoundly	[prəˈfaundli]	*adv.*	极度地；深深地，深切地，深刻地
			★ profound *a.* 极度的；深切的，深刻的
refrigeration	[riˌfridʒəˈreiʃn]	*n.*	冷藏，冷冻，制冷
			refrigerator *n.* 冰箱
relatively	[ˈrelətivli]	*adv.*	相对地；相比较而言地
▲ rhetorical	[riˈtɔrikl]	*a.*	虚夸的，空洞华丽的；修辞的，修辞学的；口头的
			▲ rhetoric *n.* 浮夸之词，花言巧语
sausage	[ˈsɔsidʒ]	*n.*	香肠，腊肠
slogan	[ˈsləugən]	*n.*	口号，标语；广告语
★ staple	[ˈsteipl]	*a.*	主要的，常产的
		n.	主要成分；主食；主要商品；主要产品
stuff	[stʌf]	*vt.*	以……填进，塞满
		n.	东西，物品；物质；材料；活动，事情
★ subsidy	[ˈsʌbsədi]	*n.*	财政补贴；津贴
sustainability	[səˌsteinəˈbiləti]	*n.*	可持续性

account for	构成（数量，比例）；解释，说明
amount to	共计；意味着
give rise to	引起，导致

 **Exercises**

Part I. Understanding the text

1. **Study the title of Text A.**
   - What are the key words in the essay title?
   - Why do you think they are the key words?

2. **Spend 5 minutes browsing the essay and answer the following questions.**
   - What's the argument refuted by Pierre Desrochers and Hiroko Shimizu in this essay?
   - What's the reason that some activists support the argument?

3. **Discuss with your partner about the possible weak points of the argument refuted by Pierre Desrochers and Hiroko Shimizu.**

Part II. Writing skills development

4. **Read this article carefully and analyze how Pierre Desrochers and Hiroko Shimizu back up their argument. Complete the following chart.**

Main argument of the two experts		
Support	Paragraph 3	Argument:
		Type of evidence:
	Paragraph 4	Argument:
		Type of evidence:
Refutation	Paragraphs 5 – 6	Argument:
		Technique of refutation:
		Type of evidence:
	Paragraph 7	Argument:
		Technique of refutation:
		Type of evidence:
	Paragraph 8	Argument:
		Technique of refutation:
		Type of evidence:

(continued)

Main argument of the two experts		
	Paragraph 9	Argument:
		Technique of refutation:
Conclusion		

5. **Read Paragraph 8 and analyze how Pierre Desrochers and Hiroko Shimizu support the view that local food production does not always produce fewer greenhouse gas emissions by providing examples and comparisons.**

Example 1: _____

_____

Example 2: _____

_____

Example 3: _____

_____

Part III. Language focus

6. **Choose the right word to complete each of the following sentences. Change the form where necessary.**

bolster	distort	notion	distraction	indicate
sustainability	advocate	obligation	detrimental	gauge

1) The United States will do what is necessary to meet its _____ to its own citizens.

2) Too much or little anxiety will always affect any performance in a _____ way.

3) All wood used in our furniture comes with a certificate saying it comes from _____ forests.

4) Mr. Williams is a conservative who _____ fewer government controls on business.

5) Timman needs to win a game to _____ his confidence.

6) When all the figures are available, it should be possible to _____ how much we'll need to spend.

7) A survey of retired people has _____ that most are independent and enjoying life.

8) Journalists were accused of sensationalizing the story and _____ the facts.

9) This will reduce _____ and help you concentrate upon your bodily feelings.

10) Humans still hold on to the absurd _____ that we are the only intelligent be-ings in the Universe.

7. Paraphrase the following sentences.

1) Economic geographer Pierre Desrochers and economic consultant Hiroko Shi-mizu challenge the notion that food miles are a good sustainability indicator.

2) Desrochers and Shimizu demonstrate that the debate over food miles is a distrac-tion from the real issues that confront global food production.

3) They warn that the food miles campaign is "providing a new set of rhetorical tools to bolster protectionist interests that are fundamentally detrimental to most of hu-mankind."

Part IV. Writing

8. Play a game of "I disagree". Generate a series of assertions of various types. Then refute each assertion using the four-step model. Try this exercise with a partner.

9. Write a paragraph to refute one of the following claims using the four-step refutation model and applying one or two of the refutation techniques that you have learned.

- Economic growth is more important than environmental protection.
- Keeping computers in dormitories does harm to freshmen.

Text **B**

Global Warming: Man-Made or Natural?

By S. Fred Singer[1]

❶   In the past few years there has been increasing concern about global climate change on the part of the media, politicians, and the public. It has been **stimulated** by the idea that human activities may influence global climate **adversely** and that therefore corrective action is required on the part of governments. Recent evidence suggests that this concern is misplaced (不适当的，不合时宜的). Human activities

---

1 S. Fred Singer is emeritus professor (名誉教授) of environmental sciences at the University of Virginia, a distin-guished research professor at George Mason University, and president of the Science and Environmental Policy Project. Dr. Singer has written or edited over a dozen books and monographs (专著，专论), including, most re-cently, *Unstoppable Global Warming: Every 1,500 Years*. This article is adapted from a lecture delivered on the Hillsdale College campus on June 30, 2007, during a seminar entitled "Economics and Environment".

are not influencing the global climate in a **perceptible** way. Climate will continue to change, as it always has in the past, warming and cooling on different time scales and for different reasons, **regardless of** human action. I would also argue that—should it occur—a modest warming would be **on the whole** beneficial.

② The most fundamental question is scientific: Is the observed warming of the past 30 years **due to** natural causes or are human activities a main or even a **contributing** factor?

③ **At first glance**, it is quite plausible that humans could be responsible for warming the climate. After all, the burning of fossil fuels to generate energy releases large quantities of carbon **dioxide** into the atmosphere. The CO_2 level has been increasing steadily since the beginning of the industrial revolution and is now 35% higher than it was 200 years ago. Also, we know from direct measurements that CO_2 is a "greenhouse gas" which strongly absorbs **infrared** (heat) radiation. So the idea that burning fossil fuels causes an **enhanced** "greenhouse effect" needs to be taken seriously.

④ But in seeking to understand recent warming, we also have to consider the natural factors that have regularly warmed the climate prior to the industrial revolution and, indeed, prior to any human presence on the earth. After all, the **geological** record shows a **persistent** 1,500-year cycle of warming and cooling **extending** back at least one million years.

⑤ A quite different question, but scientifically interesting, has to do with the natural factors influencing climate. This is a big topic about which much has been written. Natural factors include continental drift（大陆漂移）and mountain-building, changes in the Earth's orbit, volcanic **eruptions**, and solar **variability**. Different factors **operate** on different time scales. But on a time scale important for human experience—a scale of decades, let's say—solar variability may be the most important.

⑥ Solar influence can manifest itself in different ways: **fluctuations** of solar irradiance（太阳辐射）, which has been measured in satellites and related to the sunspot cycle（太阳黑点循环）; variability of the **ultraviolet** portion of the solar spectrum, which in turn affects the amount of **ozone** in the stratosphere; and variations in the solar wind（太阳风）that modulate（改变；调节）the intensity of cosmic rays（宇宙射线）(which produce cloud condensation nuclei（凝结核）, affecting cloudiness and thus climate).

⑦ Scientists have been able to trace the impact of the sun on past climate using proxy（替代值）data (since thermometers are relatively modern). A **conventional** proxy for temperature is the ratio of the heavy isotope（重同位素）of oxygen, Oxygen-18, to the most common form, Oxygen-16.

8 A paper published in *Nature* in 2001 describes the Oxygen-18 data (reflecting temperature) from a stalagmite（石笋）in a cave in Oman, covering a period of over 3,000 years. It also shows **corresponding** Carbon-14 data, which are directly related to the intensity of cosmic rays striking the earth's atmosphere. One sees there a remarkably detailed **correlation**, almost on a year-by-year basis. While such research cannot establish the detailed mechanism of climate change, the causal connection is quite clear: Since the stalagmite temperature cannot affect the sun, it is the sun that affects climate.

9 In identifying the burning of fossil fuels as the chief cause of warming today, many politicians and environmental activists simply appeal to a so-called "scientific consensus". There are two things wrong with this. First, there is no such consensus: An increasing number of climate scientists are raising serious questions about the political rush to judgment on this issue. For example, the widely touted（吹嘘的）"consensus" of 2,500 scientists on the United Nations Intergovernmental Panel on Climate Change（IPCC, 政府间气候变化专门委员会）is an illusion: Most of the panelists have no scientific qualifications, and many of the others object to some part of the IPCC's report. The Associated Press（美联社）reported recently that only 52 climate scientists contributed to the report's "Summary for Policymakers".

10 Likewise, only about a dozen members of the governing **board** voted on the "consensus statement" on climate change by the American Meteorological Society（AMS, 美国气象学会）. Rank and file（普通成员）AMS scientists never had a say, which is why so many of them are now openly rebelling. **Estimates** of skepticism within the AMS regarding man-made global warming are well over 50%.

11 The second reason not to rely on a "scientific consensus" in these matters is that this is not how science works. After all, scientific advances customarily come from a minority of scientists who challenge the majority view—or even just a single person (think of Galileo or Einstein). Science proceeds by the scientific method and draws conclusions based on evidence, not on a show of hands（举手表决）.

12 The nations of the world face many difficult problems. Many have societal problems like poverty, disease, lack of **sanitation**, and shortage of clean water. There are grave security problems arising from global terrorism and the **proliferation** of nuclear weapons. Any of these problems are vastly more important than the imaginary problem of man-made global warming. It is a great shame that so many of our resources are being diverted from real problems to this non-problem. Perhaps in 10 or 20 years this will become apparent to everyone, particularly if the climate should stop warming (as it has for eight years now) or even begin to cool.

⓭   We can only trust that reason will **prevail** in the face of an onslaught（攻击，猛攻）of propaganda like Al Gore's movie and despite the **incessant** misinformation generated by the media. Today, the imposed costs are still modest, and mostly hidden in taxes and in charges for electricity and motor fuels. If the scaremongers（散布恐慌谣言者，危言耸听者）have their way, these costs will become enormous. But I believe that sound science and good sense will prevail in the face of **irrational** and scientifically baseless climate fears.

📖 Words and Phrases

★ adversely	[əd'vɜ:sli]	*adv.*	不利地；方向相反地；敌对地
			★ adverse *a.* 不利的；方向相反的；敌对的
board	[bɔ:d]	*n.*	委员会，董事会；板，牌子；（包饭的）伙食
		vt. & vi.	上（船、车、飞机）；给……供应伙食；用板铺，用板盖
contributing	[kən'tribju:tiŋ]	*a.*	起作用的；贡献的
conventional	[kən'venʃənl]	*a.*	传统的，习惯的；墨守成规的；流于俗套的
★ correlation	[ˌkɔ:ri'leiʃn]	*n.*	相互关系
corresponding	[ˌkɔri'spɔndiŋ]	*a.*	相应的，对应的；符合的，一致的
★ dioxide	[dai'ɔksaid]	*n.*	二氧化物
			carbon dioxide *n.* 二氧化碳
enhanced	[in'hɑ:nst]	*a.*	增强的，提高的，放大的
			enhance *vt.* 提高，增加，加强
estimate	['estimət]	*n.*	估计，预测；评价，判断；概算，估价单
		vt. & vi.	估计，评价，评估
★ eruption	[i'rʌpʃn]	*n.*	喷发，爆发
			★ erupt *vi.* 喷发，爆发
extend	[ik'stend]	*vt. & vi.*	延伸，延续；给予，提供；伸展
fluctuation	[ˌflʌktju'eiʃn]	*n.*	起伏，波动，涨落
			fluctuate *vi.* 起伏，波动，涨落
★ geological	[ˌdʒi:ə'lɔdʒikl]	*a.*	地质学的；地质的
			★ geology *n.* 地质学，地质情况

▲ incessant	[in'sesnt]	*a.*	不停的，连续的，持续不断的
▲ infrared	[ˌinfrə'red]	*n.*	红外线；红外辐射
		a.	红外线的；使用红外线的
★ irrational	[i'ræʃənl]	*a.*	不合逻辑的，不合理的；失去理性的
operate	['ɔpəreit]	*vt. & vi.*	起作用；操作；运作；动手术
★ ozone	['əuzəun]	*n.*	臭氧；新鲜的空气
perceptible	[pə'septəbl]	*a.*	可感觉的，可感知的；可辨的，看得出的
			perceive *vt.* 感觉，察觉；理解
★ persistent	[pə'sistənt]	*a.*	持续的，不断的
prevail	[pri'veil]	*vi.*	占优势，占上风；盛行，流行；说服，劝服
▲ proliferation	[prəˌlifə'reiʃn]	*n.*	激增；扩散；繁殖，增生
			▲ proliferate *vi.* 激增；扩散；增生
▲ sanitation	[ˌsæni'teiʃn]	*n.*	公共卫生，环境卫生
stimulate	['stimjuleit]	*vt.*	激发；刺激；促进
★ ultraviolet	[ˌʌltrə'vaiələt]	*a.*	紫外线的；产生紫外线的
variability	[ˌveəriə'biləti]	*n.*	易变；变化性
			variable *a.* 变化的，易变的

at first glance	乍看起来；一看就
due to	由于
on the whole	总的看来；大体上
regardless of	不管，不顾

 **Exercises**

Part I. Understanding the text

1. **Study the title of Text B.**
   - What are the key words in the essay title?
   - Why do you think they are the key words?

2. **Discuss with your partner whether you think climate change is man-made or natural. What's the evidence that might be used to support your argument or to refute that of your partner's?**

Part II. Writing skills development

3. Read this article carefully and analyze how the author backs up his argument. Please finish the following chart.

Main argument of the author		
The main reason why humans could be responsible for warming the climate:		
Support	Paragraphs 4–8	Argument:
		Type of evidence:
Refutation	Paragraphs 9–11	Argument:
		Technique of refutation:
		Types of evidence:
Conclusion	Paragraphs 12–13	

Part III. Language focus

4. Complete the following sentences.

1) They have _____（延长最后期限）by twenty-four hours.

2) _____（研究人员估计）smoking reduces life expectancy by around 12 years on average.

3) City leaders hope this policy will _____（刺激经济增长）.

4) _____（存在极大的变化性）between individuals.

5) Stress, both human and mechanical, may also be a _____（起作用的因素）.

6) They fear it could have an _____（不利的效果）on global financial markets.

7) March and April sales this year were up 8 per cent on the_____（1992年同期）.

8) To some extent it is possible for parents to _____（提高婴儿智力的某些方面）.

9) According to Reynolds, _____（已存在可以感觉到的些微变化）in public attitude lately.

10) _____（存在直接的相互关系）between the best-known brands and the best-selling brands.

5. Paraphrase the following sentences.

1) Recent evidence suggests that this concern is misplaced. Human activities are not influencing the global climate in a perceptible way.

2) First, there is no such consensus: An increasing number of climate scientists are raising serious questions about the political rush to judgment on this issue.

3) We can only trust that reason will prevail in the face of an onslaught of propaganda like Al Gore's movie and despite the incessant misinformation generated by the media.

Part IV. Writing

6. Have a debate on *Whether Private Car Purchase Should Be Restricted*. The debate will consist of 2 teams, affirmative and negative, and two judges. Each team will have 2 debaters. There will be 4 roles within each debate. Members of the group will switch roles so that each person has a chance to perform each role.

Affirmative—This person is charged with arguing in support of the view.

Negative—This person is charged with arguing against the view.

Judge—This person is charged with evaluating the weight of the evidence presented, assessing the logic of the arguments, and declaring the winner of this debate.

The sequence of debate will proceed as follows:

1) *Affirmative (#1 Affirmative Debater)*: Define terms, state the main argument, and provide evidence to support the argument. (3 minutes)

2) *Negative (#1 Negative Debater)*: Define terms, state the main argument, provide evidence to support the argument, and identify errors in the affirmative's argument. (3 minutes)

3) *Affirmative (#2 Affirmative Debater)*: Respond to criticisms of the negative speaker, identify errors in logic or evidence of the negative speaker, return to the original argument, and show how it is still correct. (3 minutes)

4) *Negative (#2 Negative Debater)*: Respond to criticisms of the affirmative speaker, identify errors in logic or evidence of the affirmative speaker, return to the original argument, and show how it is still correct. (3 minutes)

5) *Judge:* Identify which conclusion is not logically supported, which ideas are unsupported by the evidence presented, and declare which side is the winner of this debate. (2 minutes)

7. Write a paragraph to refute one of the following two claims using the four-step refutation model and applying one or two of the refutation techniques that have been learned.

- Compared with 1930s, the number of lives lost in airplane crashes has increased four times. From this we can see that modern aircrafts are much more dangerous than the early ones.

- A survey of cinema audiences shows that most are in the age groups 18–25 and 45–60. It is therefore obvious that modern films do not appeal to people in the 25–45 age group.

Text C

The Environmental Argument for
Reducing Immigration to the United States

By Winthrop Staples III, Philip Cafaro [1]

❶ What to do about booming legal and illegal **immigration** rates is one of the most **controversial** topics on Americans' political agenda these days. This *Backgrounder* argues that a serious commitment to environmentalism entails ending America's population growth by **implementing** a more **restrictive** immigration policy. The need to limit immigration necessarily follows when we combine a clear statement of our main environmental goals—living sustainably and sharing the **landscape** generously with other species—with uncontroversial accounts of our current demographic（人口统计的）trajectory（轨线）and of the negative environmental effects of U.S. population growth, nationally and globally.

❷ Immigration levels are at a historic high and immigration is now the main driver of U.S. population growth. Consider some demographic history. Between 1900 and 2000, the U.S. population almost quadrupled（增长四倍）, from 76 million to 281 million people. The largest **decadal** population increase was also the most recent: a 32.7 million increase between 1990 and 2000. This population growth resulted from a mixture of natural increase and immigration.

---

1 Philip Cafaro, associate professor of philosophy at Colorado State University, is author of *Thoreau's Living Ethics* (University of Georgia Press, 2004). He is currently completing a book on the ethics of immigration, with the working title *Bleeding Hearts and Empty Promises: A Liberal Rethinks Immigration*. Winthrop Staples III is a wildlife biologist, and his master's thesis in environmental philosophy is titled *For a Species Moral Right to Exist: The Imperative of an Adequate Environmental Ethics* (Colorado State University, 2009). This article is adapted from a forthcoming article in *Environmental Ethics*.

❸   Population growth contributes significantly to a host of environmental problems within our borders. For example in the past two decades **sprawl**, defined as new development on the **fringes** of existing urban and suburban areas, has come to be recognized as an important environmental problem in the United States. Between 1982 and 2001, the United States converted 34 million acres of forest, cropland, and pasture to developed uses, an area the size of Illinois. The average annual rate of land conversion increased from 1.4 million acres to 2.2 million acres over this time, and continues on an upward trend. Sprawl is an environmental problem for lots of reasons, including increased energy consumption, water consumption, air pollution, and **habitat** loss for wildlife. Habitat loss is by far the number one cause of species endangerment in the United States; unsurprisingly, some of the worst sprawl centers (such as southern Florida and the Los Angeles basin) also contain large numbers of endangered species.

❹   A growing population increases America's large environmental footprint beyond our borders and our **disproportionate** role in stressing global environmental systems. Consider global warming. Nothing mortifies（使窘迫）American environmentalists more than our country's failure to show leadership in dealing with this, the most important environmental challenge facing the world in the 21st century. As the world's largest greenhouse gas emitter, the United States has a moral obligation to lead the world in meeting this challenge. A good start would be striving to stabilize greenhouse gas emissions at 1990 levels (the Kyoto **protocol**, rejected by the United States, calls for an initial reduction of 5% below 1990 levels). Meeting even this modest objective will prove difficult, however, if our population continues to grow.

❺   Look at the numbers. The United States' CO_2 emissions increased 20.4% between 1990 and 2005, from 4,991 to 6,009 million metric tons. That means we would have to decrease our emissions by 20.4% per person to get back to 1990 levels, *at our current population*. But if we double our population, as we are on track to do in six or seven decades, we will have to decrease **per capita** emissions 58.5% in order to reduce CO_2 emissions to 1990 levels—almost three times as great a per capita reduction. Such reductions will be much more expensive and demand greater sacrifice from Americans. They are thus less likely to happen.

❻   In order to seriously address environmental problems at home and become good global environmental citizens, we must stop U.S. population growth. It is of course possible to **spin out** scenarios in which America's population doubles, triples, or quadruples, and yet we still manage, through miracles of technological creativity or ethical self-sacrifice, to become ecologically sustainable. Perhaps, as techie（尤指计算机方面 的技术人员）magazines like *Discover* and *Wired* **periodically** suggest, we may begin building farms in high rises and let the rest of the landscape return to nature.

7   Perhaps the most important objections raised against restrictive immigration policies are that they are unjust, because they are unfair to potential immigrants. One concise way of stating this is to say that would-be immigrants have a *right* to live and work in the United States. While some immigrants' rights **proponents** argue for abolishing national borders altogether, most assert a general human right to freely move and settle without regard to national borders. Political theorist Chandran Kukathas gives the following "liberal egalitarian（平等主义的）" argument for open borders. From a proper **universal** moral point of view, he maintains, citizens of rich countries have no special **claims** to the resources and opportunities into which they have been born. "Egalitarianism demands that the Earth's resources be distributed as equally as possible," he writes, "and one particularly effective mechanism for **facilitating** this is freedom of movement." Allowing people to migrate from poor, overcrowded countries with high unemployment and little chance for economic advancement to wealthier, less crowded countries equalizes opportunities.

8   Environmentalists sometimes give specifically environmental reasons for supporting—or at least tolerating—high levels of immigration. One common argument says that we should focus on *consumption, not population* as the root cause of our environmental problems. "Don't buy big suburban houses; don't buy gas guzzlers（耗油量大的汽车）; don't put air conditioners in those houses and cars. Americans' high level of consumption is the problem—not our population." This argument is **appealing** because it seems to put the responsibility for change where it belongs: not on poor immigrants but on average Americans, who do consume too much and who could consume less without harming their quality of life. But as we have seen, it is Americans' *overall* consumption that determines our environment impact. Overall consumption equals per capita consumption multiplied by population. So if high consumption is a problem, population growth must be, too.

9   Economic arguments bring us to final class of objections to our proposal. Many pro-business proponents praise mass immigration above all for increasing economic growth. Immigration brings in poor unskilled workers willing to work physically demanding jobs for less money than native-born Americans, and highly trained professionals with the specialized skills needed by high-tech companies. It thus helps businesses meet their needs and grow. Immigration creates more domestic consumers; as Tamar Jacoby puts it: "Foreign workers emerging at the end of the day from the meatpacking（肉类加工业）plant or the carpet factory buy groceries and shoes for their children; on Saturday, they buy washing machines and then hire **plumbers** to install them." Immigration also reduces the cost of many goods and services, and this too increases overall consumption. In all these ways, immigration results in "a bigger, more productive economy." That is why the *Wall Street Journal*, the U.S. Chamber of Commerce, and other important business organs strongly support mass immigration.

❿   We have presented our reasons for limiting immigration into the United States and the most common and consequential（重要的，重大的）objections to our proposal. In the end, we return to our **primary** argument. Immigration is now the main driver of American population growth. Continued American population growth is **incompatible** with sustainability, nationally or globally. Therefore environmentalists committed to sustainability should support reducing current high levels of U.S. immigration. Not just **on pain of** contradiction, but on pain of failure.

Words and Phrases

appealing	[əˈpi:liŋ]	a.	吸引人的，有趣的；求助的，渴望同情的
claim	[kleim]	n.	主张，断言；要求
		vt.	主张，断言；提出要求，索取，索赔；值得
controversial	[ˌkɔntrəˈvə:ʃəl]	a.	引起争论的，有争议的
decadal	[ˈdekədəl]	a.	十的，十年间的
			decade n. 十年时间，十年
disproportionate	[ˌdisprəˈpɔ:ʃənət]	a.	不相称的，不成比例的
			proportion n. 部分；比例；均衡
facilitate	[fəˈsiliteit]	vt.	使（行动，过程）更容易；推动，促进
★ fringe	[frindʒ]	n.	边缘，外围；饰穗，流苏
▲ habitat	[ˈhæbitæt]	n.	（动植物等的）栖息地；生长环境
immigration	[ˌimiˈgreiʃn]	n.	移居，移民入境；移民总称
			immigrant n. 移民
implement	[ˈimplimənt]	vt.	实行，贯彻，履行
★ incompatible	[ˌinkəmˈpætəbl]	a.	与……不相容的，与……不能共存的
landscape	[ˈlændskeip]	n.	风景，景色；风景画，风景照
periodically	[ˌpiəriˈɔdikli]	adv.	周期性地；偶尔地
			periodical n. 期刊，杂志
▲ plumber	[ˈplʌmə]	n.	管道工

primary	['praiməri]	*a.*	首要的，主要的；基本的；最初的；初级的
▲ proponent	[prə'pəunənt]	*n.*	提议者，建议者；支持者
▲ protocol	['prəutəkɔl]	*n.*	（外交条约的）草案，草约；议定的条款，议定书；外交礼仪
restrictive	[ri'striktiv]	*a.*	限制（性）的，约束（性）的 restrict *vt.* 限制，约束
▲ sprawl	[sprɔ:l]	*n. & vi.*	蔓延，杂乱无序地扩展；伸开四肢坐、躺或跌下
universal	[ˌju:ni'vɜ:sl]	*a.*	普遍性的，广泛性的；通用性的

on pain of			如不……就有……的风险
per capita			每人，按人计算（地）的
spin out			使尽量延长

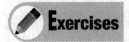 **Exercises**

Part I. Understanding the text

1. Study the title of Text C.

- What are the key words in the essay title?
- Why do you think they are the key words?

2. Discuss the following questions with your partner.

- Do you have a plan to study further abroad (e.g., US or UK) after graduation from your university?
- What are the advantages and disadvantages of studying abroad?
- Do you want to live permanently in foreign countries like US or UK? What if you can't obtain a green card just because of the fear of overpopulation and environmental problems due to growing immigration?

3. Read Paragraphs 7–9 and list the arguments used to refute restrictive immigration policies.

Moral argument in Paragraph 7: _____

_____

Environmental argument in Paragraph 8: _____

_____

Economic argument in Paragraph 9: _____

_____

Part II. Writing skills development

4. **Fill in the boxes to complete the flowchart, which illustrates the** *cause/effect* **chain developed in Paragraphs 2–6.**

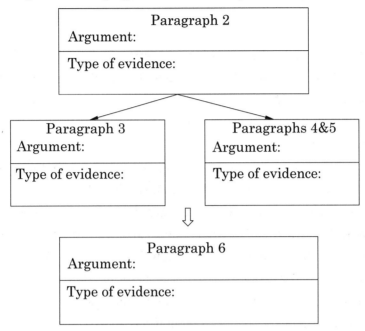

Part III. Language focus

5. **Use the proper form of the given word to complete each of the following sentences.**

   1) Although a warmer climate may sound _____, the effects of the heat can be difficult to cope with. (appeal)

   2) A recent government paper on education contains some _____ new ideas. (controversy)

   3) The Foreign Affairs Department has denied _____ that the men were tortured. (claim)

   4) Britain is to adopt a more _____ policy on arms sales. (restrict)

   5) Cost-cutting measures have _____ in most hospitals. (implement)

6. **Paraphrase the following sentences.**

   1) Nothing mortifies American environmentalists more than our country's failure to show leadership in dealing with this, the most important environmental challenge facing the world in the 21st century.

2) This argument is appealing because it seems to put the responsibility for change where it belongs: not on poor immigrants but on average Americans, who do consume too much and who could consume less without harming their quality of life.

3) Continued American population growth is incompatible with sustainability, nationally or globally. Therefore environmentalists committed to sustainability should support reducing current high levels of U.S. immigration.

Part IV. Writing

7. **Have a debate on *Whether College Students Should Take Part-time Jobs*. The debate will consist of 2 teams, affirmative and negative, and two judges. Each team will have 2 debaters. There will be 4 roles within each debate. Members of the group will switch roles so that each person has a chance to perform each role.**

Affirmative—This person is charged with arguing in support of the view.

Negative—This person is charged with arguing against the view.

Judge—This person is charged with evaluating the weight of the evidence presented, assessing the logic of the arguments, and declaring the winner of this debate.

The sequence of debate will proceed as follows:

1) *Affirmative (#1 Affirmative Debater)*: Define terms, state the main argument, and provide evidence to support the argument. (3 minutes)

2) *Negative (#1 Negative Debater)*: Define terms, state the main argument, provide evidence to support the argument, and identify errors in the affirmative's argument. (3 minutes)

3) *Affirmative (#2 Affirmative Debater)*: Respond to criticisms of the negative speaker, identify errors in logic or evidence of the negative speaker, return to the original argument, and show how it is still correct. (3 minutes)

4) *Negative (#2 Negative Debater)*: Respond to criticisms of the affirmative speaker, identify errors in logic or evidence of the affirmative speaker, return to the original argument, and show how it is still correct. (3 minutes)

5) *Judge:* Identify which conclusion is not logically supported, which ideas are unsupported by the evidence presented, and declare which side is the winner of this debate. (2 minutes)

8. **Write a paragraph to refute one of the following two claims using the four-step refutation model and applying one or two of the refutation techniques you have learned.**

   ● Military spending is detrimental to society.
   ● Science is more dangerous than religion.

Unit Summary

In this unit, you have learned four-step refutation format and various refutation techniques. The three articles in this unit are of a "Main Issue + Support + Refutation" structure. Now, do the following exercises to consolidate your knowledge.

1. How could you answer the following questions?

1) What is the four-step format of refutation?

2) What are the techniques or methods you might use while refuting others' arguments? Which ones do you prefer to apply?

2. Identify the argument which is refuted in each of the following paragraphs, and analyze the technique of refutation and types of evidence used.

1)　　The electric car industry has hit back at a new study suggesting "electric cars could speed climate change", arguing that the study understates the environmental benefits associated with electric vehicles and could undermine the embryonic market. "We have to keep going back to the basic message that electric cars are cleaner," said Barry Shrier, chief executive of Liberty Electric Cars. "Study after study has shown that the wheel-to-well emissions are much better—even if you produce electricity in the dirtiest way available using coal, life cycle emissions from electric vehicles are still 50 per cent lower than they are for internal combustion engines."

2)　　Southern Californians are now being forced to implement solutions to reduce the effects of existing causes which have created the "smog capitol of the nation" (Smith 82). There are two solutions which would solve the problem of meeting Regulation XV requirements. They are not new ideas. One is ridesharing, commonly known as carpooling, where two or more persons share the same automobile to and from work. The other is…

　　Opposition to the idea of carpools at Orchids Paper Products Company claims that there exists a lack of incentives. Among the perks is a monetary compensation of $15.00 per month. That basically covers about one week's fuel needs. Carpools would require at least four people per automobile for approximate full compensation of each month's fuel needs. There are concerns regarding personality conflict, inconvenience, and invasion of privacy. Examples of conflict include smokers vs. non-smokers, talkative persons vs. quiet (reflective) drivers, opposing driving habits, and conflicting music preferences. Carpooling becomes an inconvenience due to personal obligations like running errands before or after work, taking kids to school or the babysitter, fulfilling grocery shopping needs, or just visiting friends before going home. Potential carpoolers are also concerned whether the "other" person(s) will be on time before and after work. In regards to invasion of privacy, some people consider their automobile as personal domain where eating, drinking, smoking, and breathing is not allowed by intruders. There also exists a fear of being questioned about one's personal life.

3)   The argument is that if we are serious about fighting global-warming, there is no alternative to building new nuclear capacity. Renewables, such as wind power, have their place but few experts believe they can fill the gap in time. Also, concerns about energy security make the Government reluctant to depend even more on imported Russian gas. So nuclear it is. At the moment nuclear generation accounts for about 18% of our electricity supply, compared with 76% in France. The French seem to live perfectly happily with so many nuclear power stations, so why shouldn't we?

    Some of the arguments against are perennial. One is cost. The Government has been anxious to claim that taxpayers' money will not be involved in new nuclear generation and that the role of government is simply to facilitate the opportunity for private companies (including French ones) to build the new capacity. Skeptics say they have heard all this before, going back to the early days of nuclear power when it was boasted that nuclear-generated electricity would be so cheap to produce that it wouldn't be worthwhile to charge for it. In reality, hidden (or not so hidden) costs always end up landing on the taxpayer. Paying for the disposal of nuclear waste is one of them.

    But it is the safety issue which mostly concerns opponents of the nuclear power. Even the problem of how to dispose of the waste has not yet been solved and creates huge public alarm whenever a proposal arises to store the stuff, which has thousands of years of potential radiation toxicity, near where anyone is living.

3. **Write your essay: Use what you have learned in this unit and write an argumentative essay on any topic related to environment. At this stage, you shall be able to write an essay of 200 to 250 words.**

Prewriting

Work out the outline of the essay and ask yourself:	✔ or ✘
What is the overall stance/argument of the essay?	☐
Is the overall stance/argument obvious in Introduction and/or Conclusion?	☐
Is the main idea clear in each supporting paragraph?	☐
How many paragraphs will the essay have?	☐
Does the outline follow a logical sequence of ideas?	☐

Writing

Write the first draft alone.

Revising

Once you have the first draft of your paper completed, (peer) review it with the following questions in mind:

Does the Introduction and/or Conclusion clearly present the overall argument?

Are the ideas clearly and logically organized?

Is the main argument in each supporting paragraph supported with adequate evidence?

Are the sentences grammatical and concise?

Is coherence within and across paragraphs adequately achieved?

---

4. **Use the proper form of the given word to complete each of the following sentences.**

1) According to *Life* magazine, cars with soft smooth shapes are supposed to be _____ to females. (appeal)

2) Tom admits that playing video games sometimes _____ him from his homework. (distract)

3) All the signs _____ are that we are going to receive reasonable support from abroad. (indicate)

4) Their work includes the _____ of genes which govern the growth rate and fertility. (identify)

5) Evidence to support these _____ is still lacking. (claim)

6) The study _____ the link between poverty and malnutrition. (demonstrate)

7) My parents always seemed _____ to me, but they stayed together for over 40 years. (compatible)

8) E-commerce is a _____ recent phenomenon. (relative)

9) The economy is in danger of collapse unless far-reaching reforms are _____. (implement)

5. **Choose the right word to complete each of the following sentences. Change the form where necessary.**

assert	skeptical	notion	impose	irrational
obligation	consensus	controversial	illusion	entail

1) A recent government paper on education contains some _____ new ideas.

2) Yet although these medical theories were wrong, they weren't altogether _____.

3) He _____ that nuclear power was a safe and non-polluting energy source.

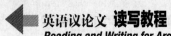

4) We will meet our international _____ to reduce harmful chimney emissions.

5) Environmental groups are _____ of the government's claims.

6) There is a _____ among teachers that children should have a broad understanding of the world.

7) I didn't want to take on a job that would _____ a lot of travelling.

8) People had bought these houses under the _____ that their value would just keep on rising.

9) Teachers should try to avoid _____ their own beliefs on their students.

10) Humans still hold on to the absurd _____ that we are the only intelligent beings in the Universe.

Glossary

Appendix

abrupt	[ə'brʌpt]	a.	突然的；唐突的；陡峭的；生硬的	U3TA
★ absurd	[əb'sɜːd]	a.	荒谬的；可笑的	U2TC
abuse	[ə'bjus]	n.	滥用（职权等）；虐待；凌辱；〈古〉欺骗	U7TC
access	['ækses]	n.	机会，权利，通路；通到	U2TB
	[æk'ses]	vt.	存取；到达；进入；使用	U2TB
accessible	[ək'sesəbl]	a.	可得到的；可进入的	U4TC
accumulate	[ə'kju:mjuleit]	vt. & vi.	积累，增加，聚集	U4TC
accumulation	[ə,kju:mju'leiʃn]	n.	积聚，累积，堆积物	U3TB
acid	['æsid]	n.	酸；＜俚＞迷幻药	U3TB
		a.	酸的；讽刺的；刻薄的	U3TB
★ activation	[,ækti'veiʃn]	n.	激活；活化作用	U2TA
			★ activate vt.& vi. 刺激；使活动；使活泼；使产生放射性	U2TA
★ actuality	[,æktʃu'æləti]	n.	现实；现存；现实性；现状	U7TC
adapt	[ə'dæpt]	vt. & vi.	使适应；改编	U2TC
addiction	[ə'dikʃn]	n.	沉溺，上瘾	U4TB
address	[ə'dres]	vt.	处理；从事；忙于；演说；写姓名地址	U2TA
		n.	地址；演讲；致辞	U2TA
adequate	['ædikwət]	a.	充足的；适当的；胜任的	U6TC
★ adherence	[əd'hiərəns]	n.	坚持；依附；忠诚	U6TC
administration	[əd,mini'streiʃn]	n.	管理；行政；实施；行政机构	U6TA
★ adolescent	[,ædə'lesnt]	a.	青春期的	U4TB
		n.	青少年	U4TB
★ advancement	[əd'vɑːnsmənt]	n.	前进，进步；提升	U7TA
★ adversely	[əd'vɜːsli]	adv.	不利地；方向相反地；敌对地	U8TB
			★ adverse a. 不利的；方向相反的；敌对的	U8TB
advocate	['ædvəkeit]	n.	倡导者，拥护者	U8TA
		vt.	提倡，主张	U8TA
affect	[ə'fekt]	vt. & vi.	影响；感染；侵袭	U2TC
▲ affluent	['æfluənt]	a.	富裕的，富足的	U1TB
agenda	[ə'dʒendə]	n.	议程	U5TB
★ aggravate	['ægrəveit]	vt.	加重（剧），使恶化；激怒，使恼火	U1TC
★ aggregate	['ægrigət]	vt.	使聚集，使积聚；总计达	U4TA
aggressively	[ə'gresivli]	adv.	侵略地；有进取心地；好争斗地	U1TB
agony	['ægəni]	n.	极大的痛苦；临死的挣扎；苦恼	U7TB
▲ ailment	['eilmənt]	n.	小病；不安	U3TC
alarming	[ə'lɑːmiŋ]	a.	令人担忧的；使人惊恐的	U6TA
			alarm n. 警报；惊慌；警告器 vt. 恐吓；警告	U6TA
alter	['ɔːltə]	vt. & vi.	改变，更改，修改	U2TA
▲ anonymity	[,ænə'niməti]	n.	匿名，笔者不明	U7TC

★	antibiotic	[ˌæntibaiˈɔtik]	*n.*	抗生素，抗菌素	U7TA
			a.	抗生的；抗菌的	U7TA
	appeal	[əˈpi:l]	*n.*	呼吁，请求；吸引；上诉	U2TB
			vt. & vi.	呼吁，恳求；上诉；有吸引力，迎合爱好	U2TB
	appealing	[əˈpi:liŋ]	*a.*	吸引人的，有趣的；求助的，渴望同情的	U8TC
	appointment	[əˈpɔintmənt]	*n.*	约会；任命；约定；任命的职位	U6TC
	approach	[əˈprəutʃ]	*n.*	方法，方式	U5TA
			vt.	处理	U5TA
	arbitrary	[ˈɑ:bitrəri]	*a.*	任意的；武断的；专制的	U3TC
	arithmetic	[əˈriθmətik]		算术；计算	U1TB
	arouse	[əˈrauz]	*vt. & vi.*	激发；引起；唤醒；鼓励	U2TB
★	artery	[ˈɑ:təri]	*n.*	动脉；干道；主流	U7TA
	artificially	[ˌɑ:tiˈfiʃəli]	*adv.*	人工地，人为地，不自然地	U2TA
★	ascribe	[əˈskraib]	*vt.*	归因于；归咎于	U3TC
	ashtray	[ˈæʃtrei]	*n.*	烟灰缸	U6TC
	aspiration	[ˌæspəˈreiʃn]	*n.*	志向，抱负	U5TB
	assert	[əˈsɜ:t]	*vt.*	断言，主张	U6TA
▲	assortment	[əˈsɔ:tmənt]	*n.*	分类；混合物	U6TA
				▲ assorted *a.* 多样混合的	U6TA
	assume	[əˈsju:m]	*vt.*	假定，设想；采取，呈现	U6TC
▲	asthma	[ˈæsmə]	*n.*	哮喘	U4TA
★	attendant	[əˈtendənt]	*n.*	服务员，侍者；随员	U6TC
			a.	伴随的；侍候的	U6TC
★	autonomy	[ɔ:ˈtɔnəmi]	*n.*	自主权；自主性；自治；自治权	U7TB
★	availability	[əˌveiləˈbiləti]	*n.*	可用性；有效性；实用性	U3TB
	available	[əˈveiləbl]	*a.*	可获得的；可购得的；有空的	U2TC
	baby-sitting	[ˈbeibisitiŋ]	*n.*	托婴服务	U6TC
	bachelor	[ˈbætʃələ]	*n.*	学士；单身汉；（尚未交配的）小雄兽	U6TA
	ban	[bæn]	*vt.*	禁止；取缔	U2TA
			n.	禁令；禁忌	U2TA
	barrel	[ˈbærəl]	*n.*	桶；一桶之量	U1TC
	bearing	[ˈbeəriŋ]	*n.*	关系；方位；举止；[机]轴承	U7TB
▲	benchmark	[ˈbentʃmɑ:k]	*n.*	基准点，参照点	U4TC
	beneficial	[ˌbeniˈfiʃl]	*a.*	有益的，有利的；可享利益的	U2TB
	better-off	[ˈbetəˌɔf]	*a.*	较富裕的；境况较好的	U6TB
▲	beverage	[ˈbevəridʒ]	*n.*	饮料	U2TA
	bidder	[ˈbidə]	*n.*	出价人，投标人	U2TB
				bid *vt. & vi.* 投标；出价；吩咐	U2TB
★	bleak	[bli:k]	*a.*	荒凉的；阴冷的；黯淡的，无希望的	U3TA
	board	[bɔ:d]	*n.*	委员会，董事会；板，牌子；（包饭的）伙食	U8TB
			vt. & vi.	上（船、车、飞机）；给……供应伙食；用板铺，用板盖	U8TB
▲	bolster	[ˈbəulstə]	*vt.*	支持，鼓励（某人）；改善，加强（某事物）	U8TA
	boom	[bu:m]	*n.*	隆隆声；繁荣；激增	U1TC
▲	bout	[baut]	*n.*	较量；发作；回合；一阵	U3TB
	brainwashing	[ˈbreinwɔʃiŋ]	*n.*	洗脑	U4TB
★	broker	[ˈbrəukə]	*n.*	（股票债券等的）经纪人；（买卖的）代理人	U1TB

bubble	[ˈbʌbl]	*n.*	泡；水泡；泡影	U1TB
bubbly	[ˈbʌbli]	*a.*	气泡的，冒泡的	U1TB
▲ buffer	[ˈbʌfə]	*n.*	缓冲器，减震器；缓冲区	U3TA
		vt.	缓冲	U3TA
burial	[ˈberiəl]	*n.*	埋葬；葬礼；弃绝	U3TC
		a.	埋葬的	U3TC
burst	[bɜːst]	*vt. & vi. & n.*	爆发，突发；爆炸	U3TB
★ bypass	[ˈbaipɑːs]	*n.*	旁路；[公路]支路	U7TA
		vt.	绕开；忽视；设旁路；迂回	U7TA
capacity	[kəˈpæsəti]	*n.*	能力，容量；生产力	U2TA
▲ carbohydrate	[ˌkɑːbəuˈhaidreit]	*n.*	糖类；碳水化合物	U3TB
cautiously	[ˈkɔːʃəsli]	*adv.*	慎重地，谨慎地	U6TB
★ censor	[ˈsensə]	*vt. & vi.*	检查	U4TB
challenge	[ˈtʃælindʒ]	*n.*	质疑，怀疑；挑战	U2TA
		vt.	向……挑战	U2TA
charge	[tʃɑːdʒ]	*n.*	控告；收费；负荷；充电	U7TC
★ chronically	[ˈkrɒnikli]	*adv.*	慢性地；延续很长地	U3TC
citation	[saiˈteiʃn]	*n.*	引用	U5TB
claim	[kleim]	*n.*	主张，断言；要求	U8TC
		vt.	主张，断言；提出要求，索取，索赔；值得	U8TC
clinical	[ˈklinikl]	*a.*	临床的；诊所的	U3TC
code	[kəud]	*n.*	代码，密码；编码；法典	U2TC
		vt. & vi.	编码；制成法典	U2TC
coil	[kɔil]	*vt.*	盘绕，把……卷成圈	U3TC
		n.	卷；线圈	U3TC
		vi.	成圈状	U3TC
coin	[kɔin]	*vt. & vi.*	创造，杜撰（新词等）；铸造；制造	U7TC
collapse	[kəˈlæps]	*vi.*	倒塌；瓦解；暴跌	U3TA
		vt.	使倒塌，使崩溃，使萎陷	U3TA
		n.	倒塌；失败；衰竭	U3TA
★ commerce	[ˈkɒmɜːs]	*n.*	贸易；商业	U2TA
commission	[kəˈmiʃn]	*n.*	委员会；佣金；委任状	U6TB
		vt.	委任；使服役；委托制作	U6TB
commitment	[kəˈmitmənt]	*n.*	承诺，保证；委托；承担义务；献身	U6TB
▲ compassion	[kəmˈpæʃn]	*n.*	同情；怜悯；怜悯之心	U7TA
▲ complacent	[kəmˈpleisnt]	*a.*	自满的；得意的；满足的	U7TA
complaint	[kəmˈpleint]	*n.*	抱怨；诉苦；委屈	U6TC
complex	[ˈkɒmpleks]	*a.*	复杂的；合成的	U2TA
		n.	复合体；综合设施	U2TA
compound	[ˈkɒmpaund]	*vt.*	混合；合成；掺合	U3TB
		n.	化合物；复合词；混合物	U3TB
		a.	复合的；混合的	U3TB
comprehensive	[ˌkɒmpriˈhensiv]	*a.*	全面的，综合的，广泛的；有理解力的；容易了解的	U8TA
compromise	[ˈkɒmprəmaiz]	*vt. & vi.*	对……妥协；和解；让步	U7TC
		n.	妥协；调和；和解；妥协方案，折中方案	U7TC
concede	[kənˈsiːd]	*vt. & vi.*	承认；让步；容许	U2TB

conflict	[ˈkɔnflikt]	*n. & vi.*	冲突，矛盾；斗争；争执	U2TA
confront	[kənˈfrʌnt]	*vt.*	面对；面临；处理，对付	U2TB
congressional	[kənˈgreʃənl]	*a.*	议会的，国会的；会议的	U4TB
▲ connotation	[ˌkɔnəˈteiʃn]	*n.*	内涵；含蓄；暗示，隐含意义	U7TB
conscience	[ˈkɔnʃəns]	*n.*	道德心，良心	U6TB
conscious	[ˈkɔnʃəs]	*a.*	意识到的；故意的；神志清醒的	U7TA
consensus	[kənˈsensəs]	*n.*	共识，一致意见	U5TC
consent	[kənˈsent]	*vt. & vi. & n.*	同意；赞成；应允；答应	U7TC
consequence	[ˈkɔnsikwəns]	*n.*	结果；后果；重要性	U2TB
★ conserve	[kənˈsɜːv]	*vt.*	节约，节省；保护，保藏，保存	U4TA
consistently	[kənˈsistəntli]	*adv.*	一致地，始终如一地；协调地	U7TC
constitute	[ˈkɔnstitjuːt]	*vt.*	组成，构成；建立；任命	U2TB
★ constrain	[kənˈstrein]	*vt.*	强迫，强使；限制，约束	U1TC
consumption	[kənˈsʌmpʃn]	*n.*	消费；消耗	U3TB
contaminate	[kənˈtæmineit]	*vt.*	污染；弄脏	U2TB
★ contend	[kənˈtend]	*vt. & vi.*	争论，争辩；（坚决）主张	U7TA
		n.	争论，争辩；竞争；战斗	U7TA
contest	[kənˈtest]	*vt.*	争辩；提出质疑	U7TB
	[ˈkɔntest]	*n.*	竞赛；争夺；争论	U7TB
contract	[kənˈtrækt]	*vt. & vi.*	感染；收缩；订约	U2TA
		n.	合同；婚约	U2TA
contraction	[kənˈtrækʃn]	*n.*	收缩，紧缩；缩写式；害病	U3TB
contradiction	[ˌkɔntrəˈdikʃn]	*n.*	矛盾；不一致；反驳	U2TC
contribute	[kənˈtribjuːt]	*vt.*	贡献，出力；投稿；捐献	U2TC
contributing	[kənˈtribjuːtiŋ]	*a.*	起作用的；贡献的	U8TB
controversial	[ˌkɔntrəˈvəːʃəl]	*a.*	引起争论的，有争议的	U8TC
controversy	[ˈkɔntrəvɜːsi]	*n.*	争论；论战；辩论	U2TA
conventional	[kənˈvenʃənl]	*a.*	传统的，习惯的；墨守成规的；流于俗套的	U8TB
★ convergence	[kənˈvɜːdʒəns]	*n.*	会聚，聚合	U5TA
▲ converse	[kənˈvɜːs]	*a.*	相反的，逆向的；倒的	U4TC
conversely	[ˈkɔnvɜːsli]	*adv.*	相反地	U5TA
convert	[kənˈvɜːt]	*vt.*	转变，变换	U5TB
▲ coral	[ˈkɔrəl]	*n.*	珊瑚；珊瑚虫	U3TA
		a.	珊瑚色的；珊瑚的	U3TA
★ correlation	[ˌkɔːriˈleiʃn]	*n.*	相互关系	U8TB
corresponding	[ˌkɔriˈspɔndiŋ]	*a.*	相应的，对应的；符合的，一致的	U8TB
★ counterpart	[ˈkauntəpɑːt]	*n.*	职位（或作用）相当的人；对应的事物	U2TB
▲ coup	[kuː]	*n.*	政变	U1TA
crash	[kræʃ]	*n.*	（商业）失败，凋敝，崩溃，破产；瓦解	U1TB
crippling	[ˈkripliŋ]	*a.*	严重损害身体的，有严重后果的	U7TB
crisis	[ˈkraisis]	*n.*	危机；危急关头；危难时刻；病危期	U2TB
cultivate	[ˈkʌltiveit]	*vt.*	培养，陶冶	U5TB
cure	[kjuə]	*vt. & vi.*	治疗；治愈	U2TA
current	[ˈkʌrənt]	*a.*	当前的；现在的；流通的，通用的；流行的	U2TB
		n.	水流；气流；电流；趋势；潮流	U2TB
decadal	[ˈdekdəl]	*a.*	十的，十年间的	U8TC
			decade *n.* 十年时间，十年	U8TC

★ deduction	[di'dʌkʃn]	n.	扣除，减除	U1TB
★ deem	[di:m]	vi.	认为，持某种看法；作某种评价	U7TB
★ defective	[di'fektiv]	a.	有缺陷的；有缺点的；有毛病的	U2TC
deficit	['defisit]	n.	不足额；赤字；亏空；亏损	U4TA
define	[di'fain]	vt. & vi.	阐明，说明；给……下定义；解释	U7TB
demonstrate	['demənstreit]	vt. & vi.	（用实例，实验）说明，示范，表演	U7TC
dentist	['dentist]	n.	牙科医生	U6TC
▲ deplete	[di'pli:t]	vt.	耗尽，用尽；使衰竭，使空虚	U2TB
▲ depletion	[di'pli:ʃn]	n.	消耗；放血；损耗	U3TB
★ deprive	[di'praiv]	vt.	剥夺对某物的所有（或使用）	U1TA
derive	[di'raiv]	vt. & vi.	源于；起源；得自	U2TA
detect	[di'tekt]	vt.	发现；察觉；探测	U2TC
★ deteriorate	[di'tiəriəreit]	vt. & vi.	恶化，变坏	U2TC
★ deterioration	[di,tiəriə'reiʃn]	n.	恶化，退化；堕落	U3TB
▲ detrimental	[,detri'mentl]	a.	有害的，不利的	U8TA
★ deviant	['di:viənt]	a.	不正常的，离经叛道的	U4TB
★ deviate	['di:vieit]	vi.	越轨；脱离	U3TC
		vt.	使偏离	U3TC
digest	[dai'dʒest]	vt. & vi.	消化；领会；领悟	U2TC
	['daidʒest]	n.	文摘；摘要	U2TC
dilemma	[di'lemə]	n.	困境，进退两难	U5TA
dim	[dim]	vi.	变暗淡，变模糊	U1TA
★ dioxide	[dai'ɔksaid]	n.	二氧化物	U8TB
			carbon dioxide n. 二氧化碳	U8TB
disaster	[di'zɑ:stə]	n.	不幸；灾难，灾祸	U2TC
★ discern	[di's3:n]	vt.	辨明，分清	U5TB
discipline	['disəplin]	n.	学科	U5TC
★ displacement	[dis'pleismənt]	n.	置换，转位，移动	U4TB
disposable	[di'spəuzəbl]	a.	一次性的，可任意处理的	U4TA
		n.	一次性物品	U4TA
disproportionate	[,disprə'pɔ:ʃənət]	a.	不相称的，不成比例的	U8TC
			proportion n. 部分；比例；均衡	U8TC
distinctive	[di'stiŋktiv]	a.	有特色的，特殊的	U5TB
★ distort	[di'stɔ:t]	vt. & vi.	扭曲，（使）变形，歪曲，曲解	U8TA
distraction	[di'strækʃn]	n.	分散注意力；使人分心的事（人）；娱乐，消遣；心烦意乱	U8TA
			distract vt. 分散注意力；使分心	U8TA
diverse	[dai'vɜ:s]	a.	不同的，多种多样的	U4TC
▲ diversity	[dai'vɜ:səti]	n.	多样性；差异	U2TB
			▲ diversify vt. 使多样化，使变化；增加产品种类以扩大	U2TB
division	[di'viʒn]	n.	除法；部门；分割	U2TB
divorce	[di'vɔ:s]	n.	离婚；分离	U6TC
		vt. & vi.	（使）离婚，（使）分……离；与……离婚	U6TC
▲ doctorate	['dɔktərit]	n.	博士学位；博士头衔	U6TA
★ doctrine	['dɔktrin]	n.	教义；学说；主义；信条	U3TC
documentation	[,dɔkjumen'teiʃn]	n.	文件证据；证明文件	U7TC

domestic	[də'mestik]	*a.*	家庭的；国内的；驯养的	U6TB
		n.	国货；佣人	U6TB
dramatic	[drə'mætik]	*a.*	突然的；令人吃惊的；戏剧的	U2TC
★ drawback	['drɔ:bæk]	*n.*	缺点；不利条件；后退；远离；退缩	U7TB
drill	[dril]	*n.*	钻子；钻孔机；播种机；训练	U3TB
		vt. & vi.	钻孔；训练	U3TB
drug	[drʌg]	*n.*	药；毒品	U2TC
★ duplicate	['dju:plikət]	*n.*	副本；复制品	U2TC
	['dju:plikeit]	*vt. & vi.*	复制；重复	U2TC
ease	[i:z]	*vt.*	减轻，缓和；使安心	U3TC
echo	['ekəu]	*vt.*	重复（他人的话等）	U5TA
★ ecological	[ˌi:kə'lɒdʒikl]	*a.*	生态的；生态学的	U2TB
economically	[ˌi:kə'nɒmikli]	*adv.*	在经济上地；节俭地；经济地	U6TC
elegant	['eligənt]	*a.*	高雅的，优雅的；讲究的	U2TA
elementary	[ˌeli'mentri]	*a.*	初级的；基本的；[化学] 元素的	U6TA
★ eligible	['elidʒəbl]	*a.*	符合条件的；有资格当选的；合格的	U6TB
		n.	合格者；适任者；有资格者	U6TB
elimination	[iˌlimi'neiʃn]	*n.*	消除；除去；淘汰	U2TC
			eliminate *vt.* 消除；排除	U2TC
★ elite	[ei'li:t]	*a.*	杰出的；名牌的	U5TB
▲ embryonic	[ˌembri'ɔnik]	*a.*	胚胎的；像胚胎的	U2TA
			▲ embryo *n.* 胚胎；晶胚；初期	U2TA
emerge	[i'mɜ:dʒ]	*vi.*	出现；浮现；暴露；摆脱	U2TC
★ emission	[i'miʃn]	*n.*	排放；辐射；排放物	U4TA
emphasize	['emfəsaiz]	*vt.*	强调；加强	U6TB
★ empirical	[im'pirikl]	*a.*	经验的；实证的	U5TA
enable	[i'neibl]	*vt.*	使能够，使成为可能	U2TC
▲ encompass	[in'kʌmpəs]	*vt. & vi.*	围绕；包含；包围；完成	U4TC
endurance	[in'djuərəns]	*n.*	忍耐；持久；耐久，忍耐力	U3TB
enduring	[in'djuəriŋ]	*a.*	能忍受的；持久的	U7TB
enhanced	[in'hɑ:nst]	*a.*	增强的，提高的，放大的	U8TB
			enhance *vt.* 提高，增加，加强	U8TB
enrich	[in'ritʃ]	*vt.*	使丰富	U5TB
ensure	[in'ʃuə]	*vt.*	保证，确保；使安全	U2TA
★ entail	[in'teil]	*vt.*	使必需；使蒙受；使承担；遗传给	U6TC
		n.	[法] 限定继承权	U6TC
entertain	[ˌentə'tein]	*vt. & vi.*	招待；怀抱；容纳	U6TC
entitlement	[in'taitlmənt]	*n.*	授权；应得权益；命名，被定名	U2TC
equivalent	[i'kwivələnt]	*a.*	相等的，相当的，等效的；等价的，等积的；[化学] 当量的	U4TA
erosion	[i'rəuʒn]	*n.*	腐蚀；侵蚀（作用）；[医] 糜烂，齿质腐损	U7TC
★ eruption	[i'rʌpʃn]	*n.*	喷发，爆发	U8TB
			★ erupt *vi.* 喷发，爆发	U8TB
essential	[i'senʃl]	*a.*	基本的；必要的；本质的；精华的	U2TB
		n.	本质；要素，要点；必需品	U2TB
establish	[i'stæbliʃ]	*vt.*	建立；创办；安置	U2TA
estimate	['estimət]	*n.*	估计，预测；评价，判断；概算，估价单	U8TB
		vt. & vi.	估计，评价，评估	U8TB

▲ ethical	['eθikl]	a.	伦理的；道德的	U2TA
			▲ ethic n. 伦理；道德规范	U2TA
ethnicity	[eθ'nisəti]	n.	种族划分；种族性	U6TB
			ethnic a. 人种的；种族的；异教徒的	U6TB
evaluate	[i'væljueit]	vt. & vi.	评价；估价；求……的值	U6TA
evolution	[ˌi:və'lu:ʃn]	n.	演变；进展；进化	U2TC
evolutionary	[ˌi:və'lu:ʃnəri]	a.	进化的	U5TA
evolve	[i'vɔlv]	vt. & vi.	发展，进化；逐步形成	U2TC
excess	['ekses]	n.	超过；超额量；多余量	U1TB
exclusively	[ik'sklu:sivli]	adv.	专有地；排外地；唯一地	U3TB
			exclusive a. 高级的；独有的；排他的	U3TB
			n. 独家新闻	U3TB
★ execution	[ˌeksi'kju:ʃn]	n.	执行，实行；完成；死刑	U3TB
★ exotic	[ig'zɔtik]	a.	非本国的，外（国）来的	U8TA
expectation	[ˌekspek'teiʃn]	n.	期待；预期；指望	U6TB
★ expire	[ik'spaiə]	vi.	终止；期满；死亡；呼气	U3TC
		vt.	呼出（空气）	U3TC
explicit	[ik'splisit]	a.	明白的；明确的；直爽的；不隐讳的	U7TC
exploitation	[ˌeksplɔi'teiʃn]	n.	开发，开采；利用；广告推销	U3TA
▲ exponentially	[ˌekspə'nenʃəli]	adv.	以指数方式	U3TA
			▲ exponent n. 指数，幂	U3TA
extend	[ik'stend]	vt. & vi.	延伸，延续；给予，提供；伸展	U8TB
▲ exuberance	[ig'zju:bərəns]	n.	活跃；愉快；茁壮	U1TB
facilitate	[fə'siliteit]	vt.	使（行动，过程）更容易；推动，促进	U8TC
falsify	['fɔ:lsifai]	vt.	证明……虚假	U5TA
fatigue	[fə'ti:g]	n.	疲劳，疲乏；杂役	U3TB
		vt.	使疲劳；使心智衰弱	U3TB
		vi.	疲劳	U3TB
		a.	疲劳的	U3TB
fee	[fi:]	n.	（加入组织或做某事付的）费；专业服务费，业务报酬；小费，赏钱	U1TB
fictional	['fikʃənl]	a.	虚构的，小说的	U4TB
fictitious	[fik'tiʃəs]	a.	虚构的；假想的；假装的；编造的	U3TC
filter	['filtə]	n.	过滤器；滤色镜；滤光器	U4TC
		vt. & vi.	过滤；渗透	U4TC
fineable	['fainəbl]	n.	终曲	U3TC
		a.	可罚款的（=finable）	U3TC
fluctuation	[ˌflʌktju'eiʃn]	n.	起伏，波动，涨落	U8TB
			fluctuate vi. 起伏，波动，涨落	U8TB
★ flush	[flʌʃ]	vt.	（以水）冲刷，冲洗；冲掉，除掉	U1TC
▲ forefront	['fɔ:frʌnt]	n.	位于最前列；处于领先地位；最前部	U7TB
forging	['fɔ:dʒiŋ]	n.	锻造	U5TB
★ formulation	[ˌfɔ:mju'leiʃn]	n.	构想；系统的阐述	U5TA
fossil	['fɔsl]	n.	化石；僵化的事物；顽固不化的人	U3TA
		a.	化石的；陈腐的，守旧的	U3TA
fragmentation	[ˌfrægmen'teiʃn]	n.	破碎；分裂；存储残片	U3TA
			fragment n. 碎片，碎块	U3TA
framework	['freimwɜ:k]	n.	构架；框架；（体系的）结构；组织	U1TB

fraud	[frɔːd]	n.	欺骗，欺诈	U7TA
▲ fraught	[frɔːt]	a.	充满……的	U5TC
★ fringe	[frindʒ]	n.	边缘，外围；饰穗，流苏	U8TC
fruitfully	['fruːtfəli]	adv.	富有成效地	U5TA
fundamental	[ˌfʌndə'mentl]	a.	基本的，根本的	U6TB
		n.	基本原理；基本原则	U6TB
★ gadget	['gædʒit]	n.	小玩意；小配件；小装置	U4TA
★ galaxy	['gæləksi]	n.	星系	U5TA
★ gauge	[geidʒ]	vt.	计量，度量；估计，判断	U8TA
		n.	厚度，直径；测量仪表；规格，尺度	U8TA
generate	['dʒenəreit]	vt.	使形成；发生；生殖	U2TA
genetic	[dʒi'netik]	a.	遗传的；基因的；起源的	U2TA
			gene n. 基因	U2TA
geographer	[dʒi'ɔgrəfə]	n.	地理学家	U8TA
geographical	[ˌdʒiːə'græfikl]	a.	地理的；地理学的	U3TA
			geography n. 地理（学）	U3TA
★ geological	[ˌdʒiːə'lɔdʒikl]	a.	地质学的；地质的	U8TB
			★ geology n. 地质学，地质情况	U8TB
giant	['dʒaiənt]	a.	巨大的；巨人般的	U2TB
		n.	巨人；巨兽；伟人	U2TB
★ gigantic	[dʒai'gæntik]	a.	巨大的，庞大的	U5TA
global	['gləubl]	a.	全球的；球形的；总体的	U2TB
▲ graft	[grɑːft]	vi. & vt.	嫁接；移植；贪污	U3TC
		n.	嫁接；移植；渎职	U3TC
grant	['grɑːnt]	vt.	授予；允许；承认；批准	U7TB
		n.	拨款；[法]授予物	U7TB
grave	[greiv]	a.	严重的	U4TB
★ grieve	[griːv]	vi.	悲痛，哀悼	U7TA
		vt.	使悲伤，使苦恼	U7TA
guarantee	[ˌgærən'tiː]	n.	保证；担保；保证人；保证书；抵押品	U7TB
▲ habitat	['hæbitæt]	n.	（动植物等的）栖息地；生长环境	U8TC
hasten	['heisn]	vt. & vi.	赶紧，赶快，使加紧；催促；促进	U7TC
★ heritage	['heritidʒ]	n.	传统，遗产；继承物；继承权	U6TB
▲ heterogeneous	[ˌhetərə'dʒiːniəs]	a.	多样化的	U5TB
household	['haushəuld]	n.	家庭，户	U1TA
★ humane	[hjuː'mein]	a.	仁慈的，人道的；高尚的	U7TA
▲ hymn	[him]	n.	赞美诗；圣歌；欢乐的歌	U6TB
		vt. & vi.	唱赞美歌	U6TB
★ hypothesis	[hai'pɔθəsis]	n.	假设，前提	U1TA
identity	[ai'dentəti]	n.	身份；同一性，一致；特性；恒等式	U6TB
ignorant	['ignərənt]	a.	无知的；愚昧的	U2TC
★ illumination	[iˌluːmi'neiʃn]	n.	解释；启发	U5TC
illusion	[i'luːʒn]	n.	幻影；幻觉；妄想，幻想；错觉	U7TC
illustration	[ˌilə'streiʃn]	n.	说明，例证，实例；图解，插画	U7TC
immediate	[i'miːdiət]	a.	直接的	U5TC
immigration	[ˌimi'greiʃn]	n.	移居，移民入境；移民总称	U8TC
			immigrant n. 移民	U8TC

▲ imminent	['iminənt]	*a.*	即将来临的；迫近的；危机的	U7TB
★ immunity	[i'mju:nəti]	*n.*	豁免；免疫力；免疫性；（税等的）免除	U7TC
impact	['impækt]	*n.*	巨大影响；强大作用；撞击；冲击力	U2TB
	[im'pækt]	*vt. & vi.*	有影响，有作用；冲击；撞击	U2TB
impaired	[im'peəd]	*a.*	受损的	U3TB
			impair *vt.* 损害，损伤，削弱	U3TB
▲ implantation	[.implɑ:n'teiʃn]	*n.*	移植；灌输；鼓吹	U3TC
			▲ implant *vt.* 移植；灌输	U3TC
implement	['implimənt]	*vt.*	实行，贯彻，履行	U8TC
import	['impɔ:t]	*n.*	进口；输入的产品；引进	U2TB
		vt.	输入，进口，引进	U2TB
impose	[im'pəuz]	*vt. & vi.*	把……强加于；迫使；推行；强制实行	U2TC
★ incentive	[in'sentiv]	*n.*	激励某人做某事的事物；诱因，动机	U1TA
▲ incessant	[in'sesnt]	*a.*	不停的，连续的，持续不断的	U8TB
★ incidentally	[.insi'dentli]	*adv.*	顺便；偶然地；附带地	U6TC
★ incompatible	[.inkəm'pætəbl]	*a.*	与……不相容的，与……不能共存的	U8TC
incredible	[in'kredəbl]	*a.*	难以置信的，惊人的	U4TB
indecent	[in'di:snt]	*a.*	下流的，不妥当的	U4TB
independent	[.indi'pendənt]	*a.*	独立的；单独的；不受约束的	U6TC
		n.	独立自主者；无党派者	U6TC
index	['indeks]	*n.*	索引；指数；指示；标志	U1TC
indicator	['indikeitə]	*n.*	标志，指示	U8TA
			indicate *vt.* 指示，指出；标志，表明	U8TA
induce	[in'dju:s]	*vt.*	导致，引起	U1TA
induced	[in'dju:st]	*a.*	感应的；诱发型	U3TA
infant	['infənt]	*n.*	婴儿；幼儿	U2TC
		a.	婴儿的；幼稚的；初期的；未成年的	U2TC
infect	[in'fekt]	*vt.*	感染，传染	U2TA
inferior	[in'fiəriə]	*n.*	低于他人者；次品；部下，属下	U4TC
		a.	下等的；差的；下级的	U4TC
▲ inflate	[in'fleit]	*vt. & vi.*	使膨胀，使物价上涨	U1TB
★ inflict	[in'flikt]	*vt.*	使遭受（损伤、痛苦等）；使……承受；给予（打击等）	U7TA
▲ infrared	[.infrə'red]	*n.*	红外线；红外辐射	U8TB
		a.	红外线的；使用红外线的	U8TB
▲ ingenuity	[.indʒə'nju:əti]	*n.*	心灵手巧；独创性；精巧	U4TB
inherent	[in'hiərənt]	*a.*	固有的；内在的；生来的	U7TB
initial	[i'niʃəl]	*a.*	初步的	U5TC
★ initiative	[i'niʃətiv]	*n.*	主动性；首创精神；主动权；主动的行动，倡议	U7TA
★ inject	[in'dʒekt]	*vt.*	注射；注入	U2TA
innocent	['inəsnt]	*a.*	无辜的；无罪的；无知的	U2TA
★ innovation	[.inə'veiʃn]	*n.*	创新，革新；新方法	U3TC
▲ innovative	['inəveitiv]	*a.*	革新的，创新的	U2TA
inquiry	[in'kwaiəri]	*n.*	探究，探索	U5TC
insert	[in'sə:t]	*vt.*	插入；嵌入	U2TC
inspection	[in'spekʃn]	*n.*	检验；视察，检查	U6TA

insufficient	[ˌinsəˈfiʃnt]	a.	不足的，不充足的	U3TB
		n.	不足	U3TB
			sufficient *a.* 足够的，充分的	U3TB
★ insulated	[ˈinsjuleitid]	a.	隔绝的，隔离的	U7TA
			★ insulate *vt.* 使隔离，使孤立；使绝缘，使隔热	U7TA
integrate	[ˈintigreit]	vt. & vi.	整合，结合，使成一体	U4TC
intensity	[inˈtensəti]	n.	强烈；强度；亮度；紧张	U3TB
interact	[ˌintərˈækt]	vi.	互相作用，互相影响	U5TA
★ intermittent	[ˌintəˈmitənt]	a.	间歇的，断断续续的	U3TB
internal	[inˈtɜːnəl]	a.	内部的；内在的；国内的	U2TC
interpret	[inˈtɜːprit]	vi.	解释；翻译	U6TB
		vt.	说明；口译	U6TB
interrupt	[ˌintəˈrʌpt]	n.	中断	U6TC
		vt. & vi.	中断；打断；插嘴；妨碍	U6TC
intervals	[ˈintəvls]	n.	间隔；音程	U3TB
★ intrinsically	[inˈtrinsikli]	adv.	本质地；固有地；内在地	U3TA
investigate	[inˈvestigeit]	vt. & vi.	调查；研究	U6TB
★ irrational	[iˈræʃənl]	a.	不合逻辑的，不合理的；失去理性的	U8TB
★ jealousy	[ˈdʒeləsi]	n.	嫉妒；猜忌；戒备	U6TC
▲ jolt	[dʒəult]	vt.	使颠簸；使摇动；使震惊	U3TA
		n.	颠簸；摇晃；震惊；严重挫折	U3TA
justify	[ˈdʒʌstifai]	vt.	证明……是正当的，为……辩护	U5TA
			justification *n.* 证实，理由	U5TA
keen	[kiːn]	a.	敏锐的，敏捷的；渴望的	U6TB
		n.	痛哭，挽歌	U6TB
landscape	[ˈlændskeip]	n.	风景，景色；风景画，风景照	U8TC
legal	[ˈliːgl]	a.	法律的；合法的；法定的	U2TC
			illegal *a.* 非法的；违法的	U2TC
legality	[liːˈgæləti]	n.	合法；合法性；墨守法规	U7TB
legalize	[ˈliːgəlaiz]	vt. & vi.	法律认可，使合法，合法化	U7TC
★ legislator	[ˈledʒisleitə]	n.	立法者	U4TB
liberty	[ˈlibəti]	n.	自由；许可；冒失	U6TC
▲ livestock	[ˈlaivstɔk]	n.	家畜，牲畜	U2TA
major	[ˈmeidʒə]	vi.	主修	U6TA
		n.	[人类] 成年人；主修科目；陆军少校	U6TA
		a.	主要的；重要的；主修的；较多的	U6TA
★ manifest	[ˈmænifest]	vt.	证明，表明；显示	U3TB
		vi.	显示，出现	U3TB
		a.	明白的；显然的，明显的	U3TB
manipulation	[məˌnipjuˈleiʃn]	n.	操作；操纵；使用	U2TC
			manipulate *vt.* 操纵；操作	U2TC
marketed	[ˈmɑːkitid]	a.	推销的；在市场上出售的	U8TA
mathematics	[ˌmæθəˈmætiks]	n.	数学；数学运算；数学专业	U6TA
mechanism	[ˈmekənizəm]	n.	机制	U5TC
medication	[ˌmediˈkeiʃn]	n.	药物；药剂；物疗法；药物处理	U7TC
★ medieval	[ˌmediˈiːvl]	a.	中世纪的；仿中世纪的；老式的	U3TC
▲ merchandise	[ˈmɜːtʃəndaiz]	n.	商品；货物	U1TC

merit	['merit]	n.	长处，优点，价值	U1TB
★ methodology	[,meθə'dɔlədʒi]	n.	方法论	U5TC
★ metropolitan	[,metrə'pɔlitən]	a.	大都会的，大城市的	U1TB
millionaire	[,miljə'neə]	n.	百万富翁；大富豪	U6TA
		a.	100 万以上人口的	U6TA
mine	[main]	vt. & vi.	在……中开采，开采	U4TA
★ minimize	['minimaiz]	vt.	把……减至最低数量（程度）；对（某事）做最低估计	U4TA
▲ mischievous	['mistʃivəs]	a.	调皮的，恶作剧的；有害的	U4TB
modify	['mɔdifai]	vt. & vi.	调整，使更适合；缓和；修饰	U2TB
▲ monopolize	[mə'nɔpəlaiz]	vt.	垄断；独占；拥有……的专卖权	U2TB
moral	['mɔrəl]	a.	道德的；精神上的；品性端正的	U2TA
			immoral a. 不道德的；邪恶的	U2TA
★ mortgage	['mɔ:gidʒ]	n.	抵押贷款	U1TB
★ mourn	[mɔ:n, məun]	vt. & vi.	哀悼；忧伤；服丧	U3TC
multiple	['mʌltipl]	n.	倍数	U1TA
★ navigate	['nævigeit]	v.	航行；驾驶；操纵	U4TC
net	[net]	a.	纯的，净的，无虚价的	U1TA
nitrogen	['naitrədʒən]	n.	[化] 氮	U3TA
★ nonrenewable	[,nɔnri'nju:əbl]	a.	不可再生的；不可更新的	U4TA
norm	[nɔ:m]	n.	基准；规范	U5TB
▲ nostalgically	[nɔ'stældʒikəli]	adv.	怀乡地；恋旧地	U3TC
			▲ nostalgic a. 怀旧的，引起对往事怀恋的	U3TC
notion	['nəuʃən]	n.	概念，观念；奇想；意图，打算	U8TA
numerous	['nju:mərəs]	a.	许多的，很多的	U2TB
▲ nun	[nʌn]	n.	修女；尼姑	U7TC
★ nurture	['nɜ:tʃə]	n.	养育；教养；营养物	U6TC
		vt.	养育；鼓励；培植	U6TC
★ nutritional	[nju'triʃənl]	a.	有营养的；滋养的	U2TC
			★ nutrition n. 营养，营养品	U2TC
obligation	[,ɔbli'geiʃn]	n.	义务，责任；承诺；恩惠	U8TA
offence	[ə'fens]	n.	攻击；违反；犯罪；过错	U3TC
★ olive	['ɔliv]	n.	橄榄；橄榄树；橄榄色	U8TA
onion	['ʌnjən]	n.	洋葱	U8TA
★ onset	['ɔnset]	n.	开始，着手；发作；进攻	U2TA
operate	['ɔpəreit]	vt. & vi.	起作用；操作；运作；动手术	U8TB
opposition	[,ɔpə'ziʃn]	n.	反对；反对派；在野党；敌对	U6TA
▲ optimal	['ɔptiməl]	a.	最理想的；最佳的	U3TB
★ orientation	[,ɔ:riən'teiʃn]	n.	方向，目标；熟悉，适应；情况介绍	U4TC
origin	['ɔridʒin]	n.	起源；原点；出身；开端	U6TB
▲ outperform	[,autpə'fɔ:m]	vt.	胜过；做得比……好；跑赢大盘	U6TB
outweigh	[,aut'wei]	vt. & vi.	比……重要	U4TA
★ overwhelming	[,əuvə'welmiŋ]	a.	压倒性的；势不可挡的	U2TC
★ ozone	['əuzəun]	n.	臭氧；新鲜的空气	U8TB
★ paperback	['peipəbæk]	n.	平装本，平装书	U4TA
▲ passionately	['pæʃənətli]	adv.	热情地；强烈地；激昂地	U6TC
			▲ passionate a. 充满热情的	U6TC

★	pasture	['pɑ:stʃə]	n.	牧草地，牧场	U1TA
★	patent	['peitnt]	n.	专利	U5TB
▲	pediatrician	[ˌpi:diə'triʃn]	n.	儿科医师（= pediatrist）	U7TA
	peer	[piə]	n.	贵族；同等的人	U6TC
			vi.	凝视，盯着看；窥视	U6TC
	perceive	[pə'si:v]	vt. & vi.	意识到，察觉；理解	U1TA
	perceptible	[pə'septəbl]	a.	可感觉的，可感知的；可辨的，看得出的	U8TB
				perceive vt. 感觉，察觉；理解	U8TB
	perfect	[pə'fekt]	vt.	使完美；使完善	U2TC
		['pɜ:fikt]	a.	完美的；最好的；精通的	U2TC
	periodically	[ˌpiəri'ɔdikli]	adv.	周期性地；偶尔地	U8TC
				periodical n. 期刊，杂志	U8TC
	permanently	['pɜ:mənəntli]	adv.	永久地，耐久地，持久地	U1TA
★	persistent	[pə'sistənt]	a.	持续的，不断的	U8TB
★	pervasive	[pə'veisiv]	a.	遍布的；弥漫的	U2TB
	pessimistic	[ˌpesi'mistik]	a.	悲观的，厌世的；悲观主义的	U3TA
★	pest	[pest]	n.	害虫；有害之物；令人讨厌的人	U2TB
	phenomenon	[fə'nɔminən]	n.	现象；奇迹；杰出的人才	U6TB
	pillar	['pilə]	n.	柱子，柱形物；栋梁；墩	U6TB
▲	pitfall	['pitfɔ:l]	n.	缺陷；陷阱，圈套；诱惑	U3TC
★	planetary	['plænətri]	a.	行星的	U3TA
	platform	['plætfɔ:m]	n.	台；站台；平台；纲领	U1TC
	plausibility	[ˌplɔ:zə'biləti]	n.	可信性	U5TA
	plausible	['plɔ:zəbl]	a.	貌似真实的，貌似有理的；花言巧语的	U3TC
▲	plumber	['plʌmə]	n.	管道工	U8TC
	poster	['pəustə]	n.	海报，广告；招贴	U7TA
▲	potent	['pəutnt]	a.	有效的；强有力的；有说服力的	U7TA
	potential	[pə'tenʃl]	n.	潜能；可能性	U2TA
			a.	潜在的；可能的	U2TA
▲	practitioner	[præk'tiʃnə]	n.	从事者；实践者；实习者；练习者	U7TC
▲	pragmatist	['prægmətist]	n.	实用主义者	U5TA
	precaution	[pri'kɔ:ʃn]	n.	预防，警惕；预防措施	U2TC
	preceding	[pri'si:diŋ]	a.	在前的；前述的	U3TB
				★ precede vt. 在……之前，先于	U3TB
				★ precedent n. 先例，范例，判例；惯例	U3TB
★	preclude	[pri'klu:d]	vt.	阻止，排除	U4TB
▲	predator	['predətə]	n.	食肉动物；掠夺者；捕食者	U3TA
	prejudice	['predʒudis]	n.	偏见	U4TA
★	prematurity	[pri:mə'tjurəti]	n.	早熟；过早；未成熟；早开花	U7TA
★	premier	['premiə]	a.	首位的；首要的	U5TB
★	premium	['pri:miəm]	n.	费用，额外补贴	U1TA
▲	preoccupation	[ˌpri:ɔkju'peiʃn]	n.	全神贯注	U4TB
	prescribe	[pri'skraib]	vt. & vi.	开药；开处方	U7TC
★	preservation	[ˌprezə'veiʃn]	n.	保存；保护；防腐	U7TB

pressing	['presiŋ]	a.	紧迫的；迫切的；恳切的	U2TB
			press vt. & vi. 压；按；逼迫	U2TB
prevail	[pri'veil]	vi.	占优势，占上风；盛行，流行；说服，劝服	U8TB
previous	['pri:viəs]	a.	先前的；以往的；稍前的	U2TC
primary	['praiməri]	a.	首要的，主要的；基本的；最初的；初级的	U8TC
principal	['prinsəpl]	n.	校长；资本；委托人，当事人；主犯	U3TC
		a.	首要的；最重要的	U3TC
prior	['praiə]	a.	优先的；在先的，在前的	U2TA
		adv.	在前，居先	U2TA
priority	[prai'ɔriti]	n.	优先；优先权；优先考虑的事	U2TB
privilege	['privəlidʒ]	n.	（因财富和地位而享有的）特权	U1TA
★ problematic	[ˌprɔblə'mætik]	a.	不确定的，有疑问的	U5TA
★ profoundly	[prə'faundli]	adv.	极度地；深深地，深切地，深刻地	U8TA
			★ profound a. 极度的；深切的，深刻的	U8TA
progressive	[prə'gresiv]	a.	进步的；先进的	U3TB
		n.	改革论者；进步分子	U3TB
▲ proliferation	[prəˌlifə'reiʃn]	n.	激增；扩散，繁殖，增生	U8TB
			▲ proliferate vi. 激增；扩散；增生	U8TB
★ prolong	[prə'lɔŋ]	vt.	延长；拖延	U7TB
★ prolonged	[prə'lɔŋd]	a.	延长的；拖延的；持续很久的	U3TB
promote	[prə'məut]	vt.	促进；提升；推销	U2TB
pronounced	[prə'naunst]	a.	断然的；显著的；讲出来的	U3TB
			pronounce vt. 发音；宣布，宣判	U3TB
▲ proponent	[prə'pəunənt]	n.	提议者，建议者；支持者	U8TC
★ proposition	[ˌprɔpə'ziʃn]	n.	企业，事业	U1TA
prospect	['prɔspekt]	n.	未来事件发生的可能性	U1TA
★ prospective	[prə'spektiv]	a.	预期的	U6TA
▲ protocol	['prəutəkɔl]	n.	（外交条约的）草案，草约；议定的条款，议定书；外交礼仪	U8TC
provision	[prə'viʒn]	n.	供应品；准备；条款；规定	U3TB
		vt.	供给……食物及必需品	U3TB
			▲ provisional a. 暂时的，临时的	U3TB
psychology	[sai'kɔlədʒi]	n.	心理学；心理状态	U6TA
★ punctuate	['pʌŋktʃueit]	vt.	不时打断；强调；加标点于	U3TB
		vi.	加标点	U3TB
pursue	[pə'sju:]	vt.	从事；继续	U5TC
▲ quaint	[kweint]	a.	（由于老式而）诱人的，奇特的	U4TA
quit	[kwit]	vt. & vi.	辞职；离开；放弃	U6TC
		n.	离开；[计]退出	U6TC
quote	[kwəut, kəut]	vt. & vi.	引述；举证用；报价	U6TB
		n.	引用	U6TB
radical	['rædikl]	a.	激进的；根本的；彻底的	U7TA
		n.	基础；激进分子	U7TA
★ radioactive	[ˌreidiəu'æktiv]	a.	放射性的	U4TA
★ radius	['reidiəs]	n.	半径范围，半径；桡骨	U4TB
rational	['ræʃnəl]	a.	理性的，合理的	U5TA
reaction	[ri'ækʃn]	n.	反应，回应；抗拒；阻碍；化学反应	U2TC

reactive	[ri'æktiv]	a.	反动的；反应的；电抗的	U3TA
			react vi. （作出）反应；反对；起化学反应（作用）	U3TA
			★ reactionary a. 保守的，反动的	U3TA
reasoning	['ri:zəniŋ]	n.	推论，推理	U5TA
★ recipe	['resipi, 'resəpi]	n.	秘诀；食谱；药方	U4TB
★ recipient	[ri'sipiənt]	n.	接受者，受领者	U6TA
recycle	[ri:'saikl]	vt.	回收利用；使再循环	U4TA
		vi.	重复利用	U4TA
refrigeration	[riˌfridʒə'reiʃn]	n.	冷藏，冷冻，制冷	U8TA
			refrigerator n. 冰箱	U8TA
★ regime	[rei'ʒi:m]	n.	机制；社会制度	U5TB
★ regulatory	['regjələtəri]	a.	调整的	U1TA
reject	[ri'dʒekt]	vt.	排斥；抵制	U2TA
relatively	['relətivli]	adv.	相对地；相比较而言地	U8TA
relevance	['reləvəns]	n.	关联，相关性	U5TB
★ reliant	[ri'laiənt]	a.	依赖的，依靠的	U7TB
▲ relic	['relik]	n.	遗迹；古董	U4TA
★ remainder	[ri'meində]	n.	剩余；[数] 余数；残余；剩余物	U7TB
remedy	['remədi]	vt.	改正；纠正；改进，补救；治疗	U1TC
▲ remittance	[ri'mitns]	n.	（尤指邮汇）汇款，汇款额	U1TA
			▲ remit vt. & vi. 汇款	U1TA
removal	[ri'mu:vl]	n.	移动；免职；排除；搬迁	U3TB
replacement	[ri'pleismənt]	n.	更换；复位；代替者	U2TA
★ reproach	[ri'prəutʃ]	vt.	责备，申斥	U6TB
		n.	责备；耻辱	U6TB
reproduction	[ˌri:prə'dʌkʃn]	n.	生殖；繁育	U5TB
reputable	['repjutəbl]	a.	受好评的；有声望的；规范的	U4TB
residency	['rezidənsi]	n.	住院医生实习期；住处	U7TA
resistant	[ri'zistənt]	a.	抵抗的，反抗的；顽固的	U2TB
▲ resonate	['rezəneit]	vt. & vi.	共鸣，共振	U4TB
▲ respirator	['respəreitə]	n.	[医] 呼吸器；防毒面具	U7TA
▲ respiratory	[ri'spiətəri]	a.	呼吸的	U2TA
restrain	[ri'strein]	vt.	抑制，压抑；限定，限制；制止	U1TC
restrictive	[ri'striktiv]	a.	限制（性）的，约束（性）的	U8TC
			restrict vt. 限制，约束	U8TC
★ retrieve	[ri'tri:v]	vt.	重新得到；恢复；检索	U3TC
		vi.	找回猎物	U3TC
		n.	检索；恢复；取回	U3TC
			★ retrieval n. 取回；补偿	U3TC
▲ retrospect	['retrəuspekt]		回顾，追溯	U4TB
returns	[ri'tɜ:nz]	n.	收益，利润	U5TB
reveal	[ri'vi:l]	vt.	泄露；显示	U2TA
▲ rhetorical	[ri'tɔrikl]	a.	虚夸的，空洞华丽的；修辞的，修辞学的；口头的	U8TA
			▲ rhetoric n. 浮夸之词，花言巧语	U8TA
★ rot	[rɔt]	n.	腐烂，腐朽	U1TC
★ routinely	[ru:'ti:nli]	adv.	惯常地；令人厌烦地	U5TB

sacrifice	['sækrifais]	n.	牺牲；祭品；供奉	U7TB
sanction	['sæŋkʃn]	n.	批准；约束力；处罚	U7TC
		vt. & vi.	批准；准许；制裁	U7TC
▲ sanitation	[ˌsæni'teiʃn]	n.	公共卫生，环境卫生	U8TB
sausage	['sɔsidʒ]	n.	香肠，腊肠	U8TA
scandal	['skændl]	n.	丑闻；丑行；流言飞语	U2TC
scarcely	['skeəsli]	adv.	缺乏地，不足地；稀有地	U2TB
★ scenario	[si'nɑ:riəu]	n.	情节；剧本；方案	U3TA
★ sceptic	['skeptik]	n.	怀疑论者；疑虑极深的人	U3TA
★ sculpt	[skʌlpt]	n.	雕刻品	U6TA
		vt. & vi.	造型；雕刻	U6TA
			★ sculpture n. 雕刻，雕刻品，雕塑；[地理]	U6TA
			刻蚀 v. 雕刻，雕塑；刻蚀	
★ sensationalized	[sen'seiʃənəlaizd]	a.	引起轰动的，骇人听闻的	U4TB
sensitive	['sensətiv]	a.	敏感的；[仪] 灵敏的；易受伤害的	U6TC
★ sentiment	['sentimənt]	n.	感情，情绪；情操；多愁善感	U7TB
shed	[ʃed]	vt.	摆脱；流出；散发；倾吐	U7TB
shrink	[ʃriŋk]	vt. & vi.	收缩，皱缩；（使）缩水；退缩，畏缩	U1TC
★ simulation	[ˌsimju'leiʃn]	n.	模仿；假装；冒充	U7TA
			simulate vt. 模仿；假装；冒充	U7TA
★ simultaneously	[ˌsiməl'teiniəsli]	adv.	同时发生地，同时进行地	U5TC
singularly	['siŋgjuləli]	adv.	异常地；非常地；令人无法理解地	U6TB
			singular n. 单数 a. 单一的；非凡的，异常的；	U6TB
			持异议的	
★ skeptical	['skeptikəl]	a.	怀疑论的，不可知论的	U5TA
★ skepticism	['skeptisizəm]	n.	怀疑论	U5TA
★ slaughter	['slɔ:tə]	n.	屠宰，屠杀；杀戮；消灭	U7TB
slip	[slip]	vi.	滑；出错，变差	U1TC
slippery	['slipəri]	a.	滑的；狡猾的；不稳定的	U7TB
slogan	['sləugən]	n.	口号，标语；广告语	U8TA
slope	[sləup]	n.	倾斜；斜率；斜坡；扛枪姿势	U3TA
		vi.	倾斜；逃走	U3TA
		vt.	扛；倾斜；使倾斜	U3TA
▲ sluggishness	['slʌgiʃnəs]	n.	萧条；呆滞；惰性，滞性	U1TC
			▲ sluggish a. 怠惰的	U1TC
soar	[sɔ:]	vi.	猛增	U1TA
span	[spæn]	n.	跨度，跨距；范围	U2TA
		vt.	跨越；持续；以手指测量	U2TA
spare	[speə]	vt.	节约，吝惜；饶恕；分出，分让	U3TB
		vi.	饶恕，宽恕；节约	U3TB
		a.	多余的；瘦的；少量的	U3TB
		n.	剩余；备用零件	U3TB
specialize	['speʃəlaiz]	vi.	专攻；专门从事	U5TB
★ spectrum	['spektrəm]	n.	范围；系列	U1TB
★ speculation	[ˌspekju'leiʃn]	n.	推测；思索；投机；投机买卖	U7TB
★ speculative	['spekjulətiv]	a.	推测的；投机的；冒险的	U7TB
sponsored	['spɔnsɜ:d]	a.	赞助的；发起的	U7TC

▲ sprawl	[sprɔːl]	n. & vi.	蔓延，杂乱无序地扩展；伸开四肢坐、躺或跌下	U8TC
▲ stagnant	['stægnənt]	a.	停滞的；萧条的	U1TC
stake	[steik]	n.	赌本；利益	U1TB
★ staple	['steipl]	a.	主要的，常产的	U8TA
		n.	主要成分；主食；主要商品；主要产品	U8TA
static	['stætik]	a.	静态的；静电的；静力的	U7TA
		n.	静力学；静态	U7TA
statistics	[stə'tistiks]	n.	统计；统计学；[统计]统计资料	U6TB
steep	[stiːp]	a.	（价格，需求）难以接受的；过高的	U1TB
stem	[stem]	n.	茎；干；船首；血统	U3TC
		vt.	除去……的茎；给……装柄；阻止；逆行	U3TC
▲ stigma	['stigmə]	n.	耻辱；污名；烙印；特征	U7TB
stimulate	['stimjuleit]	vt.	激发；刺激；促进	U8TB
★ stimulus	['stimjuləs]	n.	刺激；刺激物；促进因素	U7TC
★ strand	[strænd]	n.	股，缕；部分，方面	U2TC
		vt.	使搁浅；使滞留	U2TC
★ stray	[strei]	vi.	偏离	U4TB
stress	[stres]	vt.	强调；用重音读	U2TB
		n.	紧张；压力；强调；重音；重读	U2TB
strike	[straik]	vt. & vi.	给……以印象	U1TB
stuff	[stʌf]	vt.	以……填进，塞满	U8TA
		n.	东西，物品；物质；材料；活动，事情	U8TA
★ stunning	['stʌniŋ]	a.	使人晕倒的；极好的；震耳欲聋的	U2TA
			★ stun vt. 使震惊；打昏；使印象深刻	U2TA
▲ stunt	[stʌnt]	vt.	阻碍……的正常发展或生长	U7TB
		n.	噱头；手腕；绝技	U7TB
submit	[səb'mit]	vi.	屈从；忍受	U5TB
subsequently	['sʌbsikwəntli]	adv.	随后，其后；后来	U3TC
▲ subsidize	['sʌbsidaiz]	vt.	在财政上支持；补助，资助	U1TA
★ subsidy	['sʌbsədi]	n.	财政补贴；津贴	U8TA
substitute	['sʌbstitjuːt, -tuːt]	n.	代用品；代替者	U6TA
		vt. & vi.	替代；代替	U6TA
subtle	['sʌtl]	a.	微妙的；巧妙的；敏感的	U1TA
▲ subversive	[səb'vɜːsiv]	a.	破坏性的，颠覆性的	U5TB
suicide	['suːisaid]	n.	自杀；自杀行为；自杀者	U7TB
supplement	['sʌpləmənt]	n.	补充物；添加物；增刊	U2TC
		vt.	补充，增补	U2TC
★ supplementation	[ˌsʌplimen'teiʃn]	n.	补充；增补	U3TB
			★ supplementary a. 增补的，补充的	U3TB
survey	['sɜːvei]	n.	调查，调查表	U1TA
★ susceptible	[sə'septəbl]	a.	易受影响的；易感动的；容许……的	U2TA
sustainability	[səˌsteinə'biləti]	n.	可持续性	U8TA
sustainable	[sə'steinəbl]	a.	可持续的；可以忍受的；可支撑的	U1TC
★ swap	[swɔp]	vt. & vi.	交换	U1TC
sway	[swei]	vt. & vi.	影响；动摇	U7TB

sweeping	['swi:piŋ]	*n.*	扫除；垃圾	U3TA
		a.	扫荡的；彻底的；广泛的	U3TA
swell	[swel]	*vt. & vi.*	使（数量）逐渐增加；膨胀；肿胀	U7TB
		n.	肿胀；隆起	U7TB
symptom	['simptəm]	*n.*	征兆；症状	U3TC
synthetic	[sin'θetik]	*a.*	合成的，人造的	U2TC
		n.	合成物	U2TC
★ temperament	['temprəmənt]	*n.*	气质，性情，性格	U2TC
tendency	['tendənsi]	*n.*	倾向，趋势；癖好	U2TA
tender	['tendə]	*a.*	脆弱的；温柔的	U1TC
terminal	['tɜ:minl]	*a.*	晚期的；终点的；末端的	U2TA
		n.	末端；终点；终端机	U2TA
★ terminate	['tɜ:mineit]	*vt. & vi.*	结束；终止；满期；达到终点	U7TC
territory	['teritəri]	*n.*	领域；领土，地域；范围；版图	U6TB
★ testimony	['testiməni]	*n.*	证明；证据	U7TC
therapeutics	[.θerə'pju:tiks]	*n.*	疗法；治疗学	U3TC
therapy	['θerəpi]	*n.*	治疗，疗法	U2TC
timber	['timbə]	*n.*	木料，木材	U3TA
tip	[tip]	*vt.*	使倾斜；倾倒；给小费	U7TA
		n.	小费	U7TA
tissue	['tiʃu:]	*n.*	组织；纸巾	U2TA
tolerate	['tɔləreit]	*vt.*	忍受；默许；宽恕	U6TC
▲ tournament	['tuənəmənt]	*n.*	比赛，锦标赛，联赛	U3TB
trait	[treit]	*n.*	特性，特点；品质	U2TC
transaction	[træn'zækʃn]	*n.*	交易；执行，办理	U4TC
transfer	[træns'fɜ:]	*vt.*	转移；调动；转让	U1TA
transplantation	[.trænsplɑ:n'teiʃn]	*n.*	移植（器官等）；移栽（植物等）	U7TA
			transplant *vt.* 移植；移栽	U7TA
tremendous	[trə'mendəs]	*a.*	极大的，巨大的；惊人的	U2TB
trial	['traiəl]	*n.*	试验；磨炼；审讯；努力	U3TB
		a.	审讯的；试验的	U3TB
★ trigger	['trigə]	*vt.*	触发，引起	U5TC
★ tuition	[tju'iʃn]	*n.*	学费；讲授	U6TB
▲ tumor	['tju:mə]	*n.*	肿瘤；肿块	U2TA
ultimate	['ʌltimət]	*a.*	最终的；极限的；根本的	U7TB
★ ultraviolet	[.ʌltrə'vaiələt]	*a.*	紫外线的；产生紫外线的	U8TB
unappreciative	[.ʌnəp'ri:ʃətiv]	*a.*	不赏识的；不识抬举的	U7TA
▲ unconstitutional	[.ʌnkɔnsti'tju:ʃənl]	*a.*	违反宪法的，非立宪的	U4TC
▲ undercapitalized	[.ʌndə'kæpitəlaizd]	*a.*	投资不足的	U1TC
			capitalize *vt.* 投资于，提供资本给……	U1TC
undue	[ʌn'dju:]	*a.*	过度的，过分的；不适当的	U7TB
universal	[ju:ni'vɜ:sl]	*a.*	普遍性的，广泛性的；通用性的	U8TC
▲ unleash	[ʌn'li:ʃ]	*vt.*	解开……的皮带；解除……的束缚；发动	U3TA
		vi.	不受约束；自由自在；放荡不羁	U3TA
unobjectionable	[.ʌnəb'dʒekʃənəbl]	*a.*	不会招致反对的；可以接受的	U1TB
			objection *n.* 反对	U1TB
★ unprecedented	[ʌn'presidəntid]	*a.*	空前的；史无前例的	U3TA

	unwanted	[ˌʌn'wɒntid]	a.	有害的；不需要的；讨厌的	U7TB
	utility	[juːˈtiləti]	n.	效用；实用；功用；公共设施	U3TC
			a.	有多种用途的；通用的；实用的	U3TC
	utilize	[ˈjuːtəlaiz]	vt.	利用	U3TB
				★ utilization n. 利用	U3TB
★	vaccine	[ˈvæksiːn]	n.	疫苗；预防疫苗	U7TA
	valid	[ˈvælid]	a.	有效的，有根据的；正当的	U2TB
	variability	[ˌveəriəˈbiləti]	n.	易变；变化性	U8TB
	variable	[ˈveəriəbl]	a.	易变的，多变的；可变的；变异的	U3TB
			n.	可变物，可变因素；[数] 变量	U3TB
▲	viable	[ˈvaiəbl]	a.	可行的；能养活的；能生育的	U7TB
	virtually	[ˈvɜːtʃuəli]	adv.	实际上，实质上；虚拟	U2TA
★	visualize	[ˈviʒuəlaiz]	vt. & vi.	想象，设想；构想；使形象化	U2TC
	vital	[ˈvaitl]	a.	至关重要的，生死攸关的	U1TC
★	vocal	[ˈvəukl]	a.	激烈表达意见的；常言无忌的	U7TA
▲	volatile	[ˈvɒlətail]	a.	易变的，不稳定的；挥发的	U4TA
★	vulnerable	[ˈvʌlnərəbl]	a.	易受攻击的；易受伤害的	U2TA
	wealth	[welθ]	n.	财富；大量；富有	U2TB
	weight	[weit]	n.	重要性；影响	U7TB
★	wholesale	[ˈhəulseil]	a.	大规模的；批发的	U7TB
			n.	批发	U7TB
▲	withering	[ˈwiðəriŋ]	a.	使人畏缩的；使人害羞的；使人难堪的	U1TC
	yield	[jiːld]	vt. & vi.	产生，出产；提供；屈服；让步	U2TA
			n.	产量；产出；收益	U2TA